Deleuze and Guattari's
What is Philosophy?

D1711074

For my students
And for the opportunity to learn they continue to provide

… and …
For Elizabeth, with love

Deleuze and Guattari's
What is Philosophy?
A Critical Introduction and Guide

JEFFREY A. BELL

EDINBURGH
University Press

© Jeffrey A. Bell, 2016

Edinburgh University Press Ltd
The Tun – Holyrood Road
19 (9f) Jackson's Entry
Edinburgh EH8 8PJ

www.euppublishing.com

Typeset in 11/13pt Monotype Baskerville by
Servis Filmsetting Ltd, Stockport, Cheshire,
printed and bound in the United States of America

A CIP record for this book is available from the British Library

ISBN 978 0 7486 9252 1 (hardback)
ISBN 978 0 7486 9254 5 (webready PDF)
ISBN 978 0 7486 9253 8 (paperback)
ISBN 978 0 7486 9255 2 (epub)

The right of Jeffrey A. Bell to be identified as the author of this work
has been asserted in accordance with the Copyright, Designs and
Patents Act 1988, and the Copyright and Related Rights Regulations
2003 (SI No. 2498).

Contents

Acknowledgments

I am grateful to Southeastern Louisiana University's College of Arts, Humanities, and Social Sciences, and especially Dean Karen Fontenot, for having rewarded me with a Distinguished Teaching Professorship that allowed for greater opportunities to work on this book. Southeastern Louisiana University also supported this book through multiple Research and Travel Grants that allowed me to attend conferences and present this work while it was still in progress. I am also grateful for the generous invitations I have received to present this work, especially to Craig Lundy, Ian Buchanan, Paul Patton, James Williams, Hanping Chiu, and Tatsuya Higaki. At these events I received invaluable feedback on various early versions of the chapters in this book. I am also thankful for the many conversations I have had with scholars at other conferences and events – Henry Somers-Hall, Brent Adkins, Dan Smith, Claire Colebrook, Eugene Holland, Steven Shaviro, Joe Hughes, Eric Schliesser – and most notably to John Protevi for his friendship and support. And finally I am thankful for my students, and for the pressing questions they ask that have forced me to find the clearest way possible to express the thoughts and problems that occupy the pages of this book.

I am grateful as well for the support of Edinburgh University Press, especially to Carol Macdonald for her careful guidance and unwavering support. The anonymous reader of this book provided helpful comments, comments I incorporated and which have made this book better than it would have been otherwise. And of course I am grateful to my wife, Elizabeth, and to my daughters, Leah and Rebecca, for their continuing patience and support.

Introduction

Deleuze and Guattari's *What is Philosophy?* is a meditation on a life
well lived, and as such their book is to be placed in a long philosophical tradition. For Deleuze and Guattari, the value associated
with living life well is to be found in the nature of life itself rather
than in some purpose or end for which this life might be lived.
Aristotle can serve as our guide here, and especially Aristotle's
claim that a life well lived, a self-sufficient life, as Aristotle puts it,
"is complete without any qualification [and] is that which is chosen
always for its own sake and never for the sake of something else."[1]
The standard for how to live well is thus not to be found in something outside life, in some standard that transcends the nature of
life itself. Without a standard to apply to our particular lives and
the determinate situations within which we find ourselves, what
becomes necessary in order to live life well is that we develop a *taste*
for what works; or, as Aristotle puts it, one is to live life with an "eye
on the mean and working towards it," much as the "good artists do
their work" by attempting to create artworks where "nothing can be
subtracted from or added to them."[2] Since there is no transcendent
standard to predetermine how an artist is to go about keeping "an
eye on the mean," the problem for Aristotle, and for Deleuze and
Guattari, as we will see, is to understand the nature of a life well
lived without calling upon standards that transcend life. A life well
lived is thus much like an improvisational work – it is to be played,
and played well, but without a score that tells one precisely what or
how it is to be played. Determining how, what, when, where, and in
what circumstances a life is to be lived and lived well is the problem
that motivates Aristotle's discussions in his *Nichomachean Ethics*, and

1

it is the problem that motivates Deleuze and Guattari's efforts to understand the nature of philosophy.

There is also an important, though perhaps surprising, convergence between Deleuze and Guattari's *What is Philosophy?* and the overarching concerns one finds in Bertrand Russell's *The Problems of Philosophy*. In line with the Aristotelian claim that the value of a life well lived is not to be found in anything other than the nature of life itself, so too for Russell the value of philosophy is not to be judged relative to any practical ends or goals philosophy may help to bring about. Russell is quite forthright on this point when he argues that a full appreciation of the value of philosophy requires that we "first free our minds from the prejudices of what are wrongly called 'practical' men."[3] For the "'practical' man," Russell admits, it may be nearly impossible to convince him that "the study of philosophy is not a waste of time," and it is the practical needs of reducing "poverty and disease" that far outweigh the "goods of the mind [wherein] the value of philosophy is to be found."[4] In other words, unless philosophy is able to address problems and issues unrelated to the nature of philosophy itself – reducing "poverty and disease," for instance – then philosophy is of little use according to the "'practical' man." It is only when such practical problems have been solved, so the practical, goals-oriented person argues, that we can then begin to turn towards the benefits philosophy might have to offer. Yet even here philosophy is at a clear disadvantage, Russell notes, for although philosophy strives to attain knowledge, the effort is negligible for while "a mathematician, a mineralogist, a historian, or any other man of learning" can go on at length detailing "what definite body of truths has been ascertained by his science," the philosopher, by contrast, "will, if he is candid, have to confess that his study has not achieved positive results such as have been achieved by other sciences." In the realm of knowledge, therefore, philosophy is also found lacking. It is no wonder, then, that philosophy is shunned as an impractical, useless enterprise.[5]

There is an important lesson to be drawn from Russell's observation, Deleuze and Guattari will argue, though it is *not* the one Russell draws. For Russell, the value of philosophy lies precisely in the uncertainty brought about by "philosophic contemplation," an uncertainty that frees us from the "narrow and personal aims" of the "instinctive man [who] is shut up within the circle of his private interests" and perpetually at odds with "a great and powerful world which must, sooner or later, lay our private world in ruins."[6] Since philosophic contemplation views the world impartially, it does

2

not "divide the universe into two hostile camps – friends and foes, helpful and hostile, good and bad,"[7] and as a result philosophy is entirely useless and impractical when perceived from the perspective of our partial, private interests. For Deleuze and Guattari, however, "To say that the greatness of philosophy lies precisely in its not having any use is a frivolous answer that not even young people find amusing any more" (WP 9/QP14).[8] Their reasoning for this is that while Russell, on the one hand, is right to argue that philosophy is not to be confused with the sciences to the extent that the sciences produce a "definite body of truths," Russell nonetheless concludes that there is a greater use for philosophy insofar as it is related to "the greatness of the objects which it contemplates."[9] In other words, philosophy is held in abeyance to already existent objects, albeit "great" objects, that undermine the limited and limiting perspectives that characterize one's private interests. It is this view that Deleuze and Guattari will challenge.

For Deleuze and Guattari, however, philosophy is not a form of contemplation, even a contemplation of great objects. They are quite blunt on this point: "We can at least see what philosophy is not: it is not contemplation, reflection, or communication" (WP 6/QP 11). The reason for this is that what is presupposed by the nature of contemplation, reflection, and communication is the *object* that is contemplated, reflected upon, or communicated, whereas philosophy, Deleuze and Guattari argue, does not presuppose any already existent objects. As we will see throughout this book, Deleuze and Guattari adhere to a version of the Principle of Sufficient Reason (henceforth, PSR). For Deleuze and Guattari there must be a reason that accounts for and explains the objects of contemplation, reflection, and communication. As Deleuze and Guattari put it, "The first principle of philosophy is that Universals explain nothing but must themselves be explained" (WP 7/QP 12). Russell's call for philosophy to free us from our practical, useful interests by way of contemplating "great" objects (Universals) does not account for the nature of philosophy, for the nature of these "great" objects are themselves in need of an explanation, and it is here that the PSR becomes especially relevant. Given the importance of the PSR for the reading of Deleuze and Guattari's *What is Philosophy?* that will be offered here, let us clarify precisely the sense in which Deleuze, and Deleuze and Guattari, can accurately be said to adopt this principle.

As traditionally understood, the PSR asserts that everything has a cause or reason, and hence everything is intelligible and explicable in terms of its cause or reason. The PSR can be traced first to

Spinoza. In his early text on Descartes, Spinoza argues that "Nothing exists of which it cannot be asked, what is the cause, *or* reason, why it exists."[10] And in his *Ethics* Spinoza again argues that "For each thing there must be assigned a cause, *or* reason, as much for its existence as for its nonexistence."[11] As Michael Della Rocca argues, Spinoza's relentless adherence to the PSR leads Spinoza to affirm the intelligibility of everything.[12] Leibniz will also adopt the PSR, and he will do so explicitly in a number of places. In his *Monadology*, for instance, Leibniz argues that the reasoning that guides his philosophy

> is based upon two great principles: first, that of Contradiction . . . And second, the principle of Sufficient Reason, in virtue of which we believe that no fact can be real or existing and no statement true unless it has a sufficient reason why it should be thus and not otherwise.[13]

For those familiar with the work of Deleuze, it may seem untenable to saddle him with the PSR. There is good reason for this skepticism, for it is Deleuze, after all, who claims that in *Difference and Repetition* he is developing a philosophy of difference that sets out to understand difference in itself rather than a difference that is mediated by or subordinate to determinate identities and facts.[14] For Spinoza and Leibniz, however, it appears that the PSR entails affirming the view that for every determinate fact or thing there must be a determinate cause or reason why the fact or thing is the way it is rather than otherwise. In short, rather than embrace a philosophy of difference as Deleuze sets out to do, it appears Spinoza and Leibniz attempt to account not for difference in itself but for the intelligibility of determinate facts, and it is in the pursuit of this project that the PSR has a critical role to play.

We should take seriously, however, Deleuze's commitment to continuing to work within the tradition of Spinoza and Leibniz. As he wrote two books on Spinoza and another on Leibniz, we should not be surprised to find that Deleuze adopts a number of the moves that Spinoza and Leibniz made. Does this include adopting their adherence to the PSR? I would argue that indeed it does, but with two important qualifications. First, for Deleuze it is critical to recognize that Spinoza's and Leibniz's turn to the PSR was, according to Deleuze, motivated first and foremost by their move against Descartes. As Deleuze puts it in his first book on Spinoza, Spinoza and Leibniz were part of the "Anticartesian reaction," and this reaction is throughout, Deleuze adds, "a search for sufficient reasons: a sufficient reason for infinite perfection, a sufficient reason for clarity and distinctness, and a sufficient reason, indeed, for mechanism itself."[15] Descartes's mistake, Deleuze claims, is that he begins with predicates or the *proprium* of a subject but never adequately explains the nature of the subject itself. For instance, in his version of the ontological proof, Descartes's arguments are based on the notion of infinite perfection, "but infinite perfection is a *proprium*," Deleuze adds, "altogether insufficient to show what God's nature is, and how that nature is possible."[16] Similarly for the property of being a clear-and-distinct idea, for "'clear-and-distinct' is once more a *proprium*, an extrinsic determination of ideas which tells us nothing of the nature and possibility of the thing of which we have an idea, or of thought as such."[17] The search for sufficient reasons, therefore, the "Anticartesian reaction," is thus, on Deleuze's reading, the search for the immanent nature of the subject – for example, God or ideas, rather than the search for the proper extrinsic determinations of the subject – *proprium* – that are then used to represent the nature of the subject. According to Deleuze, "Descartes stops at the representative content of the ideas . . . he thus misses the true immanent content of ideas,"[18] and it is the search for sufficient reasons that sets out to give us this immanent content.

This search for the immanent content of ideas becomes a dominant theme in Leibniz's work, and as Deleuze himself continues to work within the "Anticartesian reaction" of Spinoza and Leibniz he will likewise turn to the work of Leibniz some twenty years after his first book on Spinoza. In the case of Leibniz, the problem is similar. What is the relation between the predicates, the *proprium*, of a subject and the subject itself? Leibniz's well-known solution to this problem is to claim that the predicates are in the subject. In other words, rather than draw out a list of extrinsic determinations in order to characterize and represent the nature of the subject – for example, the Caesar who wrote the *Gallic Wars*, crossed the Rubicon, was stabbed by Brutus, and so on; the Adam who ate from the tree of knowledge, named the animals, was the father of Cain and Abel, and so on – these extrinsic determinations are immanent to the nature of the subject itself. The predicates of Adam and Caesar, therefore, are included in their very nature. Similarly, for the world itself, it includes the Adam who sinned and the Caesar who crossed the Rubicon, for this is the world, Leibniz claims, God chose as the best of all possible worlds. A world where Adam does not sin, or where Caesar does not cross the Rubicon, would not be the best of all possible worlds, and it is God's choice that provides the sufficient reason for the nature of the world and for the subjects of this world, including the predicates and extrinsic determinations that flow from their immanent nature.[19]

Deleuze is quick to point out, however, that the predicates that are in the subject are not static, extrinsic determinations but rather are verbs that express the very nature of the subject and, by extension, the world. An important consequence follows from this fact, for Deleuze. As he states it, "That the predicate is a verb, and that the verb is irreducible to the copula and to the attribute, mark the very basis of the Leibnizian conception of the event."[20] In other words, the proper way to understand the subject is not by way of static extrinsic determinations but rather by the manner in which the subject maintains a unity throughout a dynamic process – "predication is not an attribution, because substance is not the subject of an attribute, but the inner unity of an event, the active unity of a change."[21] The sufficient reason that guarantees the inner, immanent unity of an event is, in the end, the world. With Leibniz, Deleuze argues, one finds a

> great logic of the event: the world itself is an event and, as an incorporeal (= virtual) predicate, the world must be included in every subject as a basis from which each one extracts the manners that correspond to its point of view (aspects).[22]

The world is an incorporeal event for the world is not fully actualized in each and every subject – what Leibniz calls a monad – but rather each monad expresses the world in its own manner, or from its own "point of view." For Leibniz, then, as for Spinoza, the search for sufficient reasons, and hence their adherence to the PSR, is motivated by a desire to move not from the extrinsic determinations and *proprium* of existing things to the nature of these things themselves, but rather from the immanent nature of substance (God or Nature) to the determinate manner in which this immanent substance is expressed or actualized by existing things. Deleuze follows this tradition very closely, but with one key difference, and this is my second qualification to the claim that Deleuze adheres to the PSR.

The key issue where Deleuze parts ways with Leibniz and Spinoza, and this has important implications for his understanding of the PSR, concerns the nature of unity. For Leibniz, as we saw, predication is the "inner unity of an event," a unity that in turn expresses the unity of the world or cosmos. The series of predicates in a subject, therefore, all presuppose their necessary convergence in the unity of the subject, subjects that in turn presuppose the unity of the world-event or cosmos. Deleuze makes this difference with Leibniz quite clear in the closing paragraphs of *The Fold*, when he argues that "Leibniz's monads submit to two conditions, one of closure and the other of selection."[23] With respect to the first, Deleuze points out that the monads "include an entire world that does not exist outside of them." In other words, the monads presuppose the inner unity of the cosmos or world, a world that is nothing less than the monads that express this world from their determinate points of view. The monads, therefore, are not open to other worlds, or to other ways of being, for their manner of being is always already determined by the inner unity of the world itself. This leads to the second condition – namely, selection – for on Deleuze's reading of Leibniz, "this world takes for granted a first selection, of convergence, since it is distinguished from other possible but divergent worlds."[24] By selecting the best of all possible worlds, the case is closed on other possible worlds, and thus monads may not diverge from the best of all possible worlds and be other than how they are. For Deleuze, by contrast, and as we will see in further detail in subsequent chapters, the immanent nature and substance that is the sufficient reason for the extrinsic determinations and properties of things is not an already presupposed unity, but rather multiplicity, or a substance consisting of divergent series and differences. Instead of a world of convergent series, we have for Deleuze and for Deleuze and Guattari a "world [that] is now made up of divergent series (the chaosmos)," and instead of Leibniz's monadology we have "a 'nomadology'."[25] The subsequent problem for Deleuze, then, is to account for the emergence of systematic unity in the first place. If the sufficient reason for existing phenomena is a multiplicity of divergent series, then what accounts for the apparent convergence of predicates and qualities upon the unity of a subject? It is precisely this problem that would occupy Deleuze's early work on Hume, and it is one that continues to motivate him up to his final essay, "Immanence: A Life."[26]

In Deleuze's final essay we can begin to gain a sense of the manner in which we will explore the claim that Deleuze and Guattari's *What is Philosophy?* is a meditation on a life well lived. As Deleuze begins this essay, the problem is to account for experience without presupposing either the unity or identity of the subject or object of experience. The transcendental field becomes the concept that Deleuze employs to provide such an account. One must be careful, however, as Deleuze notes, for there is an ineluctable tendency to understand the immanence of the transcendental field as being immanent to something, and thereby to place the immanence of the transcendental field in subordinate relation to that which transcends it – for example, a subject or object. What Deleuze is sketching, therefore, is a concept of pure immanence, an immanence that "is no longer immanence to anything other than itself," and for Deleuze this is the nature of "A LIFE, and nothing else. It [pure immanence] is not immanence to life, but the immanent that is in nothing is itself a life. A life is the immanence of immanence, absolute immanence: it is complete power, complete bliss."[27] A LIFE, in other words, and as we will see in subsequent chapters, is the sufficient reason for all determinate phenomena, for anything other than pure immanence itself.[28] A LIFE, however, is not a presupposed unity, the unity of the event in Leibniz's sense; rather, it is a chaosmos, a transcendental field of divergent series. The problem for life, then, is to forge a unity, to bring about a determinate, individuated phenomenon. In short, the problem for life is a matter of learning, and a life well lived, as will be argued below, is not a life of knowledge, a life in accordance with already established rules and ways of being; to the contrary, a life well lived entails extracting A LIFE from our lives as lived, the life that is the sufficient reason for all knowledge and determinate ways of being. In living this life one lives the problem of learning that is inseparable from the "absolute immanence" that is A LIFE, and in doing this we find, as Deleuze echoes Spinoza, a source of "complete power, complete bliss." This theme is integral to Deleuze and Guattari's meditation on a life well lived and it will be developed in the pages of *What is Philosophy?* and in subsequent chapters of this book.

§1

With this discussion of the PSR we can now turn to Deleuze and Guattari's account of the nature of philosophy. This will be our focus for the remainder of this introduction. As a tentative and provisional first step, we can begin with Deleuze and Guattari's claim from *A Thousand Plateaus* that "politics precedes being."[29] As they go on to clarify, "Practice does not come after the emplacement of the terms and their relations, but actively participates in the drawing of the lines."[30] In other words, we do not begin with a set of terms or individuated entities over which we battle and negotiate where they are to be situated – that is, their "emplacement"; rather, the very terms and their relations are the result of a "politics," and a politics that is always ongoing. We thus do not begin with a set of terms and entities we then subsume under a given concept, determining thereby what does or does not fall under the scope of the concept. This is the Fregean, scientific understanding of the concept that begins with being rather than politics, with that which *is* rather than with the *process* through which that which is comes to acquire the stability that makes its identity possible. In the case of scientific truths, for instance, Frege assumes that "it must be determinate for every object whether it falls under a concept or not; a concept word which does not meet this requirement on its *Bedeutung* [reference] is *bedeutungslos.*"[31] A concept may have a sense (or intension) and yet fail to have a referent (*Bedeutung*), as is often the case in literature, but if it is scientific knowledge we are after then there must be a determinate object or referent that "falls under a concept." As does Russell, Frege presupposes the objects as a *fait accompli*, and the task of science is simply one of organizing such beings – their "emplacement" – according to their proper concepts; or, as Plato described the task, it consists of carving nature at its joints.[32] But it is precisely the nature of objects themselves that needs to be accounted for rather than accepted as brute facts, and hence, following the PSR, Deleuze and Guattari set out to offer such an explanation, and one that provides the reason for beings themselves, and *politics* gives us an initial place from which these reasons may begin to emerge.

True to their claim that politics precedes being, Deleuze and Guattari turn in *What is Philosophy?* to the politics of ancient Greece in order to begin to answer the question: what is philosophy? "If we really want to say that philosophy originates with the Greeks," Deleuze and Guattari argue, "it is because the city, unlike the empire or state, invents the *agon* as the rule of a society of 'friends,' of the community of free men as rivals (citizens)" (WP 9/QP 14). In an empire or state, opposing claims are resolved by appealing to a hierarchy of ruling elites. The rulers of empires and states are the ones who pass judgment on which claims and opinions (*doxa*) are valid and worthy of being acted upon. With "Athenian democracy," by contrast, Deleuze and Guattari claim that "this is not the case . . . [and] (h)ence the necessity for Plato to put things in order and create authorities for judging the validity of these claims: the Ideas as philosophical concepts" (ibid.). The "Ideas as philosophical concepts" are precisely the created authorities that serve to pass judgment on the validity of contested claims. Anticipating points to be discussed in subsequent chapters, we can say that what is crucial for the emergence of philosophy in Athens is not the *place* where it occurred, the city-state of Athens, but rather the *problematic place,* or better the *problem space*, that is inseparable from the politics of Athenian democracy, and it was this *problem space* that allowed for the creation of "Ideas as philosophical concepts" which emerged as a solution to the problem space that will hold sway over subsequent generations of philosophers.[33]

I will return to the theme of philosophy's emergence in Athens in a later chapter (Chapter 4), but for the moment it is to be noted that by creating the concept of Ideas in response to the problem space that was Athenian politics, Plato exemplifies what Deleuze and Guattari take to be the nature of philosophy itself – namely, the creation of concepts. Deleuze and Guattari are quite straightforward on this point and in the opening paragraphs of *What is Philosophy?* they answer the very question that serves as the title of their book: "philosophy is the art of forming, inventing, and fabricating concepts" (WP 2/QP 8). A few pages later they qualify this answer by adding that "philosophy is not a simple art of forming, inventing, or fabricating concepts, because concepts are not necessarily forms, discoveries, or products. More rigorously, philosophy is the discipline that involves *creating* concepts" (WP 5/QP 10). Recalling our earlier discussion of Russell, we can say that Deleuze and Guattari would agree with Russell's claim that philosophy is not to be understood in terms of a "definite body of truths"; rather, philosophy instills a sense of uncertainty that frees us from the prison of private interests. In short, philosophy injects a problem space into the comfortable and familiar world of everyday truths, beliefs, and expectations. The ultimate purpose of philosophy for Russell, however, is not the creation of concepts in response to this problem space but rather an expanded understanding of the nature of reality itself. Philosophy, in other words, is for Russell simply a handmaiden to the sciences, a contemplative activity that motivates further scientific enquiry by bringing to light the uncertainty intrinsic to problem spaces, and problem spaces that then come to be solved by way of new scientific discoveries and inventions.[34]

Russell's understanding of philosophy has had a largely unquestioned influence in the Anglophone philosophical tradition, though Deleuze and Guattari view Russell's philosophy as a rival to philosophy rather than as philosophy proper. "[P]hilosophy," Deleuze and Guattari claim, "has encountered many new rivals," of which they list "the human sciences, and especially sociology," followed by the challenges of "epistemology, of linguistics, or even of psychoanalysis and logical analysis" (WP 10/QP 15). What each of these rivals has in common is that it set out to create concepts that will help to facilitate more accurate and comprehensive representations of reality, and thus add to our "definite body of truths." Understood in this way, philosophy may be seen as a discipline that creates concepts, but concepts that are subservient to the extensive properties and qualities of the world, properties and qualities that our best scientific theories will accurately represent and track. Philosophy thus serves to add, albeit indirectly, to our definite body of knowledge by creating the concepts that will give us the means to represent aspects of the world that had previously been hidden from view. Philosophy becomes a research discipline, which is not surprising, for ever since the university reforms in Germany at the turn of the nineteenth century, a primary task of researchers, in contrast to teachers, has been to contribute new knowledge to one's field. In preparing a dissertation proposal, for instance, a prospective doctoral candidate must show that their research will add new knowledge and insight to the body of truths of their discipline.

Whether it is the human sciences, epistemology, or linguistics that are among the many disciplines vying to add to our body of knowledge, what we do not have here, according to Deleuze and Guattari, is philosophy but rather "rivals" to philosophy. The series of "successive challenges" to philosophy, of which these disciplines are examples, comes to its "most shameful moment," Deleuze and Guattari lament, "when computer science, marketing, design, and advertising, all the disciplines of communication, seized hold of the word *concept* itself and said: 'This is our concern, we are the creative ones, we are the *ideas men (concepteurs)*!'" (WP 10/QP 15). In our time, they argue, it is the marketing executive who takes on the mantle of being the creative one, the one who creates concepts, and yet such creativity is put to work securing market share, quantifiable profits, and an ever-expanding distribution and saturation of one's products. From Russell and the sciences to the advertising executives in the marketing department, what we are left with is an impoverished understanding of philosophy and no sense of what it means for philosophy to be the "art of forming, inventing, and fabricating concepts." What we are left with, instead, is a series of rivals to philosophy who place the creation of concepts in subservience to securing a firm and ever expanding grasp of the extensive properties and qualities of the world.

In contrast to the understanding of concepts and philosophy offered by the false rivals to be found among the scientists and marketing executives, Deleuze and Guattari praise, perhaps somewhat surprisingly for those familiar with Deleuze's work, the approach of the post-Kantians, especially Schelling and Hegel. It is Schelling and Hegel, Deleuze and Guattari argue, who rightly recognize the "self-positing" reality of the concept, or the sense in which the concept "depends on a free creative activity [that] is also that which, independently and necessarily, posits itself in itself: the most subjective will be the most objective" (WP 11/QP 16). As a self-positing, "autopoetic" (ibid.) reality, the concept is not placed in a subservient relationship to extensive properties and qualities, much as a happy, self-sufficient life for Aristotle (or, as we saw for Deleuze, the "complete bliss" associated with the pure immanence of A LIFE) is never lived for the sake of something else and is thus a life in want of nothing. The reason for the praise of Schelling and Hegel, therefore, is that they extend the Aristotelian argument to the nature of reality itself, arguing that the extensive properties and qualities of the world are to be understood in terms of the autopoetic, self-positing nature of the concept. We thus find a sharp contrast between the Hegel/Schelling approach to concepts and the scientific approach endorsed by Russell. This is unsurprising, given Russell's own philosophical development, for Russell's own approach to philosophy was largely forged in the kiln of an anti-Hegelian, anti-idealist critique, and especially the idealism of Russell's day that was especially evident in the work of F. H. Bradley. There has been much written of late on this history, and we will review it in more detail later (Chapter 2, §3), but for our current purposes it is worth highlighting that key to the difference between Russell and Bradley is that whereas the latter accepts the PSR, the former rejects it. Russell will deny the reality of a self-positing, autopoetic reality that is the PSR for the facts regarding the extensive properties and qualities of the world.[35] Russell will accept instead that there are certain inexplicable brute facts, and it is on the basis of these facts that our explanations regarding the world are to begin.

Because Deleuze and Guattari embrace a version of the PSR they will follow Schelling and Hegel and argue that it is an autopoetic, infinite reality that is the PSR that accounts for the determinate facts of the world. Despite this move and their praise for Hegel, however, Deleuze and Guattari go on to claim that Hegel's account succeeds only "at the cost of an indeterminate extension of philosophy," and an extension that "left scarcely any independent movement of the arts and sciences remaining" (WP 12/QP 17). In other words, Hegel (for reasons to be discussed later) subsumes all creative processes under the autopoetic process of an absolute Spirit, and as a result Hegel has "reconstituted universals" (ibid.) and restored the representational model of thought whereby the elements of this autopoetic process, such as those involved in philosophy, science, or art, become "no more than ghostly puppets" (ibid.) that merely *re-present* the autopoetic process of absolute Spirit. It is at this point, in the closing lines of their introduction, that Deleuze and Guattari propose their alternative understanding of the concept. In contrast to the Russellian subservience of the concept to scientific discovery, or in its extreme form to "commercial professional training" and the exploits of the marketing executive, *and* in contrast to Hegel's "encyclopedia of the concept" whereby all determinate reality becomes subsumed under the purview of a "pure subjectivity," Deleuze and Guattari propose instead "the more modest task of a *pedagogy* of the concept, which would have to analyze the conditions of creation as factors of always singular moments" (ibid.). For the remainder of this introduction I will begin to explore the manner in which Deleuze and Guattari set out, in *What is Philosophy?*, to create the concept of learning that is presupposed by their "modest task of a pedagogy of the concept."

§2

To begin clarifying the importance that a "pedagogy of the concept" has for Deleuze and Guattari, we can return to Plato's famous problem of the *Meno*. The dialogue (*Meno*) begins with a pedagogical problem: can virtue be taught? If one assumes that it can be taught, then the student who learns to be virtuous does so at the feet of their master, for it is the master who knows the nature of virtue and imparts this wisdom to their students. Socrates, however, confesses that he knows "literally nothing about virtue,"[36] and therefore he cannot place himself in the role of teacher or master but sees himself rather as one who seeks to learn the nature of virtue. But then we come to the problem – if Socrates does not know the nature of virtue, how will he come to recognize it if he does not know what he is looking for? There are many who claim to know the nature of virtue, justice, and so on, but as any reader of Plato will know, through the course of the various dialogues with Socrates this knowledge is ultimately revealed to be nothing but opinion and is not the objective knowledge or standard they initially claimed it to be. This leads Socrates to his famous conclusion that if he is wise it is because he knows he lacks the knowledge others believe they possess. Socrates is thus not in a position to teach others the nature of virtue; nor is anyone else able to do so, Socrates concludes. Even if we were by chance to come upon someone who does know the true nature of virtue, we would still have the problem of accounting for how we come to recognize their claims as true unless we already know what it is we are looking for and hence the standard that differentiates true from false claims regarding virtue. To restate this in the terms discussed above, what we lack is the authority to differentiate between true and false opinions.

Plato's famous solution to this problem is to argue that we do indeed know what it is we are looking for – we already know the true nature of virtue, justice, beauty, and so on – but we have simply forgotten it. If we were to encounter the truth, we would immediately recognize it as what we already knew, much as one recognizes a name one had on the tip of their tongue to be the name they were struggling to remember just a few seconds before. This solution has come to be called Plato's theory of recollection, and it bears striking similarities to the two approaches towards concepts discussed above – namely, those of Russell and Hegel/Schelling. On the one hand, the truth that has been forgotten and needs to be recollected can be understood to be a forgotten fact, an already existent fact (or Idea for Plato) that needs simply to be recollected rather than created. The pedagogy of the concept in this context would thus consist of facilitating access to this already existent fact that is not yet known or recognized as such.[37] On the other hand, and as the Platonic dialogues make clear, the facts that need to be recollected are already within one's self, and it is therefore a form of self-recognition, or a self-positing, that is necessary if we are to grasp the true nature of virtue, and so on. Yet in this case it is, as we have seen, the form of the self as a "reconstituted universal" that is the already existent form that prefigures and predetermines the facts that come to be known and learned.

In their proposal that philosophy be understood more modestly as a "pedagogy of the concept," Deleuze and Guattari set out to offer an alternative to the Russellian and Hegelian approaches. To state the alternative briefly, one is to place learning into a problem space, and more precisely into the singular conditions of this problem space, rather than place learning in relationship to existent facts (Russell) or to the autopoetic returning into itself of a pure subjectivity (Hegel). Learning, in short, entails coming to grips with the singular elements or signs that constitute the problem space, and it is this problem space that allows for the possibility of learning. Deleuze offers the example of learning to swim to illustrate this process:

The movement of the swimmer does not resemble that of the wave, in particular, the movements of the swimming instructor which we reproduce on the sand bear no relation to the movements of the wave, which we learn to deal with only by grasping the former in practice as signs. That is why it is so difficult to say how someone learns: there is an innate or acquired practical familiarity with signs, which means that there is something amorous – but also something fatal – about all education. We learn nothing from those who say: "Do as I do". Our only teachers are those who tell us to "do with me", and are able to emit signs to be developed in heterogeneity rather than propose gestures for us to reproduce. In other words, there is no ideo-motivity, only sensory-motivity. When a body combines some of its own distinctive points with those of a wave, it espouses the principle of repetition which is no longer that of the Same, but involves the Other – involves difference, from one wave and one gesture to another, and carries that difference through the repetitive space thereby constituted. To learn is indeed to constitute this space of an encounter with signs. . . .[38]

As this passage illustrates, learning takes place "in the relation between a sign and a response," with signs involving heterogeneity in "at least three ways."[39] There is the heterogeneity between the sign and the object that bears them – between singular points (that is, signs) of contact between the body and singular points of buoyancy, currents, and so on, of the water; there is the heterogeneity between the sign and the Idea or problem space this sign incarnates – in the case of swimming we have the problem space of coordinating and producing the conjunction of signs of body and water such that one is able to learn how to swim; and finally there is the relation between the sign and the response they elicit. The latter is the process of taking up the sign in a synthesis whereby the sign comes to be drawn together with other signs – what Deleuze and Guattari will call a plane of consistency (as we will see in Chapter 1) – which in turn facilitates the possibility of learning. To learn to swim is thus not a matter of reproducing what the swimming instructor does on the sand, but rather of working with the singular points and signs of the instructor's gestures on the sand as one puts one's own body in relation to the singular points of the waves and currents of the water. While learning to swim one comes to acquire a familiarity with the singular points and signs where certain gestures, kicks, and so on, achieve an equilibrium of consistency that matches the intensity of the waves and currents, and so on. In learning to drive a stick shift car, to offer another example, it is not a matter of understanding the rule that one must press the clutch to switch gears and then release the clutch while pressing on the accelerator to engage the gear. Although this is certainly true, and one can say that this is what one knows how to do when they have learned to drive a stick shift car, for Deleuze what is key to the learning process is the encounter with the singular points and signs associated with one's feet, hands, pedals, and the position of the car on the road, and so on – releasing the clutch at just the right time, at just the right speed, and with the foot exerting the appropriate amount of pressure on the gas pedal to assure a smooth acceleration or change of gear. It is for this reason that Deleuze argues that in learning to swim "there is no ideo-motivity, only sensory-motivity."

Turning now to philosophy as a pedagogy of the concept, we will see that here too it involves a "sensory-motivity," or a particular taste for the singular points and signs that constitute the problem space that allows for the creation of concepts, much as the singular points of our body and water were the conditions for the problem space that allowed for the possibility of learning how to swim. Similarly, for the philosopher who "invents and thinks the Concept" (WP 3/ QP 8), the wisdom of the philosopher is not, Deleuze and Guattari argue, one of knowing an abstract, general truth but rather it "designate(s) a type of competent intimacy, a sort of material taste and potentiality, like that of the joiner with wood – is the potential of wood latent in the good joiner; is he the friend of the wood?" (WP 3/QP 9). In creating their works, the good joiner is indeed a friend of the wood and they have the ability to work with the singular points of the wood – its hardness, grain patterns, and so on. The joiner does not follow a rule that predetermines how to work on a piece of wood; rather, they have a taste for the singular points and signs that elicit the response from the joiner such that they work with the idiosyncrasies of this particular piece of wood – they note the spacing of the grains, the hard and soft spots, knots, and so on. Likewise for the philosopher, they are a friend of the concept and through "a sort of material taste and potentiality," a "sensory-motivity," they too are able to draw from the singular points and signs the problem space or plane of immanence, as this will be called by Deleuze and Guattari, that then allows for the possibility of creating a concept.

Many of these themes will be discussed at length in later chapters, but to indicate briefly the contours these arguments will take we can begin with the friend, who for Deleuze and Guattari is an example of the "conceptual personae" that philosophy needs in order to create concepts ("We will see that concepts need conceptual personae" [WP 2/QP 8]). If a piece of woodworking, for example, needs a joiner who is a friend of the wood, and if philosophical concepts need a philosopher who is a friend of the concept, then what is this relationship of friendship between joiner/philosopher and woodwork/concept? For Deleuze and Guattari, most importantly, this relationship is not an external relationship, and hence a conceptual persona is not to be understood as an "extrinsic persona," or as a character who serves as "an example or empirical circumstance" associated with a particular time or place. To the contrary, Deleuze and Guattari claim that a conceptual persona is a distinctive conjunction and assemblage of singular points and signs that give life to a plane of immanence and problem space that elicits the response that is nothing other than the autopoetic process inseparable from the creation of concepts. When a joiner becomes a friend of the wood, or a philosopher a friend of the concept, they enter into a heterogeneous series of conjunctions and syntheses whereby one cannot separate out the joiner from the woodwork, the philosopher from their concept, the swimmer from the water; rather, we have a plane of immanence, or a problem space that is inseparable from the creative process itself, and from the resulting abstractions that identify and separate the creator (joiner/philosopher) from the created (woodwork/concept). As the problem space that allows for the creative processes that give rise to concepts, the "conceptual personae," Deleuze and Guattari claim, give life to the problem space and it is this life (or A LIFE) that is "intrinsic to thought, a condition of possibility of thought itself, a living category, a transcendental lived reality" (WP 3/QP 9).

If the friend is the conceptual persona "that is even said to reveal the Greek origin of philo-sophy" (WP 2/QP 8), as Deleuze and Guattari argue, then this is precisely because the friend is not "an extrinsic persona, an example or empirical circumstance," but rather the "presence that is intrinsic to thought" (WP 3/QP 9). The friend as conceptual persona brings together singular points and signs in a way that allows for the concept of philosophy to emerge for the Greeks – *philo-sophia*, a friend or lover (*philo*) of wisdom (*sophia*). This conceptual persona, however, is not, *à la* Leibniz, a unity of the event immanent to the concept, but to the contrary, it involves other divergent series and possibilities as it always already implies its own variations, or relations to other elements and to other singular points and signs. For example, Deleuze and Guattari claim that, "if the philosopher is the friend or lover of wisdom, is it not because he lays claim to wisdom, striving for it potentially rather than actually possessing it?" (WP 4/QP 9). But if it is the case that the friend implies other claimants regarding wisdom, then the friend brings in tow a "third party who ... becomes a rival," and hence friendship here involves a "competitive distrust of the rival as much as amorous striving for the object of desire" (ibid.). "The basic point of friendship," then, as Deleuze and Guattari conclude, is "that the two friends are like claimant and rival (but who could tell them apart?)" (ibid.). Are the friends equal in their relationship to wisdom, or are they rivals in dispute over who has the legitimate right to be a claimant to wisdom? For Deleuze and Guattari, "Friend, lover, claimant and rival are transcendental determinations that do not for that reason lose their intense and animated existence, in one persona or in several" (WP 4/QP 10). In other words, friend, lover, claimant, and rival constitute the problem space from which the concept of philosophy comes to be created in ancient Greece, a problem space that is related to the problem space associated with Athenian democracy, as discussed earlier, though in this instance the conceptual persona involves the problem space associated with the "condition(s) of possibility of thought itself, a living category, a transcendental lived reality."

Returning to where we began, we will see in subsequent chapters that this "transcendental lived reality" is what Deleuze and Deleuze and Guattari will refer to as a life (A LIFE for our purposes) to be extracted from our lives as lived, an extraction that results in nothing less than living a life of thoughtful, engaged, creative learning and thought. To trace and chart the relations between A LIFE as transcendental lived reality and our lives as lived is to confront the problem of a life well lived, a life of thoughtful learning. This is the problem space that conditions *What is Philosophy?*, and in developing their arguments in response to it, Deleuze and Guattari will highlight what they call the "three great forms" (WP 197/QP 186) of thought – namely, philosophy, science, and art. What characterizes each of these three great forms is the manner in which the transcendental lived reality becomes the problem space in which various creative (that is, learning) processes become possible. These creative processes will result in concepts for philosophy (Chapters 1 to 4), functives for science (Chapters 5 and 6), and percepts and affects for art (Chapter 7). The creative processes of the "three great forms" of thought are inseparable from the transcendental lived reality – A LIFE – and a life well lived, therefore, will be a life that thrives on the heterogeneity of the singular points and differences between art, science, and philosophy, and the learning these differences provoke in response to the fundamental problem that is living a life.

§3

In Chapter 1 we will set the stage for subsequent chapters since much of what Deleuze and Guattari say in *What is Philosophy?* hinges upon their theory of concepts. As we have seen, a concept is not, *à la* Frege and Russell, a way to delineate between those things which do and do not fall under a given concept (for example, those objects that fall under the concept 'horse', for example); nor are concepts simply resources that facilitate human communication; rather, concepts are creations inseparable from the problem space that is the condition of possibility for thought itself. Put differently, concepts are self-organized dynamic systems that provoke and are provoked by problems. The real, we will argue, is the problem space of multiplicities, and the concepts that are inseparable from problem spaces are themselves realities – multiplicities – rather than representations of reality; moreover, we will see that concepts are, in what is for Deleuze and Guattari a nod to Hegel, infinite realities. This similarity is key to understanding Deleuze and Guattari's project, just as it is critical to understanding the difference between their projects, which will be discussed when we examine the Hegel example in Chapter 4. The remainder of the first chapter will look at the two examples Deleuze and Guattari use to clarify the arguments one finds in their first chapter (and we will do the same for each of the examples from their other chapters). By looking at the example of Descartes's cogito (example 1) and Plato and Kant's concept of Ideas (example 2), we will be able to see how Deleuze and Guattari's theory of concepts can be fruitfully applied to cases from the history of philosophy.

Chapter 2 will turn to the theme of the PSR. In his 1968 doctoral presentation lecture, published under the title "The Method of Dramatization," Deleuze begins by arguing that the traditional Socratic question – what is x?; for example, justice, beauty, love, and so on – is not an adequate way to delineate the nature of Ideas as problem spaces. A better line of questions would be, "who? how? how much? where and when? in which case?"[40] In philosophy's attempt to discern the reasons of things, it will not be a matter of discovering and stating the simple essences of things, of definitively answering a "what is x?" question. For Deleuze and Guattari, the reasons philosophy seeks will continually create differences, or philosophy will consist of a series of problematic, divergent series that continually return to the "who? how?" . . . , and so on, questions. As we clarify what this means for Deleuze and for Deleuze and Guattari, and look at how this is presented in *What is Philosophy?*, the importance of the PSR will become clear. Deleuze's thought is infused with Spinozism from beginning to end, and Spinoza's embrace of the PSR is, as we have seen, a crucial move that Deleuze and Guattari adopt (though with variations, as we have seen). The ultimate reason, finally, that philosophy can give and that is in line with the PSR, is difference itself, or multiplicities as problematic planes of immanence (as we will see) that are literally for Deleuze the difference that makes the difference between things. To think this difference, however, entails creating concepts in the wake of filtering the infinite speeds of chaos, of running the indeterminate chaos through a sieve, and this is what the plane of immanence provides. Stated differently, the plane of immanence is precisely the problem space that allows for the creation of concepts.

Chapter 3 will look at the nature of philosophy, or the concept of philosophy, from the perspective of two of the important questions discussed in Chapter 2 – namely, how? and who? More precisely, this chapter will address the significance of the notion "conceptual personae" and hence expand upon our earlier discussion. Conceptual personae constitute one-third of what Deleuze and Guattari refer to as "the philosophical trinity" of immanence, insistence, and consistency (WP 77/QP 74). Whereas the plane of immanence accounts for the problem spaces that are inseparable from the consistency of created concepts, conceptual personae provide the dynamism or life of conceptual practice itself – the how and who of the creation of concepts. As will have been discussed in Chapter 2 when we detail the PSR, the ultimate reason for actualized entities and forms is a series of heterogeneous and intensive differences. As Deleuze argues repeatedly throughout his writings, however, these intensive differences come to be covered over and hidden by the extensities and qualities they make possible. In the case of conceptual personae, similarly, we will see that they are the intensive differences or mediators (*intercesseurs* in French) that make possible the identity of the philosopher as philosopher, and yet they come to be hidden by the extensive qualities and properties of the philosopher and the philosophical school that may come to be associated with their name. As Deleuze and Guattari put it, the "philosopher is only the envelope of his principal conceptual persona and all the other personae who are the intercessors, the real subjects of his philosophy" (WP 64/QP 62).

Chapter 4 continues with the theme of the previous chapter and approaches the task of philosophy from the questions, where and when? and in which case? In this chapter, these questions lead us to an investigation of the historical conditions of philosophy. This theme has been discussed elsewhere in the literature on Deleuze, and our discussion here will draw upon this literature only to the extent that it helps us to address Deleuze and Guattari's arguments about the history of concepts themselves. Of particular concern in this context will be Deleuze's Humean understanding of habit. A major conclusion of this chapter will be that a history of concepts, as Deleuze and Guattari conceive it, would not be a standard history of philosophy or history of ideas, if by this is meant a restatement of ideas and concepts that have already been put forth and argued for; to the contrary, the history of concepts that Deleuze and Guattari envision will entail a disruption of established habits such that the intensive differences and problem spaces immanent to these habits may in turn problematize these habits and thus provoke thought and the creation of new concepts. A history of concepts, in other words, is nothing less than another way of doing philosophy.

Chapter 5 will explore Deleuze and Guattari's claim that there is a key difference between philosophy and science. Science, they argue, works with functives rather than concepts. Some have viewed this distinction between science and philosophy as problematic, or as overly simplistic, especially given the important role the minor and nomad sciences play (in contrast to the major and royal sciences) in *A Thousand Plateaus* (we will return to this distinction in the Conclusion). In this chapter we will argue that the simplistic distinction is only problematic if it is perceived from the scientific perspective, or from the perspective of propositions that entail a functional reference to the actual world (what Deleuze and Guattari call the "plane of reference"). From the perspective of problems, however, as discussed in Chapters 2 and 3, philosophical concepts provide the metaphysics necessary for science (in agreeing with Bergson, Deleuze claims that "modern science has not found its metaphysics ... It is that metaphysics that interests me"[41]), and it is minor/nomad science that best embraces and exemplifies the metaphysics of problems. This point becomes clearest when one looks at the importance of chaos theory and dynamic systems theory for Deleuze and Guattari. Just as philosophy institutes a plane of immanence that acts as a sieve of chaos and allows for the consistency necessary for the creation of concepts, dynamic systems theory also recognizes the need for a consistency at the "edge of chaos" that is necessary for the emergence of new forms.[42] The difference, however, is that while philosophy seeks to retain the "infinite speeds" of chaos in order to establish the consistency necessary to create the concepts that provoke thought, science "relinquishes the infinite" (WP 118) in order to set up functions on the plane of reference. As a science, therefore, a dynamic system works with functions that have reference to the spatio-temporal dynamisms of the actual world; as philosophy, a dynamic systems metaphysics draws from the actual the "infinite speeds" of chaos in order to create concepts that do not serve to represent the actual world but rather to provoke thought. The two approaches are not mutually exclusive; to the contrary, and as will be argued in this chapter, the scientific approach presupposes the philosophical (or problematic), even when the philosophical comes to be covered over and hidden by the successes of the sciences.

Chapter 6 will address Deleuze and Guattari's claim that logic is "essentially and necessarily" reductionist. This occurs, Deleuze and Guattari argue, when philosophers attempt to transform concepts into functions, or when logic converts concepts into propositional functions. What is reduced, we will see, is difference itself. To appreciate the importance of Frege and Russell in Deleuze and Guattari's account, and to get a better sense of their critique of analytic philosophy, we will first explore the important innovations that Frege and Russell developed in logic that provided tools that could better serve to capture the varied relations between things (including the changing relations between subjects and their predicates). The result came to be called the logic of relations, and it gives rise to what Deleuze and Guattari call the propositional function. The advantage of the logic of relations and propositional functions over the traditional logic of syllogisms, at least from the perspective of Deleuze and Guattari in *What is Philosophy?*, is precisely that it is better able to express in logical form the *differences* between things. A consequence of this move, however, and one that would come to characterize much of twentieth-century analytic philosophy, is that philosophy would come to be dominated by an emphasis upon propositional logic and its functional relationship to states of affairs. What is dismissed, or hidden and covered over, however, to return to a recurring theme of this book, are the non-propositional and pre-individual singular points that constitute the problem spaces that make possible the actualized states of affairs, as well as the propositions that refer to these states and to their various properties. In short, in this chapter we will draw up a brief history of the concept of propositions in analytic philosophy.

It is quite appropriate that art is the focus of the last full chapter of *What is Philosophy?* Given the emphasis Deleuze and Deleuze and Guattari place upon creation throughout their work, it is unsurprising that the arts will frequently supply Deleuze with a number of examples that he will use as he comes to develop his own sense of what is involved when philosophy creates concepts. Central to the efforts of the arts, it will be argued, is the creation of percepts and affects. Such percepts and affects serve as a sieve or filter of chaos, and thus they do not allow the chaos to consume the work; nor do they allow the chaos (as does science with the infinite) to be relinquished. The creative path of the artist is thus quite similar to that of the philosopher, but as Deleuze and Guattari make clear, the artist's work is to create percepts and affects which are irreducible to any role they may play in a representational framework, much as philosophical concepts are irreducible to the Fregean concepts discussed in Chapter 1.

In the Conclusion we will expand upon one of the central points that is stressed in the conclusion to *What is Philosophy?*, which was in turn a thread running throughout this critical guide and introduction – namely, chaos. Rather than rehearse the arguments and discussions of earlier chapters, we will close by pointing towards problems that may prompt future work, and in fact are currently prompting such work. Most notably, we will point towards work within dynamic systems theory to show how Deleuze and Guattari have provided the metaphysics the sciences need. We will also draw to a close our theme that *What is Philosophy?* is a meditation upon what constitutes a life well lived. This will indicate how the creation of concepts, or how a thoughtful, engaged life of learning, can lead to a rethinking of our lives as lived in all their social, political, and historical variety. Many of these themes will have been discussed in earlier chapters, but in closing we hope to raise these problems again and differently, and, motivated by the concept of philosophy as laid down here and in *What is Philosophy?*, we hope to set philosophy to work.

NOTES

1. Aristotle, *Nichomachean Ethics* 1097a36–7, trans. Hippocrates Apostle (Grinnell: Peripatetic Press, 1984).
2. Ibid., 1106b10–14.
3. Bertrand Russell, *The Problems of Philosophy* (Oxford: Oxford University Press, 1959), p. 158.

4. Ibid.
5. Stephen Hawking, in his book *The Grand Design* (New York: Bantam, 2012), argues that since "philosophy has not kept up with modern developments in science, particularly physics" (p. 5), it has not therefore been able to address the questions that had traditionally been within the purview of philosophy. Hawking's conclusion is: "philosophy is dead" (ibid.). Neil deGrasse Tyson has recently reiterated a similar point about philosophy (see this *Huffington Post* story: http://www.huffingtonpost.com/massimo-pigliucci/neil-degrasse-tyson-and-the-value-of-philosophy_b_5330216.html; last accessed May 16, 2014).
6. *The Problems of Philosophy*, p. 158.
7. Ibid.
8. Throughout the text, WP refers to the English-language edition of *What is Philosophy?* and QP to the French edition, *Qu'est-ce que la philosophie?*
9. *The Problems of Philosophy*, p. 159.
10. Benedict de Spinoza, *Collected Works of Spinoza*, Vol. 1, trans. and ed. Edwin Curley (Princeton: Princeton University Press, 1985), p. 246, Axiom 11 of Principles of Descartes' Philosophy.
11. Ibid., *Ethics* 1P11Dem., p. 417.
12. See Michael Della Rocca, *Spinoza* (Routledge: New York, 2008), p. 1: "Spinoza's philosophy is characterized by perhaps the boldest and most thoroughgoing commitment ever to appear in the history of philosophy to the intelligibility of everything." This commitment, Della Rocca later explains, "can best be articulated in terms of his commitments to the Principle of Sufficient reason and to his naturalism" (p. 4).
13. G. W. F. Leibniz, *Monadology* §31–2, trans. George Montgomery (La Salle: Open Court, 1988), p. 258.
14. See Gilles Deleuze, *Difference and Repetition*, trans. Paul Patton (New York: Columbia University Press, 1994), p. xix: "We propose to think difference in itself independently of the forms of representation which reduce it to the Same, and the relation of different to different independently of those forms which make them pass through the negative."
15. Gilles Deleuze, *Expressionism and Philosophy: Spinoza*, trans. Martin Joughin (New York: Zone, 1990), p. 228.
16. Ibid., p. 323.
17. Ibid.
18. Ibid., pp. 323–4.
19. The same is largely true for Spinoza as well, on Deleuze's reading. See *Expressionism in Philosophy: Spinoza*, p. 135: "The cause as sufficient reason is what, being given, means that all the thing's properties are also given, and, being withdrawn, means that all the properties are withdrawn with it."

20. Gilles Deleuze, *The Fold: Leibniz and the Baroque*, trans. Tom Conley (Minneapolis: University of Minnesota Press, 1993), p. 53.
21. Ibid., p. 55.
22. Ibid., p. 53.
23. Ibid., p. 137.
24. Ibid.
25. Ibid.
26. See my *Deleuze's Hume: Philosophy, Culture and the Scottish Enlightenment* (Edinburgh: Edinburgh University Press, 2009).
27. Gilles Deleuze, "Immanence: A Life," in *Pure Immanence: Essays on A Life*, trans. Anne Boyman (New York: Zone, 2001), p. 27.
28. We will use the all-capitals form of A LIFE to highlight Deleuze's argument that it is "the immanence of immanence, absolute immanence."
29. Gilles Deleuze and Félix Guattari, *A Thousand Plateaus: Capitalism and Schizophrenia*, trans. Brian Massumi (Minneapolis: University of Minnesota Press, 1987), p. 203.
30. Ibid.
31. Gottlob Frege, "Comment on Sinn and Bedeutung," in *The Frege Reader*, ed. Michael Beaney (Oxford: Blackwell, 1997), p. 178. The standard translation of *bedeutungslos* is "meaningless" but that implies a word will have no sense; Frege's point is precisely that it may lack reference, and hence be *bedeutungslos* while still having sense, as in the case of fiction.
32. See *Phaedrus* 265e: "That of dividing things again by classes, where the natural joints are, and not trying to break any part, after the manner of a bad carver." In *The Collected Dialogues of Plato*, trans. Lane Cooper, ed. Edith Hamilton and Huntington Cairns (Princeton: Princeton University Press, 2005).
33. As Whitehead said, "The safest general characterization of the European philosophical tradition is that it consists of a series of footnotes to Plato" (*Process and Reality* (New York: Free Press, 1979), p. 39).
34. It is no secret that Russell sought to align philosophy with the sciences. See especially Russell's essay, "On Scientific Method in Philosophy," in *Mysticism and Logic and Other Essays* (London: George Allen & Unwin, 1910). See also the work of the new realists, work that was inspired by Russell, in Edwin B. Holt, Walter T. Marvin, W. P. Montague, Ralph Barton Perry, Walter B. Pitkin, and Edward Gleason Spaulding, "The Program and First Platform of Six Realists," in *Journal of Philosophy and Psychology* VII (1910), which was a manifesto published by six philosophers in support of efforts to adopt the methods of science in philosophy. This essay was later expanded into a book by the same authors, *The New Realists* (New York: Macmillan, 1912).
35. For more on this see especially Michael Della Rocca's "Taming of Philosophy," in *Philosophy and its History*, ed. Mogens Lærke, Justin E. H. Smith, and Eric Schliesser (Oxford: Oxford University Press, 2013).

36. *Meno* 71a, in *The Collected Dialogues of Plato.*
37. St Augustine follows Plato on this. See his essay "The Teacher," in *Augustine: Earlier Writings* (Westminster: John Knox Press, 1953), p. 100: "When the teachers have expounded by means of words all the disciplines which they profess to teach, the disciplines also of virtue and wisdom, then their pupils take thought within themselves whether what they have been told is true, looking to the inward truth": that is, to the truth already within one. "Our real Teacher . . . who is so listened to, who is said to dwell in the inner man, namely Christ" (p. 95).
38. *Difference and Repetition*, p. 23.
39. Ibid., p. 22.
40. Gilles Deleuze, *Desert Islands and Other Texts 1953–1974*, trans. Michael Taormina (New York: Semiotext[e]), p. 96.
41. Gilles Deleuze, cited in Robin Mackay, ed., *Collapse Vol. II: Speculative Realism* (Falmouth: Urbanomic, 2007), p. 41.
42. For more on the importance of dynamic systems theory in Deleuze, and especially the notion of the edge of chaos, see my *Philosophy at the Edge of Chaos: Gilles Deleuze and the Philosophy of Difference* (Toronto: University of Toronto Press, 2006). See also Manuel DeLanda, *Intensive Science and Virtual Philosophy* (London: Bloomsbury Academic, 2005).

1

What is a Concept?

If the distinctive task of philosophy is to create concepts, or, as Deleuze and Guattari argue, if "the concept belongs to philosophy and only to philosophy" (WP 34/QP 37), then let us start with the obvious question: what is involved in creating a concept and why do concepts belong "only to philosophy"?

To begin, let us return to the example of the joiner from the Introduction. The joiner "lays claim to wood" and says "'I am a friend of wood'" (WP 9/QP 14), and as a friend of wood the joiner *knows* wood; they *know* a variety of techniques for joining wood – which woods work best for given circumstances, which joints to use, glues, and so on. A good joiner, therefore, or a joiner who can make a strong claim to wood, knows the right way to go about doing what it is that joiners do. Similarly for the "forester, the lumberjack, and the carpenter" (ibid.) who also lay claim to wood – they too, if they can make a strong claim to wood, will know what is necessary in order to do what foresters, lumberjacks, and carpenters do. We can even imagine some of what it is necessary to know – a forester, for instance, would know how to identify sick trees, forest fire risks, and so on. But what does the philosopher know who lays claim to the concept? More importantly, what does the philosopher know that gives them a strong and exclusive claim to the concept?

We must be careful here, for while it is indeed important for joiners, and so on, to acquire the knowledge they will need in order to perform their duties, what is of primary interest for Deleuze and Guattari is not the knowledge or set of rules one is able to apply in any given circumstance, but rather it is the learning process that resulted in the acquisition of this knowledge. To recall our earlier example of learning to drive a stick shift car, while it may be easy to state the rule one is to follow in shifting gears (press on the clutch to change gears, and release the clutch and press the accelerator to engage the gear, and so on), the learning process itself is not nearly as simple as the stated rule, as anyone who has learned to drive a stick shift car will know. Finding the precise point of transition between releasing the clutch and pressing the accelerator can be quite difficult to do, and it is a problem that can be compounded if one is starting on a hill where the shift into first gear needs to be accomplished quickly if one is to avoid rolling back down the hill! The interaction between these various elements – clutch, accelerator, incline of the road, and so on – involves singular inflection points that, on first encounter, are surprising and unfamiliar; the learning driver, as a result, will frequently be seen lurching down the road, or they might stall the car while attempting to shift into first. In time, the learner becomes habituated to these singular points as these points come to be related to one another in a consistent manner that then become routinized as one comes to know how to drive a stick shift car. With these habits in place, the knowledgeable driver is even able to drive an unfamiliar car and adjust quickly to its tighter or looser clutch.[1] It is at this point that the driver can make a strong claim to being a friend of the stick shift car, or they are in possession of the knowledge necessary to do what stick shift drivers do – they may even be able to state what it is they know in the form of a simple rule, "release the clutch while pressing on the accelerator."[2]

The point for Deleuze, however, and this is stressed in *Difference and Repetition*, is that learning is a distinct process from knowledge and ought not to be confused with, or placed in subservience to, knowledge – in other words, learning is not simply the means to the end of acquiring knowledge. As Deleuze puts it, "Learning is the appropriate name for the subjective acts carried out when one is confronted with the objectivity of a problem (Idea), whereas knowledge designates only the generality of concepts or the calm possession of a rule enabling solutions."[3] Once one knows how to drive a stick shift car, one can lay claim to "the calm possession of a rule," but learning is quite a different story, for it is the encounter with singular points (signs) – hand *and* stick shift, foot *and* pedals, car *and* road, and so on – that, for Deleuze, constitutes the "objectivity of a problem (Idea)." How can hand *and* stick shift, foot *and* pedal, car *and* road be brought together such that I can drive down the road without lurching or stalling the car? This is the objectivity of the problem. Of course, in learning to drive a stick shift car, one knows in advance what the solution to the problem will be – and, given time, one will overcome the problem space of the encounter and be able to engage the gears and successfully drive the car. Examples such as this feed the assumption that questions and problems are subservient to the answers and solutions that resolve them, or as Deleuze puts it, "solutions tend to abruptly replace the movement of problems with the rigidity and stasis of a true cover up."[4] We know in advance what a successful driver of a stick shift car does, and thus once one has attained that state of knowledge the problem space of learning is replaced and forgotten in a "true cover up."

If we shift to another example, and to one more in line with what is involved in creating concepts, then we can begin to clarify the sense in which problems have an objectivity that is distinct from and not a means to the solutions that resolve them and cover them up in the process. Let us take Leibniz's example of the veins in the block of marble which he uses to argue for innate ideas and to criticize Locke's claim that all knowledge comes from experience, or that the mind is a blank slate (*tabula rasa*) upon which all our experience and subsequent knowledge are recorded. When the sculptor comes to a block of marble, Leibniz asks whether this block is indeed a *tabula rasa* that is "entirely neutral as to whether it assumes this shape [of Hercules] or some other," or whether there might be "veins in the block which marked out the shape of Hercules rather than other shapes."[5] Understood in this way, the sculptor does not simply impose the shape they want to create upon a neutral block of marble; rather, the sculptor works with and discovers the veins in the marble, its singular points and thresholds, and in doing so they come to reveal the shape that was already innate in the marble. "This is how ideas and truths are innate in us," Leibniz concludes, "as inclinations, dispositions, tendencies, or natural potentialities, and not as actualities; although these potentialities are always accompanied by certain actualities, often insensible ones, which correspond to them."[6] The objectivity of the problem, therefore, is not encountered as an obstacle or hindrance that stands in the way of realizing a predetermined end – such as the example of learning to drive a stick shift car might lead one to believe – but the problem consists of the singular points and signs (for example, veins) that are encountered along the way. The sculptor follows the veins without knowing where this process will lead. This is the "movement of problems" that is covered up and hidden by the "rigidity and stasis" of solutions, and yet even in Leibniz's example we have the "rigidity and stasis" of the hidden Hercules, the already completed shape that needs simply to be revealed by the labors of the sculptor. Deleuze and Guattari, by contrast, argue that the objectivity of the problem is objective and real precisely because it does not prefigure or predetermine the actuality that will come to be and then disappear within the solution as the actualization process is completed (for example, once the Hercules sculpture is complete). The "problematic structure," Deleuze argues, "is part of objects themselves [that is, the actualized solutions], allowing them to be grasped as signs, just as the questioning or problematizing instance is a part of knowledge allowing its positivity and specificity to be grasped in the act of learning."[7] In other words, the problematic structure does not vanish with the actuality of objects but remains as the "signs" that may elicit further responses and give rise to problems and to further learning. Learning itself, moreover, is inseparable from the actual encounters with and between actual objects – an actual foot and pedal, for instance – and it is for this reason that we can say that *something* is being "grasped in the act of learning."

A concept, as we will now begin to detail, is inseparable from a "problematic structure," or a problem space, and it is the objectivity and reality of this problematic structure that account for why concepts are such provocateurs of thought. To begin to clarify these points, and in particular to illustrate the relationship between problems and concepts, we can turn to Hume, and in particular to the section on "abstract ideas" from *A Treatise of Human Nature.*

§1

Hume begins his section on abstract ideas stating his intention to defend Berkeley's claim that general or abstract ideas "are nothing but particular ones, annexed to a certain term, which gives them a more extensive signification, and makes them recall upon occasion other individuals, which are similar to them."[8] When I consider the concept or abstract idea of a baobab tree, for example, according to Berkeley I am simply thinking of a particular baobab tree – perhaps the tree as I recall it from the film *Lion King* – and then I am capable of connecting this particular image and idea to the term, "baobab tree," a term which can then be extended to other similar examples. To use another example, when my daughters first learned to use the word "cat," or "kiddykat" to be precise, they used the word not only to refer to other cats but they also called the raccoon on our back patio a "kiddykat." Berkeley's explanation, which Hume largely supports, is that the word is being extended to examples similar to the particular idea and image of a cat from which they began. With time and experience (and parental correctives), my daughters learned to differentiate between "cats" and "raccoons." The strength of Berkeley's approach, according to Hume, is that it enables us to avoid a dilemma regarding the relationship between the abstract idea and the content from which this idea is abstracted. On the one hand, the "abstract idea of a man," to use Hume's example, cannot represent "men of all sizes and all qualities"; nor, on the other hand, can it represent no particular qualities at all. If an abstract idea were to be expected to do the former, then it would entail "an infinite capacity in the mind," but since this is impossible according to Hume, "it has been commonly infer'd in favour of the latter" possibility, that abstract ideas are not about anything in particular.[9] Hume will argue against the second possibility as well, for the abstract idea is indeed about something. To resolve the dilemma, Hume will argue that while "the capacity of the mind be not infinite," he will nonetheless claim that "we can at once form a notion of all possible degrees of quantity and quality, in such a manner at least, as, however imperfect, may serve all the purposes of reflexion and conversation."[10]

Without retracing all the steps of Hume's arguments, we can focus on Hume's founding principle that "all ideas are deriv'd from impressions, and are nothing but copies and representations of them," and thus since we cannot have an impression that does not have a "determinate quantity and quality, the case must be the same with its copy or representative (that is, with an idea)."[11] Agreeing with Berkeley, therefore, Hume concludes that "Abstract ideas are therefore in themselves individual, however they may become general in their representation." An abstract idea becomes general in its representation as we acquire a sense of all the "possible degrees of quantity and quality in such an imperfect manner as may serve the purposes of life," and we do this through becoming habituated in our ability to apply the "same name" to several objects that resemble each other, regardless of "whatever differences we may observe in the degrees of their quantity and quality, and whatever other differences may appear among them."[12] What happens, then, when we conceive an abstract idea is that the word, although it is not "able to revive the idea of all these individuals," or even the indeterminate number of individuals to which it could apply (for this would involve an infinite capacity of mind), what it does do is that it "revives the custom" or habit which "produces any other individual one, for which we may have occasion." Hume thus offers a pragmatic solution to the dilemma – through habituation we grasp enough of the quality and quantity of an abstract idea that is necessary for the purposes of life, and in conversation with others our habits usually lead us to use the right word, though, as was the case with my daughters, we may need to be corrected.

Hume's solution to the dilemma, however, and as the last point intimates, opens the door to skepticism, as Hume himself recognizes. When discussing the influence of "general rules" as a form of "unphilosophical probability," or prejudice, Hume offers the example of a prejudice of his time – to wit, that an "Irishman cannot have wit, and a Frenchman cannot have solidity."[13] One will continue to maintain such prejudices, Hume argues, even "tho' the conversation of the former [Irishman] be visibly agreeable, and of the latter [Frenchman] very judicious."[14] In accounting for such prejudices, Hume argues that they arise for the same reason we come to our judgments regarding cause and effect – that is, they are "deriv'd from habit and experience; and when we have been accustom'd to see one object united to another, our imagination passes from the first to the second, by a natural transition, which precedes reflection, and which cannot be prevented by it."[15] In other words, much as habit and human nature will lead us "by a natural transition, which precedes reflection" to assume that where there is smoke there is fire, or lead us to extend the use of the word "cat" to a raccoon, so too will we extend our prejudices and judge, despite appearances to the contrary, that the witty and conversational Irishman and judicious Frenchman must nonetheless "be dunces or fops in spite of sense and reason."[16] If habit and experience are the source of all our knowledge and judgments, therefore, then what assurances do we have that the habits and judgments we have acquired reflect the nature of the world as it really is? In short, we have no such assurances, and Hume famously ends the first book of his *Treatise* lamenting,

> My memory of past errors and perplexities, makes me diffident for the future. The wretched condition, weakness, and disorder of the faculties, I must employ in my enquiries, increase my apprehensions. And the impossibility of amending or correcting these faculties, reduces me almost to despair, and makes me resolve to perish on the barren rock, on which I am at present, rather than venture myself upon that boundless ocean, which runs out into immensity.[17]

Hume thus confronts the problem space for knowledge, a problem space that looks for its solution in extension, though a solution Hume despairs of finding, for what he is left with is the concept of belief, and belief for Hume is nothing less than the strength and vivacity with which one idea is associated with another.[18] This belief, however, may, as Hume was well aware, be ill founded, if not outright delusional. Amidst the "boundless ocean" of A LIFE and the infinite fund of potential experiences that "runs out into immensity," our limited and finite encounters have given rise to a set of habits and "abstract ideas" that may well become undone as a result of future encounters that come with the vast, boundless ocean of future experience. For Hume, therefore, the philosopher is one who is constantly in tension with their natural propensities, their established habits. Through reflection upon these habits, the philosopher hopes to induce a healthy skepticism that problematizes these habits and thereby facilitate the creation of concepts that are not simply the products of habit but are the result of reflecting upon and offering *corrections* to the abstract ideas our habits give rise to. Despite these efforts, there are no assurances that the philosopher has gotten it right; they may still be suffering from delusion.[19]

For Deleuze and Guattari, however, the concept is not to be understood in terms of its extension, and hence the problem is not one of correcting our habits in order to get the extension right. For Deleuze and Guattari, it is the task of science to get the extension right. There is, however, more than extension, as Frege importantly recognized when he argued for the distinction between intension and extension, or what he referred to as the sense (*Sinn*)/ reference (*Bedeutung*) distinction. This distinction becomes exceedingly important to Frege's own project and will have a tremendous influence upon twentieth-century Anglo-American philosophy. To clarify the distinction, Frege offers what is now his famous example of the morning star and evening star. When they were thought of as two different stars, the reality, unbeknownst to those who thought they were different, was that they were simply thinking about the same object (extension) in two different ways (intension). This distinction also helps to clarify what is at work in fictional stories where one can understand the sense (intension) of the narrative even if there is no corresponding person or state of affairs to which this narrative refers (extension). Is the sacking of Troy simply a fictional tale told by Homer that lacks an actual referent to events that happened in the world, or did it actually happen?[20] Despite this distinction, Frege called upon philosophy to be concerned with propositions in the scientific sense; that is, they are to work with propositions and set out to determine the extensions that function as the truth conditions of a proposition. The proposition, "The King of France is bald," for example, would be true if there were a King of France who is bald. We will explore this theme in much greater detail in Chapter 6, but for the moment it should be stressed that Deleuze and Guattari reject a purely extensional approach to the concept, and propose instead an alternative. Their reasoning is as follows:

> Confusing concept and proposition produces a belief in the existence of scientific concepts and a view of the proposition as a genuine 'intension' (what the sentence expresses). Consequently, the philosophical concept usually appears only as a proposition deprived of sense. This confusion reigns in logic and explains its infantile idea of philosophy. Concepts are measured against a 'philosophical' grammar that replaces them with propositions extracted from the sentences in which they appear. We are constantly trapped between alternative propositions and do not see that the concept has already passed into the excluded middle. The concept is not a proposition at all; it is not propositional, and the proposition is never an intension. (WP 22/QP 27)

As we will explore later in Chapter 6, the "infantile idea of philosophy" Deleuze and Guattari rail against is the assumption that the philosophical concept can be reduced to syntactics alone – that is, to an extensional system of rules, customs, and habits (a "philosophical" grammar) without any concern for the semantics or "intension" of the concept. Quine is perhaps the most famous proponent of the extensional approach. This is especially evident in Quine's well-known essay on Carnap, where Quine challenged Carnap's distinction between internal and external questions.[21] Put briefly, for Carnap there is a role for intension but it is to be understood systemically with respect to other aspects of the language. For Carnap there are internal questions regarding a language, which consist of determining the systemic relationship between the terms of the language, and there are external questions which consist of determining whether or not a language is successful at telling us about the world. While Carnap does maintain the intension/extension distinction, the intension of a term, Quine argues, remains subordinate to the extensional role of representing the world. Quine's move to challenge the internal/external distinction thus rests upon what Quine sees as Carnap's move to make internal questions reducible to external questions.[22] In Deleuze and Guattari's view, however, a concept is solely intensional and is not to be confused with the extensional nature of propositions, or with the extensional bifurcation that comes with this – that is, the law of the excluded middle whereby either a proposition or its negation is true.

As Deleuze and Guattari will argue, it is the intensional concept as objectivity of a problem that is the condition for the possibility of propositions in the first place, and hence for the law of the excluded middle they bring in their wake. To begin to gain a foothold on the arguments Deleuze and Guattari offer to support this claim, it is important first to understand the transcendental turn in philosophy, a turn that Kant famously initiated in response to Hume's skepticism (it was Hume, Kant claimed, who woke him from his dogmatic slumber). There has been a tremendous amount written on Deleuze's own version of the transcendental turn – namely, his transcendental empiricism – which we will have occasion to encounter again in later chapters. For the purposes of this chapter, and to point towards the nature of the concept and what creating concepts might entail, we will turn now to the philosopher Deleuze and Guattari recognize as one who did give due weight to the intensional nature of the concept (recall the contrast we made in the introduction between Russell and Hegel/Schelling) – we turn to Hegel.

§2

Turning to Hegel might be a surprising move in a book about Deleuze and Guattari; after all, the differences between their two projects are quite substantive. Deleuze sets out to pursue a philosophy of difference that does not reduce difference to being simply a mediation of opposites (as Hegel argues), and at numerous points Deleuze and Deleuze and Guattari refer to their projects as anti-Hegelian.[23] Despite their stolidly anti-Hegelian stance, Deleuze and Guattari do follow Hegel in one very important respect – like Hegel, they claim that the nature of the concept does not consist of its extensional relationships (as it did for Hume, Frege, Russell, Quine, and many others) but rather what is essential to the concept is its immanent, intensional (or intensive, as Deleuze and Guattari will also refer to it) self-positing. To sketch Hegel's theory of concepts, and to contrast Hegel's theory with Deleuze and Guattari's Spinozist theory, let us turn first to Hegel's critique of Spinoza.[24]

At the heart of Hegel's critique of Spinoza is the issue upon which Hegel and Spinoza agree – in short, they agree that there is a simple, absolute substance. Where Hegel and Spinoza disagree is on how Spinoza understands the nature of this absolute substance. In particular, Hegel will argue that Spinoza ventures down the wrong path when he distinguishes between the absolute substance that is conceived through itself and the modes or individual substances that are not conceived through themselves but by way of another – proximately by other modes and ultimately by the nature of absolute substance. On Hegel's reading of Spinoza, then, "We have before us two determinations, the universal or what has being in and for itself, and secondly the determination of the particular and singular, that is, individuality."[25] A consequence of this move for Hegel is that a singular thing "does not have genuine actuality," and thus the absolute substance for Spinoza is an "abstract unity," removed from individuality; hence "there is then no development, no life, no spirituality or activity."[26] What Spinoza must do, and what Hegel believes he has done with his system, is to show how the particular and the individual are the very *life* of the absolute substance, part of its self-development. Hegel does praise Spinoza for recognizing the importance of the One absolute substance: "The great merit of the Spinozist way of thinking in philosophy is its renunciation of everything determinate and particular, and its orientation solely to the one." In the final analysis, however, Hegel argues that this One "is something utterly fixed and immobile."[27] What is needed for philosophy, Hegel concludes, is to conceive the One as self-development – "This," Hegel claims, "is a fundamental concept in all speculation – return into self within the other."[28]

In further developing this "fundamental concept in all speculation" of a return into self within the other, Hegel makes an important distinction between the good and bad infinite. The bad infinite results when one has not yet returned "into self within the other," and the other remains just that, other. For example, if in counting to any number, as high as you please, the bad infinite assumes I can add another number, or for every number, n, there is an-*other* number, $n + 1$. As Hegel states it in the *Jena Logic*, the bad infinite is "just an alternation of the positing and sublating of the limit and of the self-equivalent unity. Because there is immediately in each of them the requirement of the other, both continue *in infinitum*."[29] In other words, as long as we have the alternation of a finite limit and the other, n + 1, beyond it rather than the recognition of each in the other, then we have the continuing alternation *in infinitum*, or we have the bad infinite. The good infinite, by contrast, is "not a series that always has its completion in some other yet always has this other outside itself"; to the contrary, "the other is in the determinate itself; it is a contradiction, absolute on its own account: and this is the true essence of determinacy."[30] The good infinite, therefore, is, from the perspective of the fundamental conception in all speculation, the "return into self within the other," or infinity is the "absolute contradiction" that is "not a 'beyond', but simple connection, pure absolute movement, being-outside-itself within being-within-itself."[31] Hegel's theory of the concept follows from this latter point. The concept is not tied to an external other to which it is related – *it is not extensional* – but it is itself an "absolute contradiction," or the movement of the "being-outside-itself within being-within-itself." A concept is a pure and absolute self-movement (or self-positing, as Deleuze and Guattari put it), and the extensional relations between concepts and the states of affairs to which they refer are to be understood in light of this fundamental self-movement.[32] For Hegel, then, "the real concept" is nothing less than the fact that it has "become itself from its being other, or that in its being other it is itself."[33]

We can now restate Hegel's critique of Spinoza. When Spinoza argues that God is an absolutely infinite substance, Hegel claims that Spinoza conceives of the infinite substance in terms of the bad infinite. As an abstract unity that does not return to self by way of the otherness of determinacy, Spinoza's theory of absolute substance remains mired in abstraction and the bad infinite. Deleuze and Guattari, however, remain deeply committed to a Spinozist project, and they openly praise Spinoza on numerous occasions, referring to him as both "the prince of philosophers" (WP 48/QP 49) and the "Christ of philosophers" (WP 60/QP 59). Are Deleuze and Guattari thus subject to Hegel's critique? Do they succumb to an abstract conception of the One, as philosophers such as Alain Badiou argue, and to a notion of the bad infinite?[34]

At first sight, it might appear that Deleuze and Deleuze and Guattari are indeed susceptible to a Hegelian critique. In *Difference and Repetition*, for instance, when discussing the relationship between problem-questions and solutions, Deleuze argues that "there are no ultimate or original responses or solutions, there are only problem-questions, in the guise of a mask behind every mask and a displacement behind every place."[35] A problem-question, as we saw earlier, becomes hidden in the true cover up of the solution, and yet behind each cover up and mask there is yet another, and so on *in infinitum*. Deleuze is explicit on this point: "Behind the masks, therefore, are further masks, and even the most hidden is still a hiding place, and so on to infinity."[36] In a related manner, Deleuze argues later in *Difference and Repetition* that, for every phenomenon that appears, there is an intensive difference or differential, what Deleuze calls a doubled difference, that lay masked or hidden, and this differential involves its own terms that likewise mask further intensive differences or differentials, and so on *in infinitum*. Deleuze refers to this "state of infinitely doubled difference which resonates to infinity *disparity* [*disparité*]," and "Disparity," Deleuze claims in true Spinozist fashion, "is the sufficient reason of all phenomena, the condition of that which appears."[37] Is this not simply what Hegel calls the bad infinite – the alternating relation between problem-questions and solutions, or between phenomena and intensive differences, that continues *in infinitum* without returning the other into the self that it is?

Hegel's critique has the potential to become especially damning as we come to realize the importance of the infinite in *What is Philosophy?* To take the most important case of many instances where the infinite plays a role, the infinite is integral to Deleuze and Guattari's very understanding of a concept: "The concept is defined by the inseparability of a finite number of heterogeneous components traversed by a point of absolute survey at infinite speed" (WP 21/QP 26). An equally important notion within *What is Philosophy?*, as we will see in later chapters, is chaos. For reasons to be discussed below, a concept must be a "fragmentary whole," Deleuze and Guattari argue, for "only on this condition can it escape the mental chaos constantly threatening it, stalking it, trying to reabsorb it" (WP 16/QP 21). And chaos itself is defined in terms of the infinite: "In fact, chaos is characterized less by the absence of determinations than by the infinite speed with which they take shape and vanish" (WP 42/QP 44). So how do Deleuze and Guattari understand the infinite in these cases? Are they susceptible to a Hegelian critique of succumbing to the bad infinite?[38]

To show that Deleuze and Guattari have not fallen into an extensional view of concepts that relies upon a notion of the bad infinite, we will need to show how they understand the manner in which a concept is self-positing and how, more importantly, this entails an understanding of difference that is not the difference of opposing terms, which is how they believe Hegel understands difference; rather, it is a difference in itself that is the transcendental condition ("a transcendental lived reality," or A LIFE, as this was discussed in the Introduction) for the possibility of identifiable terms and the exclusive, mutually opposing relations between them.[39] To develop these arguments, Deleuze drew heavily from the calculus, and these arguments will tie in to much of what Deleuze and Guattari say about concepts, the infinite, and chaos. It is to this topic that we now turn, for by doing so, we will find ourselves further along the way in clarifying what Deleuze and Guattari take to be the nature of philosophical concepts and what is involved in creating them.

§3

To highlight the significance of the calculus for Deleuze, and the role it will play in the understanding Deleuze and Guattari have of concepts that is neither extensional (*à la* Russell and Frege) nor a Hegelian intensional unity of opposites, we can begin with an important, though often overlooked, argument of José Benardete. In his book *Infinity: An Essay in Metaphysics*, Benardete draws heavily upon what he calls the Zeno procedure, or what for Deleuze and Guattari we might call the problem space of the Zeno procedure. The problem, in short, is whether one can successfully carry out an infinite task in a finite amount of time – for example, if I count one star in the first half-minute, another in the next quarter-minute, another in the next eighth of a minute, and so on *in infinitum*, will I have counted an infinite number of stars at the end of a minute? For Kant, the answer is clearly no, for we cannot synthesize an infinite number of representations[40]; for Hegel, similarly, the problem is misstated for it presupposes the bad infinite, the infinite that relies upon there being one count followed by an-*other* count, followed by another, and so on *in infinitum*. But is there another alternative, an alternative that neither succumbs to the bad infinite nor takes refuge in Hegel's unity of opposites? Benardete offers an example to show that there is indeed another alternative. Benardete states the example of a stick of wood that has a Z written on the right hand end of the stick. If one performs a Zeno procedure on this stick, the result, as Benardete states it, is the following:

> Is it at all possible to sever the infinitesimal tail from the rest of the stick? The answer is, yes. Let us first cut the stick in half and inscribe the number 1 on the right-hand end of the butt-end of the left-hand piece. Now let us throw the left-hand piece into a box, leaving the right-hand piece on the table. Next, we shall cut this latter piece again in half, inscribing the number 2 on the right-hand butt-end of the new left-hand piece . . . Once more we shall cut the Z piece in half, &c. ad infinitum. At the end of the minute we shall have an infinite number of pieces in the box, each being of some rational length, and lying on the table there will be a single infinitesimal chip with the Z plainly marked on one side.[41]

Most significantly for our purposes, Benardete adds that while we have the infinitesimal lying on the table, "there was no specifiable cut which severed the infinitesimal chip from the rest of the stick."[42] In other words, Benardete is arguing that "there is no actual point of separation (be it rational or irrational) between the infinitesimal tail [that is, the Z chip] of any closed continuum and the main body," and yet, as his example is intended to show, we nonetheless have a separable infinitesimal. The conclusion to draw, according to Benardete – and Deleuze and Guattari, as will be argued here, is that the infinitesimal is not to be confused with the processes and procedures we identify with extensive magnitudes – for example, with specifiable cuts and points of separation. The way to understand such infinitesimals, therefore, is as intensive magnitudes that are real but are yet not the extensive magnitudes of the stick; nor are they to be identified with each of the specifiable, determinate cuts of the stick. It is this infinitesimal that offers us the alternative Deleuze himself seeks,[43] for the infinitesimal is neither a minimal extensive magnitude, an irreducible and determinate point that brings an infinite regress to an end (*it is what is left over* after *an infinite regress and not the end point that is included within the regress itself*); and the infinitesimal is obviously not an extensive continuum or totality, for the infinitesimal (the Z chip) is precisely what is eliminable from the stick *after* an infinite totality of cuts! The infinitesimal is also immune to Hegel's charge of the bad infinite for precisely the reason that it is not an extensive magnitude in relation to a determinate other, to an-other extensive magnitude, and so on *in infinitum*. The infinitesimal sidesteps the bad infinite and is, rather, as Deleuze will argue, the condition for the possibility of extensive relations between terms.

Deleuze's turn to the calculus, and in particular the role differentials play in the calculus, dovetails quite significantly with Benardete's arguments. Deleuze will argue, along the same lines as Benardete, that differentials are intensive magnitudes that are inseparable from and yet irreducible to an infinite series.[44] More precisely, Deleuze adopts the Leibnizian conception of differentials. In the differential relation dy/dx, for example, as y and x become infinitely small, we end up with $dy = 0$ and $dx = 0$ (or $dy/dx = 0/0$, as it was commonly written in the seventeenth and eighteenth centuries). As x and y become infinitely small, we end up doing away with the terms themselves but not with the differential relation itself (the infinitesimal or Z chip). In fact, key to the calculus and Deleuze is the very notion that, at the limit, as the determinate terms tend towards zero, they do not result in the indeterminate and undifferentiated, as would ordinarily be the case when a determinate quantity is divided by zero; rather, what we end up with is an intensive difference (Benardete's Z chip) that is not to be confused with extensive quantities and differences. This is the differential relation or infinitesimal that subsists even when the terms have been eliminated, or, as Deleuze will frequently put it, the relation is irreducible (or external, as he will often say) to the terms.[45]

With the differential in hand, we are a short step away from what I will argue is at the core of Deleuze's metaphysics – namely, his theory of multiplicity. What gets us from differentials (infinitesimals) that are irreducible to their determinate, extensive terms to a multiplicity is the fact that, for Deleuze, differentials – intensive differences – presuppose other differentials, and so on *ad infinitum*. For example, as x and y become infinitely small and approach zero in the differential relation dy/dx, we end up with a differential relation that is irreducible to the determinate, extensive terms of the differential itself, but the differential can come to be identified with the limit of the relations. In other words, the differential relation can come to be seen as identical to the determinate, extensive limit that is reached as x and y become zero, or in the differential relation $dy/dx = z$, it is the determinate value or limit z that takes on – in a true cover up – the identity of the differential relation as x and y become infinitely small. Z may be, for example, the determinate slope of the trigonometric tangent on a circle, or the determinate slope of any curve.[46] On this reading, therefore, every determinate, finite term can be understood as the limit of a differential relation. Deleuze, however, is interested in the absolute nature of the infinite, the absolutely infinite or unlimited (*a-peiron* in Greek[47]). As a result, each determinate finite phenomenon is not simply to be understood as the determinate limit of a differential relation, but more importantly for Deleuze, each of the terms of this relation is itself the limit of yet another differential relation, and so on *ad infinitum*. In other words, and as the fundamental theorem of the calculus argues, the derivative of a function gives us the determinate slope of the tangent, and this can become in turn the antiderivative or integral that is the infinite sum of infinitesimals.[48] This relation between a determinate phenomenon (the slope of the tangent one reaches through the derivative of a function) and an infinite sum of intensive differences and infinitesimals (the integral) is what Deleuze, as we have seen, calls disparity. To be clear, however, Deleuze is not doing calculus; he is doing philosophy, and moreover the calculus should not be seen as the model one should adopt in making sense of Deleuze's thought. The main reason for this is that Deleuze rejects the notion of limits that is central to the calculus as well as set theory (see Chapter 5, example 10) and adopts instead a Spinozist metaphysics of infinite substance without limits. Determinate, finite limits are the illusory quasi-effects of the differentials, of the infinitesimals in Benardete's sense.[49] When Deleuze and Guattari discuss the components of a concept, therefore, they do indeed argue that these components "remain distinct," but they add that

> something passes from one to the other, something that is undecidable between them. There is an area *ab* that belongs to both *a* and *b*, where *a* and *b* "become" indiscernible. These zones, thresholds, or becomings, this inseparability, define the internal consistency of the concept. (WP 19–20/QP 25)

The infinitesimal or differential, as well as the integral and infinite sum of infinitesimals, is precisely the "area *ab*," and this area is not a determinate third term or limit upon which *a* and *b* converge, a finite minimum for instance; nor is it a determinate sum and totality of infinitesimals, a maximum. It is, rather, the intensive, intensional condition for the possibility of differentiating between *a* and *b*. What allows for the possibility of this "area *ab*," for the "internal consistency of the concept" that conditions the possibility for the actualization of determinate, individuated terms, and hence the differences between *a* and *b*, for instance, is A LIFE, a problematic multiplicity. This point cannot be stressed enough, and in *Difference and Repetition* Deleuze will indeed stress this point and argue, in true Spinozist fashion, that multiplicity (or "disparity"[50]) is the sufficient reason of all that appears, "the true substantive, substance itself."[51]

From Deleuze's perspective, therefore, Hegel is right to criticize the bad infinite, but for Deleuze this is because the bad infinite presupposes the extensive relation between a determinate finite limit and the determinate other that is beyond it, rather than, as Hegel argues, because the self has failed to incorporate its opposed other as itself. Hegel's view, moreover, continues to rely upon the primacy and reality of the limits themselves, for it is the opposition of limits that constitutes absolute contradiction for Hegel, or the real concept. For Deleuze, by contrast, the limits are not real but are only the abstract, ideal limits that a multiplicity resists or staves off (we will discuss this further in Chapter 2). As an assemblage of differentials (infinitesimals), moreover, a multiplicity is not to be confused with the determinate, spatio-temporal properties and qualities with which they come to be identified. Each and every determinate phenomenon thus presupposes as its sufficient reason – and hence Deleuze and Deleuze and Guattari's adherence to the Principle of Sufficient Reason – an assemblage of differentials (infinitesimals), or what Deleuze will also call singularities and signs (as we have seen). If a given phenomenon were to be self-identical and did not presuppose disparity or multiplicity as its sufficient reason, then we would have a brute, determinate phenomenon or fact, a fact without a reason other than an-other fact, and so on *ad infinitum.* This approach, however, entails accepting brute facts and the primacy of finite limits (this is even true, as we will see below, with respect to Cantor's understanding of the transfinite [see Chapter 5, example 10]), while at the same time rejecting the PSR along with the infinite. Although this is precisely the approach of Russell, Moore, and most of the post-Kantian tradition, Deleuze's embrace of a Spinozist theory of absolute, infinite substance and the PSR leads him to follow a different path. Every phenomenon, Deleuze argues, consciously echoing Leibniz's theory of monads, is related to every other phenomenon, and this in turn is because of the nature of multiplicities, the true substance.[52]

We are now in a position to return to the subject of concepts themselves, for although Deleuze and Guattari begin by discussing the nature of concepts, they begin in the midst of an ongoing effort that each had been engaged in, both separately and together, for the better part of thirty years – namely, the effort to develop a metaphysics of multiplicity. As we turn to the opening lines of the first chapter of *What is Philosophy?*, the problem space of multiplicities as A LIFE (recall the Introduction), the sufficient reason of all determinate, extensive differences, should now begin to resonate:

> There are no simple concepts. Every concept has components and is defined by them. It therefore has a combination. It is a multiplicity, although not every multiplicity is conceptual. There is no concept with only one component. Even the first concept, the one with which philosophy "begins," has several components, because it is not obvious that philosophy must have a beginning, and if it does determine one, it must combine it with a point of view or a reason. (WP 15, translation modified/QP 21)

Let us now return to the questions with which we began this chapter – what is involved in creating a concept and what, precisely, is created that belongs "only to philosophy"?

§4

To understand the significance of Deleuze and Guattari's claim that every concept has components and is "defined by them," let us return to our earlier discussion from the Introduction regarding Deleuze and Guattari's effort to develop a pedagogy of the concept that is neither scientist (*à la* Russell, et al.) nor idealist (*à la* Hegel). In this chapter and the Introduction we have stressed the importance of learning, and how learning, as Deleuze put it in *Difference and Repetition*, is "the appropriate name for the subjective acts carried out when one is confronted with the objectivity of a problem (Idea), whereas knowledge designates only the generality of concepts or the calm possession of a rule enabling solutions."[53] In *What is Philosophy?*, concepts are always connected to problems – "All concepts are connected to problems without which they would have no meaning and which can themselves only be isolated or understood as their solution emerges" (WP 16/QP) – and problems, or Ideas, are always multiplicities: "Ideas are multiplicities: every idea is a multiplicity or a variety."[54] We thus have our own multiplicity of terms – or own problem space, so to speak – in that problems, concepts, Ideas, and multiplicities are all in some sense differentiated and yet connected. The difficulty is to learn how Deleuze and Deleuze and Guattari connect these elements. This is the objectivity of the problem that confronts us now.

To confront this problem let us return to the problem of learning. The key process involved in learning is hard to pinpoint, hard to discuss, and more dramatically, Deleuze argues, there "is something amorous – but also something fatal – about all education."[55] In learning to drive a stick shift car, it is not sufficient simply to be told by the instructor to "do as I do," or follow the rule as stated and/or exemplified by the instructor's actions. What one encounters in learning to drive a stick shift car is the task of connecting various elements – the hand, foot, clutch, accelerator, slope of the road, and so on. Similarly, in learning to swim, it is a matter of establishing connections between the various parts and motions of one's body with the resistance, currents, and buoyancy of the water. As Deleuze argues, "To learn to swim is to conjugate the distinctive points of our bodies with the singular points of the Objective Idea in order to form a problematic field."[56] The problematic field is precisely that which arises when the elements are presented as needing to be connected in some way – this is the "Objective Idea" that results when the elements are drawn or filtered into a field of relevance, what Deleuze and Guattari will call a plane of immanence. In the encounter with the "Objective Idea," the problem or Idea needs then to be drawn into what Deleuze and Guattari call a plane of consistency, or the "area *ab*," as discussed earlier. It is precisely the plane of consistency that allows for the actualization of learning as the solution to a problem. In the case of swimming or driving, the relevant singular points (or signs) constitute the objectivity of the problem or Idea. For in driving a stick shift car it is the hand, stick shift, accelerator, clutch, and so on, that constitute the multiplicity and assemblage of singular points, the objectivity of a problem (Idea) that then needs to be drawn into a plane of consistency that then allows for the realization of a new skill. To restate this in accordance with a theme discussed earlier, the plane of consistency is the "intension" or sense that is irreducible to the extensional relationship between a problem as identified and its solution. Deleuze offers the example of a monkey who "learns" to find the food it wants, which is always in a box of a particular color. Initially, the monkey is confronted with the objectivity of the problem – there is the food, the boxes of many different colors, the hunger that piques the interest in finding the food – and these, among others, are the singular points that constitute the multiplicity or problem space that confronts the monkey. At first the monkey picks up boxes at random, but, Deleuze notes, "there comes a paradoxical period during which the number of 'errors' diminishes even though the monkey does not yet possess the 'knowledge' or 'truth' of a solution in each case."[57] It is at this point that the objectivity of the problem is drawn into a plane of consistency, where the elements and components are brought together in a consistent way to constitute the "intension" of the problem, though not yet the solution. And it is here that there is something "amorous – but also something fatal – about all education." The amorous aspect captures the bringing together of elements into a plane of consistency. At the same time, it is also possible that the elements fail to be brought together and that we thus fail to learn – which could indeed be fatal in the case of learning to swim. It is the failure to create a plane of consistency that can either lead to chaos and total breakdown or lead to a return to the already existent strata and established way of doing things. This is why learning is always fragile, dangerous, or even potentially fatal, in that there may be too many components to be drawn into a plane of consistency – the problem may be overwhelming – and the result would be a failure to establish any connections, and this is precisely how Deleuze and Guattari define chaos:

> The plane of immanence is like a section of chaos and acts like a sieve. In fact, chaos is characterized less by the absence of determinations than by the infinite speed with which they take place and vanish. This is not a movement from one determination to the other but, on the contrary, the impossibility of connection between them ... Chaos makes chaotic and undoes every consistency in the infinite. (WP 42/QP 44)

In order to learn, therefore, the focus must be on a selection of components – a filtering of chaos, so to speak – for it is this filtering or "sieve" that allows for the possibility of the consistency necessary to become actualized as knowledge and learned behavior. The pedagogy of the concept, therefore, requires a similar plane of immanence, a similar filtering, or it is "a fragmentary whole," Deleuze and Guattari argue, for "Only on this condition can it escape the mental chaos constantly threatening it, stalking it, trying to reabsorb it" (WP 16/QP 21).

In its effort to create concepts, therefore, philosophy sets out to learn, and in doing so the concern is first to encounter the objectivity of a problem – a multiplicity (Idea) – and then draw together the elements of a concept into a plane of consistency. Philosophy is not, however, a matter of discussing the elements themselves, of debating their proper arrangement or whether they are to be included among the concept's repertoire. Such discussions already presuppose that the elements themselves have been identified, whereas the differentials and intensive differences, as we have seen, are precisely the pre-individual conditions for the possibility of identifying such elements. These intensive differences (disparity, multiplicity, and so on) are the "sufficient reason of all phenomena"; in short, they are the condition for the possibility of discussing the terms that have come to be identified. It is for this reason that Deleuze and Guattari argue, in what is an oft-cited remark, that "Every philosopher runs away when he or she hears someone say, 'Let's discuss this'" (WP 28/QP 32). As they go on to clarify, "the best one can say about discussions is that they take things no farther, since the participants never talk about the same thing" (ibid.). What is at issue for Deleuze and Guattari are problems, and the plane of consistency that is drawn in response to the objectivity of the problem. As a multiplicity, a problem is nothing less than infinitely doubled difference and disparity, the sufficient reason for all that appears, and for this reason the problem as problem is "undiscussible" (ibid.), for every discussion already presupposes that a position has been staked relative to the problem, something determinate has been established, while the problem itself is not to be confused with such determinate positions. The staking of positions belongs to "scientific enunciation," as Deleuze and Guattari call it, for the position one stakes in such discussions is relative to a state of affairs or situation that the discourse or discussion is about. Philosophy, however, is "not a discursive formation" and the "concept is not discursive" (WP 22/QP 27). Conversations and discussions, therefore, "always comes too early or too late, and when it comes to creating, conversation is always superfluous" (WP 28/QP 32). The key, therefore, is to create concepts in connection with the objectivity of a problem, but in doing so we presuppose planes of consistency and multiplicities that are "undiscussible." The best we can do when criticizing another philosopher is therefore not to discuss their work but rather to create a concept that draws from other components, from other problems. As Deleuze and Guattari argue,

> To criticize is only to establish that a concept vanishes when it is thrust into a new milieu, losing some of its components, or acquiring others that transform it. But those who criticize without creating, those who are content to defend the vanished concept without being able to give it the forces it needs to return to life, are the plague of philosophy. (ibid.)

It is this last point that is essential: namely, the need to give a concept "the forces it needs to return to life." It is not the actualized elements and components that are the concern for Deleuze and Guattari, the established discourses and positions one "learned" in graduate school. It is not a matter of staking a position relative to one or more of these "learned" positions, or of defending and extending the discourses associated with them. To the contrary, it is the life of the concept, the "transcendental lived reality" (A LIFE) that is "intrinsic to thought, a condition of possibility of thought itself" (WP 3/QP 19), that is the proper concern of philosophers and what they grapple with when they create concepts. When it comes time to discussion, the "transcendental lived reality" has already become hidden or masked by the true cover up of solutions and discourses along with the positions they stake in reference to events and states of affairs. The relationship between this "transcendental lived reality" and the creation of concepts that is proper to philosophy will become the theme of the next chapter, but first, in the interest of the pedagogy of the concept, we will briefly examine the two examples Deleuze and Guattari bring to the first chapter in order to clarify the nature of philosophical concepts. This will further our effort to draw together the connections we are in the process of making.[58]

Example 1

If we are able to say that our life is a life well lived, then what justifies our claim? Perhaps, despite our best intentions to live well and do what is best, we are seriously misguided and thus our life is not a life well lived. The recognition of this possibility can be traced back to Socrates, at least, who raised the problem with Meno of whether anyone could do evil knowingly.[59] Socrates argues that one would not knowingly do evil, and thus one who does evil is simply not aware of what is truly good when they do what they do, or perhaps it is because they think it is in their best interest to do what they did while all the while they are ignorant of what is truly in their best interests. But can we ever know what our true good is, and how would we ever recognize it as such? This problem, commonly referred to as the problem of the *Meno*, has a long history in the philosophical tradition.

Descartes picks up the thread of this problem but provides an important new perspective upon it – in short, he creates a new concept in response to this problem. As Descartes begins his *Meditations*, he recognizes that for years he had "detected how many were the false beliefs that I [Descartes] had from my earliest youth admitted as true, and how doubtful was everything I had since constructed on this basis."[60] Descartes then sets out to take advantage of the time he has at his disposal to provide a true and proper foundation for his knowledge and, one would hope, a foundation for recognizing that the life one lives is indeed a good life.

According to Deleuze and Guattari, the cogito – "a concept of self" – is the concept Descartes creates to address the problem of the *Meno*. What is crucial to this concept is that it reworks the problem that vexed Socrates and Meno. Rather than pursue the Socratic attempt to discover the proper definition and concept that would enable one to capture the objective nature of justice, beauty, the good, and so on, Descartes, Deleuze and Guattari claim, develops his concept on a different plane, a "Cartesian plane [that] consists in challenging any explicit objective presupposition where every concept refers to other concepts (the rational-animal man, for example)" (WP 26/QP 31). Instead of finding the proper concept, Descartes creates the concept of the prephilosophical plane, the plane that "demands only a prephilosophical understanding, that is, implicit and subjective presuppositions: everyone knows what thinking, being, and I mean (one knows by doing it, being it, or saying it)" (ibid.). One thus does not begin with a concept or set of concepts whereby one is able to differentiate the true from the false; to the contrary, one begins with a prephilosophical understanding of reality and the cogito is precisely the concept of this reality – the philosophical concept of, paradoxically, the prephilosopical reality.

As Deleuze and Guattari set forth Descartes's concept of the cogito as an example of a philosophical concept, they claim that it has three components – "doubting, thinking, and being" (WP 24/QP 29) – and the concept itself "condenses at the point I, which passes through all the components in which I' (doubting), I'' (thinking), and I''' (being) coincide" (WP 25/QP 29). In other words, for Deleuze and Guattari there is an indiscernible becoming, the "area *ab*," where "something passes from one [component] to the other, something that is undecidable between them . . . where a and b 'become indiscernible'" (WP 19–20/QP 25) – and in passing indiscernibly between the components the consistency of the "area *ab*" allows for the elements to crystallize as the philosophical concept of the cogito. In doubting, for instance, our prephilosophical grasp of doubting elides indiscernibly into thinking. Doubting and thinking are different – they are different components – but the passage from doubting to thinking presupposes an "area *ab*" where doubting and thinking become indiscernible. Similarly for the passage from thinking to being, I already have a prephilosophical grasp of what it means to think and what it means to be, and moreover I am already aware as well that when I think I am, I am someone who is thinking, and thus on Deleuze and Guattari's reading of Descartes there is an "area *ab*" where thinking and being become indiscernible. The I that condenses the three components is precisely the point of absolute survey, the point that is not an external vantage upon the three components but rather the internal consistency, the area *ab*, which is presupposed by the three determinate and distinct components, and it is for this reason that this is a point of absolute survey and infinite speed – that is, it is immanent to the finite (or *in*-finite) as that which allows for the possibility of finite, determinate components, and the basis for understanding the components as components of the concept.

The concept of the cogito, however, is not a world unto itself but is connected to other concepts by "bridges or crossroads," such as the idea of infinity being among my ideas "leading from the concept of self to the concept of God," and this concept in turn "throws out a bridge or branches off to a concept of the extended, insofar as it guarantees the objective truth value of our other clear and distinct ideas" (WP 26/QP 30). It is with this latter bridge that we return to the problem with which Descartes began his *Meditations* – to wit, whether we can provide a proper foundation for our claims to know that which is true and differentiate this truth from all the other truths that had been mistakenly held to be true. It is precisely at this point that Deleuze and Guattari claim that Descartes departs most dramatically from the philosophical tradition. In line with Descartes's effort to create a concept of the prephilosophical plane that challenges any explicit objective presuppositions, Descartes provides a basis for truth solely within the prephilosophical reality of the subject, the cogito.

The biggest change Descartes initiates, then, and as has been canonized within the historical tradition by the tendency to place Descartes at the beginning of modern philosophy, is how Descartes transforms the relationship between objectivity and time. In the context of Descartes's concept of the cogito, for example, objectivity does not preexist the conditions of the subject, the conditions of the cogito. The objectivity of the external world, including the truths that determine whether our life is well lived or not, will be connected by bridges to the conditions of the prephilosophical plane associated with the cogito. The objectivity of our claims, in other words, will be *simultaneous* to the subjective conditions of the grasp of this objectivity rather than it being understood, as it was traditionally, as the recognition of a truth that preexisted our grasp of it. Instead of the independent objectivity of truth, it is consequently the certainty of our subjective grasp that becomes the benchmark of objectivity. Deleuze and Guattari make this point explicit as they conclude their brief sketch on Descartes's concept of the cogito: "Objectivity here will assume a certainty of knowledge rather than presuppose a truth recognized as preexisting, or already there" (WP 27/QP 31). If Descartes is truly representative of a break in philosophy, a break earmarked by the distinction between ancient/medieval *and* modern philosophy, then it is because the former holds to an objectivity of a preexisting truth while the latter understands objectivity in terms of the certainty – that is, Descartes's "clear and distinct ideas" – of our subjective grasp. The former approach, however, requires its own concepts, and as for the latter the cogito is the concept Descartes created in light of his particular problem space.

Suggested reading for example 1
    Plato, *Meno*
    René Descartes, *Meditations on First Philosophy.*

Example 2

One thing that becomes increasingly clear as one progresses through
the pages of *What is Philosophy?*, though one can gather as much
from the other works of Deleuze and Deleuze and Guattari as
well, is that the history of philosophy is not a history of progress, a
history of theories that are built upon and improve their predecessors. Descartes's concept of the cogito, therefore, is not an advance
on the work of Plato, for instance, but instead Descartes creates a
concept that cannot even be created on the Platonic plane, or it is
in response to an entirely different problem space. In brief, whereas
Descartes creates the concept of the cogito on a prephilosophical
plane where objectivity is simultaneous to the conditions of givenness to the subject – in the form of "clear and distinct" ideas – Plato
creates a concept of the Idea that presupposes a plane of anteriority,
or a time of the object that precedes its givenness to the subject. As
Deleuze and Guattari put it, the anterior time that Plato puts into
the concept results "in the form of a difference of time capable of
measuring the distance or closeness of the concept's possible con-
structor" (WP 29/QP 33). In other words, whereas there is no temporal difference for Descartes between the givenness of an object to
the cogito and the certainty and truth whereby this object is given,
for Plato there is a temporal difference between the givenness of the
object and the objective-ness (Deleuze and Guattari use the French
neologism *objectité*) that already precedes this givenness and is
"capable of measuring the distance or closeness" between the object
or concept as given and constructed and its preexistent objective-
ness. "This is the Idea," Deleuze and Guattari argue, "the Platonic
concept of the Idea" which presupposes the Platonic plane where
"truth is posed as presupposition, as already there" (WP 29/QP 33).

As with Descartes's concept, or as with any philosophical concept,
Plato's concept of the Idea has its own components. According to
Deleuze and Guattari, these components are: "the quality possessed
or to be possessed; the Idea that possesses it first, as unparticipable;
that which lays claim to the quality and can only possess it second,
third, fourth; and the Idea participated in, which judges the claims"
(WP 30/QP 34). If we take the example of the good life, such as a
life lived in accordance with justice and fairness, then the Idea as
unparticipable is the anteriority of any givenness. My actions may

reflect justice and fairness, which is the quality my life claims to possess, and this quality is the first component. However, the Idea is that which possesses this quality first, in anteriority, as the objectiveness whereby claims are to be judged. The possession of the quality by the Idea is the second component. Then there is the life as lived that lays claim to being a just and fair life, to possessing the quality of justice and fairness. Between this life as lived, the pure quality of justice and fairness, and the Idea that possesses this quality and in which the life as lived participates, there is an indiscernible "area *ab*" that passes between them. Although the components of the concept are distinct, there is an indiscernible "becoming" that passes between them such that the pure quality, the Idea that possesses this quality, and the life as lived that lays claim to this quality, become indiscernible. And finally there is the "Idea participated in," and the temporal distance this Idea presupposes, that enables the quality of the life as lived to be judged in accordance with whether and to what extent this life does possess the quality to which it lays claim to. This fourth component, along with the other three, become crystallized and condensed in an absolute survey that is the Platonic concept of the Idea.

We are now in a better position to understand Deleuze and Guattari's claim that Descartes's concept of the cogito was not an advance upon the Platonic concept of the Idea but rather a concept that could not have been created on the Platonic plane, for the Platonic plane presupposes the consistency of an entirely different set of components that are incompatible with those of Descartes. In fact, as Deleuze and Guattari put it,

> For Descartes to create this concept [of the cogito], the meaning of 'first' must undergo a remarkable change, take on a subjective meaning; and all difference of time between the idea and the soul that forms it as subject must be annulled. (WP 30/QP 34)[61]

The lesson Deleuze and Guattari draw from the examples of Descartes and Plato, then, is that "a concept always has components that can prevent the appearance of another concept or, on the contrary, that can themselves appear only at the cost of the disappearance of other concepts" (WP 31/QP 34). The Cartesian cogito, therefore, displaces the Platonic Idea, and the Cartesian cogito itself, as it comes to be addressed by subsequent philosophers, will in turn become subject to disappearance and transformation as philosophers such as Kant add components and take on different problems.

In the case of the latter, Deleuze and Guattari argue that "Kant constructs a 'transcendental' plane that renders doubt useless and changes the nature of the presuppositions once again" (WP 31/ QP 35). Whereas the Platonic plane presupposed a temporal difference between a truth and the soul for which this truth is given, and Descartes presupposed the prephilosophical plane where the idea and the soul are given at the same time, Kant presupposes a different plane altogether. The reason for this is that, given the Cartesian plane, we do not know how an undetermined "I am" (the component of being) becomes determinable and acquires the determinations it comes to have – for example, determinations such as I, Jeffrey Bell, can claim that I am this thinking being, thinking through Kant, Descartes, and Deleuze in August, 2014. Without addressing this problem, Kant argues that "nothing warrants such a claim of the 'I'" (ibid.). The problem subsequently for Kant, and the plane his philosophy presupposes, is how the undetermined existence that "I am" becomes determinable and determinate. Kant's answer is: "I am only determined in time as a passive and phenomenal self, an always affectable, modifiable, and variable self" (ibid.). The result is a concept of the cogito with four components:

> I think, and as such I am active; I have an existence; this existence is only determinable in time as passive self; I am therefore determined as a passive self that necessarily represents its own thinking activity to itself as an Other that affects it. This is not another subject but rather the subject who becomes an other. (WP 31–32/QP 35)

In addition to the two Cartesian components of thinking and being we have the being that I am being determined in time and hence a passive self, the third component, which then becomes the object of critical reflection and becomes the representation of an active subject (fourth component). With Kant's concept of critical reflection, then, we have the distinction between I and self, and the interplay between recognizing the I in the self that is the determinate self as synthesized in time. Hegel, as we have seen, generalizes this process to the absolute nature of reality as the becoming of self in other (see Introduction). In contrast to Plato, therefore, where the plane presupposes the anteriority of time and Ideas preexist their givenness to the soul, and Descartes, where the ideas exist "'at the same time' as the soul" (WP 30/QP 34), for Kant "time becomes *form of interiority*" (WP 32/QP 35), or the manner in which the self becomes determinate. With time as the form of interiority comes space as the form of exteriority whereby objects are given in time to

a passive subject in the process of becoming synthesized and determinate (see example 3 for the notion of horizon as the limit for this
process of synthesis).

With the first two examples, we can begin to add clarity to
Deleuze and Guattari's approach to the history of philosophy. As
we have seen, we cannot presume that philosophers are already
working from the same set of presuppositions, the same plane and
problem space, and hence we cannot use the same standards for
judging the success or failure of one philosopher over another. It
is for this reason, among many others, that Deleuze and Guattari
raise the alarm against discussions and conversations, arguing that
they already come too late. By the time a conversation becomes
possible, a shared plane of discourse is presupposed that hides and
displaces the problem that motivated the conceptual creations that
are the work of philosophers. The value of a philosopher, therefore,
is not to be determined by the extent to which they produce a consensus that can become the subject of a discussion or roundtable,
but rather their concepts are to be valued to the extent that they
problematized the lived, established ways of thought and engender
a process of connection that breeds further conceptual innovations. Deleuze and Guattari are quite forthright on this point: "The
history of philosophy means that we evaluate not only the historical
novelty of the concepts created by a philosopher but also the power
of their becoming when they pass into one another" (WP 32/QP
35–6). Plato, Descartes, and Kant have each created concepts novel
to their own historical period but they have also created concepts
that in part engendered the creations of subsequent philosophers.
The nature of this process of creation and historical influence
between philosophers, complicated as it is, is the subject of the next
example.

Suggested reading for example 2
> Plato, *Parmenides*
> Immanuel Kant, *Prolegomena to any Future Metaphysics.*

NOTES

1. A related example can be found in Merleau-Ponty's *Phenomenology of
   Perception*, trans. Colin Smith (New York: Routledge & Kegan Paul,
   1958), p. 146. Merleau-Ponty uses the fact that the skilled organist can
   quickly adjust to a new organ, even if it has a different layout of keys
   and pedals, in such a way that it cannot be accounted for, Merleau-

Ponty claims, by representational learning but rather is made possible by the felt, kinaesthetic adjustments of the body.

2. There is an interesting parallel here with the work of Jason Stanley. In his important essays and book on practical knowledge, Stanley has argued that practical knowledge, or "know how," is a form of propositional knowledge, or "knowing that." In response to skeptics, Stanley points out that "knowing that" does not mean that one actually states one's knowledge in a linguistic form. One may even be incapable of doing so. What is important is that one's action is predictably guided by a propositional rule. See Jason Stanley and John Krakauer, "Motor Skill Depends on Knowledge of Facts," *Frontiers in Human Neuroscience* (August 29, 2013). Deleuze and Guattari would agree, though their primary interest is the learning process itself rather than the propositional rules this learning makes possible.

3. Gilles Deleuze, *Difference and Repetition*, trans. Paul Patton (New York: Columbia University Press, 1994), p. 164.

4. Ibid., p. 166.

5. G. W. F. Leibniz, *New Essays on Human Understanding* (Cambridge: Cambridge University Press, 1996), p. 52.

6. Ibid.

7. *Difference and Repetition*, pp. 63–4.

8. David Hume, *A Treatise of Human Nature*, ed. L. A. Selby-Bigge and P. H. Nidditch (Oxford: Clarendon Press, 1978), 1.1.7.1 [conventional referencing by book, part, section, and paragraph], p. 17.

9. Ibid. 1.1.7.2, p. 18.

10. Ibid.

11. Ibid. 1.1.7.3, p. 18.

12. Ibid., 1.1.7.7, p. 20.

13. Ibid., 1.3.13.6, p. 146.

14. Ibid., 1.3.13.7, pp. 146–7.

15. Ibid.

16. Ibid.

17. Ibid. 1.4.7.1, p. 264.

18. In the Preface to the English-language edition of *Empiricism and Subjectivity* (New York: Columbia University Press, 1991), Deleuze claims that belief was one of the key concepts Hume created. For more on this theme see Chapter 3 below.

19. See my *Deleuze's Hume* (Edinburgh: Edinburgh University Press, 2009), where I touch on the significance of this point for Deleuze's reading of Hume.

20. With Heinrich Schliemann's (albeit problematic and controversial) discovery of the ancient city of Troy, the fictional events of Homer's *Iliad* became factual.

21. By siding with Carnap's emphasis on intension in contrast to Quine's extensional approach, Deleuze and Guattari's philosophy provides

an important window onto debates that have been with both analytic and continental philosophy largely from the beginning. The history of the split between analytic and continental philosophy, and the importance of Carnap in this history, have been the subject of much current research. In particular, see Michael Friedman's work, *Parting of Ways: Carnap, Cassirer, and Heidegger* (New York: Open Court, 2000), and Peter Gordon's *Continental Divide: Heidegger, Cassirer, Davos* (Cambridge, MA: Harvard University Press, 2012).

22. As Hao Wang shows in his *A Logical Journey: From Gödel to Philosophy* (Cambridge, MA: MIT Press, 2001), Gödel was critical of Carnap's attempts to reduce mathematics to a logical syntax without fully accounting for the nature of mathematical objects themselves. As Wang shows, Gödel spent fifteen years (1943–58) developing a conceptual realism that directly challenged the Carnapian tendency to hold that "mathematics is syntax of language" (p. 76).

23. In the Preface to the Italian edition of *A Thousand Plateaus*, for instance, Deleuze and Guattari claim that "The ambition of *A Thousand Plateaus*, however, is post-Kantian in spirit (though still resolutely anti-Hegelian)." On a light-hearted note, in an interview with Jeanette Colombel, she notes that Deleuze is "merciless with Hegel," and asks, "Why is that?" Deleuze's response was, "Why not Hegel? Well, somebody has to play the role of traitor" (*Desert Islands and Other Texts 1953–1974*, trans. Michael Taormina (New York: Semiotext(e), 2004), p. 144). Deleuze is no doubt referring to the historical fact that Hegel studies were dominant at the time of his own mentoring, and thus to go against Hegel was in effect an act of heresy against the dominant orthodoxy of his time. He then adds that he is troubled by "What is philosophically incarnated in Hegel ... [namely] the enterprise to 'burden' life, to overwhelm it with every burden, to reconcile life with the State and religion, to inscribe death in life – the monstrous enterprise to submit life to negativity, the enterprise of resentment and unhappy consciousness" (ibid.). For reasons to be discussed further in later chapters, we will see that these are very good reasons for Deleuze to take an "anti-Hegelian" stance.

24. One of the dividing lines in contemporary continental philosophy is drawn between those who largely accept Hegel's critique of Spinoza (Žižek, Badiou, Meillassoux, Johnston) and those who do not (Deleuze, Althusser, Foucault, Balibar).

25. G. W. F. Hegel, *Lectures on the History of Philosophy*, ed. Robert F. Brown, trans. Robert F. Brown and J. M. Stewart (Berkeley: University of California Press, 1990), p. 154.

26. Ibid. Hegel will make the charge of "abstract unity" more explicit in the closing lines of his section on Spinoza: "The reproach that Spinoza does not distinguish God from the finite is therefore of no account, since Spinoza casts all this [finite being] into the abyss of One Identity" (p. 163).

27. Ibid., p. 155.

28. Ibid., p. 156.

29. G. W. F. Hegel, *The Jena System, 1804–5: Logic and Metaphysics*, trans. John W. Burbidge and George di Giovanni (Montreal: McGill–Queen's University Press, 1986), pp. 32–3.

30. Ibid., p. 35.

31. Ibid.

32. Among many places, see Hegel states the thesis most simply in his *Science of Logic*, trans. A. V. Miller (Atlantic Highlands, NJ: Humanities Press International, 1995), p. 108: "From becoming there issues determinate being, which is the simple oneness of being and nothing. Because of this oneness it has the form of immediacy. Its mediation, becoming, lies behind it; it has sublated itself and determinate being appears, therefore, as a first, as a starting-point for the ensuing development."

33. *Jena System*, p. 10.

34. This is one of Alain Badiou's central criticisms of Deleuze. See *Deleuze: The Clamor of Being*, trans. Louise Burchill (Minneapolis: University of Minnesota Press, 2000), p. 10: "And, contrary to the commonly accepted image (Deleuze as liberating the anarchic multiple of desires and errant drifts), contrary even to the apparent indications of his work that play on the opposition multiple/multiplicities . . . it is the occurrence of the One . . . that forms the supreme destination of thought and to which thought is accordingly consecrated."

35. *Difference and Repetition*, p. 107.

36. Ibid.

37. Ibid., p. 222.

38. Later we will discuss the transfinite and Deleuze and Guattari's critique of Cantor's understanding of the infinite (see Chapter 5, example 10). There are thus multiple understandings of the infinite. The point here, however, is to stress the distinction between the good and bad infinite, as Hegel understands it, in order to lay out Deleuze and Guattari's understanding of the infinite as an intensive infinite. This theme will recur throughout subsequent chapters.

39. In his Preface to *Difference and Repetition*, Deleuze is quite forthright in stating that the tone of his book is one of a "generalized anti-Hegelianism; difference and repetition have taken the place of the identical and the negative, of identity and contradiction. For difference implies the negative, and allows itself to lead to contradiction, only to the extent that its subordination to the identical is maintained" (p. xix).

40. See Kant's first antinomy, *Critique of Pure Reason*, trans. Norman Kemp Smith (London: Macmillan, 1929), A428/B456: "In order, therefore, to think, as a whole, the world which fills all spaces, the successive synthesis of the parts of an infinite world must be viewed as completed, that is, an infinite time must be viewed as having elapsed in the enumeration of all co-existing things. This, however, is impossible."

41. José A. Benardete. *Infinity: An Essay in Metaphysics* (Oxford: Clarendon Press, 1964), pp. 272–4. John Hawthorne and Brian Weatherson have recently addressed Benardete's arguments as they relate to this example (see "Chopping Up Gunk," *The Monist* 87, no. 3 (2004), 339–50). In the context of discussing the supertask of cutting gunk to infinity, the problem they uncover is one that arises if we attempt to marry a theory of gunk (that is, an infinitely divisible substance) to the supertask of cutting a piece of matter that always occupies an extended volume of space. If the infinitesimal does not occupy an extended, specifiable volume, as Benardete argues, or if it is an intensive difference and differential, as Deleuze will argue, then gunk is compatible with Benardete's arguments. As Hawthorne and Weatherson argue: "If we are allowed *parts that lack finite extent*, then it will be consistent to adopt Benardete's picture of the outcome" (342, emphasis mine). I argue elsewhere that the Deleuzian interpretation of Benardete offered here ultimately rejects gunk.
42. Ibid., p. 274.
43. Benardete will see his own argument as an effort to find a third alternative between the view of reality as constituted of basic minima that are irreducible extensive points and a continuum that is infinitely divisible (that is, gunk).
44. There is a further reason to find in Benardete an anticipation of Deleuze's project, for in his account of the difficulties the finitists have with the actual infinite, Benardete cites the difference between mathematics and ontology, with the latter lending itself most naturally to the notion that a finite movement accomplishes an infinite process. Benardete points out that "Variables in mechanics not only converge toward their limits, in many cases they actually reach them. The 'rigorous' formulation of the calculus in finitist terms is seen to become possible only on the basis of a radical abstraction from those very ontological facts – above all, the facts of motion – which the calculus was originally intended to mathematize" (*Infinity*, p. 27). It is for this reason that Deleuze indeed returns to the early formulations of calculus, as we will see, for he finds in this effort an accomplice in his own effort to develop a philosophy of becoming, or ontology of motion, as Benardete might put it.
45. This is a theme to which we will return repeatedly in subsequent chapters. It is one of the chief lessons Deleuze takes from Hume. The causal relation, for example, is not to be found in the terms themselves, as Hume famously argues. A causal relation will only be found in a contemplative relation or habit of mind that is external to the terms.
46. I borrow this example from Dan Smith, *Essays on Deleuze* (Edinburgh: Edinburgh University Press, 2012), p. 246, though this example and others like it are common knowledge to those familiar with calculus.
47. This accounts in part for Deleuze's interest in the pre-Socratics, espe-

cially Anaxagoras. See Deleuze's essay, "The Fissure of Anaxagoras and the Local Fires of Heraclitus," in the *Desert Islands* collection.

48. This is basic to the calculus, and no doubt familiar to those adept at calculus. For a history of the development of the calculus and the concepts of derivatives and integrals, see Boyer's *The History of the Calculus and its Conceptual Development* (New York: Dover, 1959).

49. I use the term quasi-effect in order to avoid the tendency to think of causal relations in external terms – for example, A acts as external cause which brings about determinate and distinct effect B – and thereby to assume that differentials are in a relationship that is irreducible to the determinate limits they make possible.

50. *Difference and Repetition*, p. 222.

51. Ibid., p. 182.

52. See G. W. Leibniz, *Monadology* (La Salle: Open Court, 1988), §56: "Now this connexion or adaptation of all created things to each and of each to all, means that each simple substance has relations which express all the others, and, consequently, that it is a perpetual living mirror of the universe."

53. *Difference and Repetition*, p. 164.

54. Ibid., p. 182. See also ibid., p. 162: "Not only is sense ideal, but problems are Ideas themselves."

55. Ibid., p. 23.

56. Ibid., p. 165.

57. Ibid., p. 163.

58. One may skip the examples if one wishes and move on directly to the next chapter. The examples are written such that they can be read as a series on their own and independent of the rest of this book, although they are intended here, as they no doubt were by Deleuze and Guattari in *What is Philosophy?*, to be helpful at fleshing out the chapters. One could argue that the examples offered in *What is Philosophy?* serve a role similar to the *scholia* in Spinoza's *Ethics* – they are separate from the geometric presentation of the arguments and constitute a second track, so to speak.

59. See Plato's *Meno*, where the possibility of recognizing virtue and doing evil knowingly are important themes.

60. René Descartes, "Meditations on First Philosophy," in *The Philosophical Works of Descartes*, trans. Elizabeth S. Haldane and G. R. T. Ross (Cambridge: Cambridge University Press, 1967), p. 144.

61. In a parenthetical comment Deleuze and Guattari add that this is why Descartes was critical of the Platonic theory of reminiscence, "in which," Deleuze and Guattari claim, Descartes "says that innate ideas do not exist 'before' but 'at the same time' as the soul" (WP 30/QP 34).

2

Why Philosophy?

In the previous chapter we began to lay out the manner in which Deleuze and Guattari offer a theory of concepts that avoids the extensional understanding of concepts one finds in Frege, Russell, and the sciences, while at the same time avoiding the absolute idealism of Hegel whereby a concept is an absolute self-positing "return into self within the other."[1] The problem from Deleuze and Guattari's perspective with each of these approaches is that *either* they presuppose an already existent object to which concepts refer (for extensional theory), or they presuppose the predetermining substantial form of the universal self into which the other returns (for the idealist theory). For Deleuze and Guattari, by contrast, the problem is precisely one of accounting for the emergence and individuation of an identifiable object in the first place, whether an already existent object or the predetermining formal unity of a universal self. Rather than presuppose such identities, Deleuze and Guattari push the Principle of Sufficient Reason to the point where identity itself is to be accounted for rather than assumed as a brute, metaphysical reality. To do this, Deleuze and Guattari propose a "pedagogy of the concept," and it is with learning that we began to see their account of the individuation of identity begin to take shape.

As the trajectory of these arguments has developed, we were led to one of Deleuze's key philosophical concepts – namely, multiplicity. It is multiplicity that is the sufficient reason of all phenomena, "the true substantive, substance itself."[2] As the condition presupposed by real, individuated identities, multiplicities constitute the "transcendental lived reality" – or A LIFE as this was discussed in the Introduction – that is the "condition of possibility of thought itself" (WP 3/QP 19), the condition for philosophy itself but only, and this is critical, if learning is successful and chaos is avoided such that the elements and signs that constitute the objectivity of a problem can be drawn into a plane of consistency. This is difficult; in fact, it is the very problem of life itself, the problem (again, as we saw in the Introduction) of how A LIFE as a transcendental field of divergent series (chaosmos) can be transformed into a plane of consistency that allows for the emergence of determinate, individuated phenomena. In short, the problem of life is a problem of learning, and philosophy and the creation of concepts are inseparable from this problem.[3] As the difficulty of learning is hard to grasp until one is in the midst of attempting to conjugate the singular points and elements into a plane of consistency that facilitates successful learning, so too philosophy is a difficult enterprise of connecting and conjugating components in response to the problem of life and the demands of thought – the demands, as we will see, of extracting A LIFE from our lives as lived, a thought from opinion. Philosophy contributes to this effort and in this chapter we will begin to lay out a number of the components involved in this effort, and show how they constitute the objectivity of the problems associated with philosophy that is then, upon learning, drawn into a plane of consistency that will account for why one might do philosophy. Let us turn, then, to the first of these components: namely, Deleuze and Guattari's work on Kafka and the importance of asking the right questions.

§1

At the beginning of Franz Kafka's unfinished novel, *The Trial,* Joseph K. awakes to find himself "arrested one fine morning."[4] K., as he is referred to from this point forward in the book, is at a loss to account for his arrest. "Someone," he assumes, "must have been telling lies" about him, and yet two men are there to arrest him. Confronted with his own arrest, K. finds himself unconcerned with what the men might take from him, for the "things which he might possess" were of little concern to him at this point and what was "far more important to him was the necessity to understand his situation clearly; but with these people beside him he could not even think."[5] What K. was unable to think, the problem space he could not even begin to draw into a plane of consistency and hence solve, was the reason for his arrest, the determinate facts or charges that brought the two men to his flat. K. was simply left wondering "Who could these men be? What were they talking about? What authority could they represent?"[6] It is K.'s encounter with this problematic situation that underlies the ensuing narrative of *The Trial.* K. does not spend the rest of the book attempting to counter and defend himself against the charges for which he has been arrested. K. never knows what these charges were; there are no determinate facts or claims that K. knows of that support and provide the reasons for his arrest. What K. sets off to discover, then, are the conditions for his own arrest, but each condition he discovers sends him to a further condition in the next room, down the hall, and so on, and thus the novel takes on an interminable quality.

This interminable quality of *The Trial,* Deleuze and Guattari argue, is a consequence of Kafka's efforts to give full justice to the objectivity of the problem, to a problem that is A LIFE of pure immanence without transcendence. "It is in this sense," Deleuze and Guattari claim, "that *The Trial* is an interminable novel. An unlimited field of immanence instead of an infinite transcendence."[7] To state the point differently, K. is not in a position to disprove the charges against him. Had he known the charges, he could then set out to dispute them – it could not have been him, for instance, for he was with someone else that night, as witnesses can attest, and so on. What K. sets out to do instead is to find the determinate conditions themselves, but in doing so he repeatedly encounters further conditions. In short, K. continually encounters the problematic plane of immanence, and it is this problematic plane that sends K. down the path of further conditions, or the path of disparity and infinitely doubled difference (see previous chapter).

At this point it will be helpful to contrast K.'s plight with that of the person learning to swim or drive a stick shift car. As we have seen, in learning to swim one must draw the singular points and signs of water, waves, body, and so on, into a plane of consistency if one is to acquire the skill and knowledge associated with swimming. Part of the problem associated with learning to swim is that one does not know in advance precisely how the elements are to be conjugated. This was the objectivity of the problem – being told what to do, or being shown (do what I do) does not suffice on its own, for such demonstrations and established rules are simply further elements to be drawn into the plane of consistency. K.'s situation, by contrast, is even more enigmatic, for he does not even begin to know what elements he needs to address in order to "learn" the charges for which he is being arrested. In the case of the aspiring swimmer or stick shift driver, they are able to begin the process of learning to swim or drive, and there is a determinate and known end to be achieved as a result of this process. I will be able to do *that* once I have learned this. K., by contrast, cannot even begin to learn the charges; he is forever in the process of discerning the conditions whereby he can begin to learn the reasons for his arrest. For K., therefore, it is a perpetual, unlimited process and trial.

In their book on Kafka, Deleuze and Guattari develop this contrast and it becomes integral to their understanding of assemblages and the plane of immanence. What Kafka initiates, they argue, is a writing style that transforms "a *method* (*procédé*) in the social field into a *procedure* as an infinite virtual movement."[8] K., for instance, does not follow an established methodology or set of rules and laws in order to challenge the charges he faces. By virtue of the fact that K. faces the problematic conditions of his arrest, he is launched upon an infinite virtual movement that leads him into the path of disparity, into the intensive "transcendental lived reality," and it is this movement, Deleuze and Guattari argue, that will "at the extreme invoke the machinic assemblage of the trial (*procès*) as a reality that is on its way and already there."[9] In other words, at the extreme the trial will undo one's determinate life as lived, which is precisely what happened to K., and what is revealed in such circumstances is the transcendental condition and multiplicity that is always already there as the condition of both possibility and impossibility for this determinate life. A multiplicity is the condition of possibility for a determinate life insofar as it becomes a machinic assemblage that avoids actualizing either of two extremes. Understood in this way, a machinic assemblage is a dynamic, autopoetic system. As a dynamic system a machinic assemblage maintains its functioning as long as it staves off collapsing either into chaos or into a stasis of already established, determinate strata. A machinic assemblage is thus what could be called a system at the edge of chaos in that it maintains a dynamic equilibrium that avoids falling either into chaos or stasis.[10] Stated otherwise, and in terms that have been employed here, a machinic assemblage is an active, dynamic process of learning. A machinic assemblages is thus not a set of ideal limits but rather it staves off these limits, the extremes, in order to maintain its functioning in reality. Machinic assemblages (or, simply, assemblages as they come to be referred to by Deleuze and Guattari in *A Thousand Plateaus*) are also inseparable from a problem space that brings crucial questions to the table. As Deleuze and Guattari note, "Since the assemblage functions really in the real, the question becomes:

how does it function? What function does it have?"[11] These questions are in fact the appropriate philosophical questions when one is encountering the objectivity of a problem or the functioning of an assemblage on a plane of immanence. As Deleuze argued in his "Method of Dramatization" lecture, when the subject is "'multiplicity' [or Idea], when used as a substantive," as the sufficient reason of all phenomena – then the appropriate question is not the Socratic "what is x?," where the answer will be the determinate, simple essence that defines the nature of x; rather, Deleuze argues that it is better to ask a series of questions: "who? how? how much? where and when? in which case?" These questions, Deleuze claims, better enable us to "sketch the genuine spatio-temporal coordinates of the Idea"; or, they better enable us to learn, among other things, how assemblages function, and in which cases and circumstances, and the limits they must avoid, the thresholds to stave off, if they are to continue functioning or avoid transforming into another dynamic assemblage.[12]

Early in the "Plane of Immanence" chapter from *What is Philosophy?*, Deleuze and Guattari argue that a concept is an assemblage. "Concepts are concrete assemblages, like the configurations of a machine, but the plane is the abstract machine of which these assemblages are the working parts" (WP 36/QP 39). The abstract machine is the opposition between the poles of chaos and stasis, and each pole of this opposition "functions as the absolute horizon" (ibid.) that is staved off in the real functioning of assemblages. Reality, or multiplicity as the "true substantive," is the problematic plane of immanence that staves off the ideal, abstract poles of the abstract machine – namely, chaos and stasis – and therefore the nature of reality is a chaosmos whereby the question then becomes one of determining when, under what conditions, how much, and so on, an assemblage can be pushed before it exceeds its functioning powers and capacities and ceases to work. Assemblages are therefore the "working parts" of the abstract machine precisely because they manage to avoid being drawn too far towards either of the two poles. As the working parts of the abstract machine, assemblages are nonetheless always drawn towards *both* the absolute horizon of chaos that deterritorializes the assemblages *and* the horizon of territorialization and stasis wherein processes become stratified into a determinate set of rules and methods. Assemblages are thus always at risk, and the working of assemblages is therefore not one of following a set of rules but rather of engaging in cautious experimentation, a continual process of trial and error, a continual learning.

It is just this experimentation and turning away from a strict, rule-based method that Deleuze and Guattari find in the writings of Kafka. On the one hand, there is the abstract machine of escape and capture. There is the becoming-animal that enables Gregor (from "The Metamorphosis") to escape his stifling work schedule and family commitments, and there is the ape in "A Report to an Academy" who is able to escape his cage when he learns to speak English. At the same time there is "the transcendental law that blocks the way out"[13] by a process of reterritorializing capture, such as when Gregor is brought back within the sphere of the family ("the re-Oedipalization of Gregor, the platonic apple that his father throws at him"[14]), or the stifling etiquette and rules of those in high society that the learned ape must now live with and among. Between the poles of this abstract machine, Kafka's texts develop characters and relations between characters that become assemblages that are in perpetual trial, avoiding the poles of the abstract machine. According to Deleuze and Guattari,

> Because the whole story of K. (in *The Trial*) revolves around the way in which he enters more deeply into an unlimited postponement, breaking with all the formulas of a superficial acquittal [that is, Kafka's writings avoid the poles of the abstract machine of guilt *or* innocence]. He thereby leaves the abstract machine of the law that opposes law to desire, as body is opposed to spirit, as form is opposed to matter, in order to enter into the machinic assemblage of justice – that is, into the mutual immanence of a decoded law and a deterritorialized desire.[15]

§2

Let us build upon Deleuze and Guattari's reading of Kafka in order to develop their understanding of philosophical method. We can do so by continuing with the abstract machine/machinic assemblage duality that looms large, as we have seen, in Deleuze and Guattari's reading of Kafka's writing "procedure." What is at work in this duality is a continuation of Deleuze's effort to argue for difference in itself – what Deleuze calls "disparity" (as we have seen [see above, p. ??]) – as the sufficient reason for all phenomena, an effort Deleuze continues in his work with Guattari. In the context of their book on Kafka, it is the abstract machine that is the difference that is the sufficient reason for all determinate, individuated *reality*. The difference between the abstract poles of the abstract machine – the pole of chaos and absolute deterritorialization and the pole of stasis and territorialized strata – is not a difference between determinate poles but rather it is an interminable, non-explicated difference, a difference that is implicated but must remain forever staved off by each and every machinic assemblage. It is, as we have seen, the "transcendental lived reality" (A LIFE) that is the sufficient reason for the determinate, explicated differences between individuated terms and entities, or for the determinate assemblages that are the "working parts" of the abstract machine. It is for this reason that Deleuze claims that insofar as difference (disparity) is the sufficient reason for all phenomena, then this reason is inexplicable.[16] In short, difference, or the abstract machine, is not inexplicable in the sense that it involves an *absence* or *lack* of reason. Deleuze and Deleuze and Guattari wholly support, as we saw in the Introduction, a version of the PSR that further tracks and develops the "Anticartesian reaction" Deleuze finds in Spinoza and Leibniz. What this entails for Deleuze and for Deleuze and Guattari is that every phenomenon has a sufficient reason for its determinate, individuated being, though this reason is an inexplicable difference, a transcendental pure immanence – namely, A LIFE. This reason, therefore, is inexplicable because it is not a determinate, individuated reason. The philosopher is thus in a situation much like that of K. from *The Trial* – there is no determinate reason one can find that provides the reason for the phenomenon one wants to account for (for example, K.'s arrest). Similarly, for the Spinozism of Deleuze and Guattari there are no determinate reasons, or set of reasons, that one can appeal to that provide the sufficient reason for all phenomena. This reason is difference-in-itself, or it is the abstract machine, but this reason is never explicated within determinate phenomena but rather is masked and hidden in the true cover up that is determinate, individuated reality.

The abstract machine is therefore the condition for the possibility of assemblages and multiplicities,[17] for the "working parts of the abstract machine" (WP 36/QP 39) that are what "really functions in the real."[18] As either of the two poles becomes increasingly realized, the working assemblage ceases functioning. Put differently, inseparable from an assemblage that "really functions in the real" is the breakdown of the assemblage. The condition for the possibility of determinate phenomena, therefore, the "sufficient reason of all that appears,"[19] is problematic multiplicity that staves off chaos and stasis, or it is the "area *ab*" that is not to be confused with either "a" (chaos) or "b" (stasis). What follows from this understanding of the PSR, as we will now see, is a reworked version of Kant's notion of the transcendental illusion.

§3

As we have argued, Deleuze and Guattari pursue a relentless Spinozism in that they affirm the immanence of difference as the sufficient reason for all determinate, individuated phenomena. Much as Spinoza was seen by Deleuze and Guattari to be "the prince of philosophers" for being perhaps "the only philosopher never to have compromised with transcendence and to have hunted it down everywhere" (WP 48/QP 50), so too do they seek to challenge those who take the transcendent and determinate to be the condition when it is precisely that which is conditioned. It is at this point that Deleuze and Guattari continue the Kantian critique that challenges and undermines the claims of those who succumb to what Kant calls the transcendental illusion. According to Kant, the transcendental illusion occurs when we "take the subjective necessity of a connection of our concepts, which is to the advantage of the understanding, for an objective necessity in the determination of the things themselves."[20] For Deleuze, the transcendental illusion comes when one confuses that which is already individuated and hence capable of being the subject of representational thought as that which is the condition that accounts for the individuation of phenomena. For Deleuze and Guattari, by contrast, it is the problematic conditions, or A LIFE as pure immanence, that are the condition for the possibility and impossibility of each and every assemblage, and hence for the determinate identities that explicate the conditions of these assemblages. In creating concepts, therefore, the philosopher produces an assemblage (WP 36/QP 39: "Concepts are concrete assemblages") that both problematizes the presupposed identity that makes representational thought possible while at the same time allowing for the emergence of new individuated identities, and hence for new representational thoughts. This is why philosophy will remain an indispensable and integral component of the effort to think, for inseparable from representational thought are various machinic assemblages (concepts as multiplicities) that allow for the possibility of representational thought while simultaneously guaranteeing the problematization and demise of this thought.

In *Difference and Repetition*, Deleuze claims that there is a fourfold root of representation, with each of these roots being an instance of the transcendental illusion as he develops it. These four roots are identity, analogy, opposition, and resemblance, and the transcendental illusion occurs when one assumes that difference is conditioned by the fourfold root of representational thought rather than difference itself being, as Deleuze argues, the sufficient reason for all identity, including the identity of each of these four roots.[21]

Identity

In representational modes of thought, *identity* looms largest with respect to the determinable concept, such as the determinable genus color, for instance. From this perspective, determinate differences are understood relative to the identity of this determinable concept. Representational differences are thus mediated by the identity of an undetermined determinable, and this determinable is undetermined precisely because it itself lacks determinate content.

To clarify, let us take the determinable color. When I say that the color of my shirt is different from the color of my pants, it is the determinable concept color that remains the same while the determinate instances of this self-same concept are precisely what differ. Among examples of this representational approach in the philosophical tradition, we could turn to Aristotle, Kant, and a host of others who reduce representational differences to the mediating identity of an undetermined concept. For Aristotle, as Deleuze shows in *Difference and Repetition*, this undetermined concept is the genus that mediates specific differences; and for Kant, it is the *noumena* that mediates the differences of an indefinite series of representations (Kant's solution to first antinomy).[22]

Analogy

As we move on to the second of the four roots of representation, the mediating role of identity as analogy figures most prominently within judgments. Since different judgments will usually apply or differentiate between different determinable concepts, the basis for the difference between determinable concepts themselves is understood, Deleuze argues, by analogy.

To offer an example, Wilfred Sellars has argued that every judgment always already inhabits what he calls the space of reasons, and thus every concept is always already inferentially related to other concepts. The judgment that my shirt is purple, for instance, is inferentially connected to, and yet different from, other judgments, such as this shirt is colored, it is not yellow, or Jeff's fashion sense is lacking for who wears purple shirts, and so on. All these judgments presuppose, as an analogue, the being or totality of the space of reasons, and it is this space of reasons that makes the different judgments possible. We thus do not learn concepts one at a time, Sellars argues, but we come to learn their place within the already presupposed space of reasons.[23] John McDowell has more recently continued largely in this same Sellarsian tradition and has argued for what he calls a "world-disclosing experience" that provides the basis for differentiating between the propriety of our judgments, in short for differentiating between which judgments do and do not carve at the joints.[24] This "world-disclosing experience" is necessary, McDowell argues, if we are to avoid a "frictionless spinning in a void" which would result if the spontaneity of our judgments were to be left unchecked. Robert Brandom, finally, also falls into this tradition, a tradition he rightly traces back to Hegel, and for him the analogue to his inferentialism is the community, or a social holism, much as for Hegel it was, as we saw, the formal unity of the self into which the other returns as itself.

Opposition

For Deleuze, the mediating role of identity with respect to representational differences between predicates in relation to their subjects occurs by way of the opposition of predicates within a subject. The maximal difference, therefore, is opposition in a subject, and it is the identity of the subject that mediates these representational differences.

As Aristotle, and Hegel much later, argued, the greatest difference would be between predicates of a self-same subject. For Aristotle, a self-same subject cannot have opposing predicates predicated of it at one and the same time, and in one and the same way, although it is the same subject that can have these predicates at different times and in different ways. A subject cannot be both hot and cold, light and heavy, fast and slow, for example, though it can be hot at one time and cold later, fast now, slow earlier, and so on. Similarly for Hegel, with his notion of absolute contradiction: it is one and the same Absolute Spirit that resolves the maximal difference between universal and particular, being and becoming. In contemporary philosophy it is the proposition, as it is generally understood, that is the identity that mediates the law of the excluded middle whereby a proposition is either true or the negation of the proposition is true. It is the subject, the proposition in this case, that bears these contrary, opposing predicates and yet it itself remains one and the same.

Resemblance

The final mediating role of identity in representation occurs with respect to perception, where representational differences are subordinated to the identity of a continuum of resemblance.

69

The difference between the color of my shirt and the color of my pants, for example, can be subordinated to a continuum of resembling colors. The two colors, as represented separately, are thus abstracted from this continuum and the representational difference between them is in the end mediated by the continuity of resemblance. Even Hume, whom one would least suspect of affirming the identity of a continuum, relies upon this presupposed identity. It is the continuity of resemblance that accounts for Hume's discussion, in the appendix to his *Treatise*, where he notes that although blue and green are different colors – "different simple ideas," as he puts it – they bear more resemblance to one another than blue and scarlet, and this is a resemblance "without having any circumstance the same."[25] In other words, one can recognize the resemblance without a third idea or a common component, for if there were a common component the simple ideas would not be simple. The continuity of resemblance is thus a primitive for Hume, and it is the basis for mediating perceptual differences.

In each of these four cases, what is presupposed is a brute fact, an unquestioned and unaccounted for identity, whether this be the undetermined concept, a space of reasons, an underlying subject or proposition, or the continuity of resemblance. Deleuze, by contrast, breaks with a broad swath of twentieth-century philosophy and reaffirms the PSR; a fundamental consequence of this reaffirmation is the rejection of brute, self-identical facts. Let me briefly recap on an important aspect of this history, for it will both help us to situate Deleuze and Guattari's project into the context of the contemporary philosophical landscape, and help to prepare the way for further understanding Deleuze and Guattari's arguments regarding the distinctive nature of philosophy.

§4

As has been argued on a number of occasions, though more commonly of late, an important motivating factor for the philosophical work we now identify as analytic philosophy stems from an effort to reject and move beyond the absolute idealism that was common in the latter half of the nineteenth century. In a series of foundational essays, Bertrand Russell and G. E. Moore will challenge key aspects of Bradley's philosophy, Bradley being the most prominent idealist at that time and thus the ideal target.[26] One of Bradley's pivotal claims that Russell and Moore will reject is that relations are not real since they cannot, if we adhere to the PSR as Bradley does, be grounded and hence explained. Relations are inexplicable, Bradley argues, and hence are to be done away with if we are to accept as truth only that which can be explained and accounted for. Why are they inexplicable? This is where Bradley's famous, or notorious (depending on your perspective), regress argument enters the scene. As Michael Della Rocca has summarized the argument, if there is a relation R between "a" and "b," we cannot ground R in "a" alone, for then this would be arbitrary. Why not "b" rather than "a"? It would also be arbitrary, and for the same reason, if were we to attempt to ground R in "b"? If we account for R in terms of a unique relation "ab," however, then we have yet another relation that is used to account for the relation R, a relation that itself needs to be explained, and hence we are off on our regress.[27]

According to Russell, Bradley's regress argument gets off the ground only as a result of "the rejection of brute or inexplicable relations and [an affirmation of] . . . the PSR."[28] It is because Bradley rejects brute facts and endorses the PSR that he is led to reject relations. Russell, by contrast, rejects the PSR and accepts brute and inexplicable relations. As Russell puts it, Bradley's view depends

> upon some law of sufficient reason, some desire to show that every truth is "necessary". I am inclined to think that a large part of my disagreement with Mr. Bradley turns on a disagreement as to the notion of "necessity". I do not myself admit necessity and possibility as fundamental notions: it appears to me that fundamentally *truths are merely true in fact,* and that the search for a "sufficient reason" is mistaken.[29]

Moore will largely follow Russell on this point, arguing that: "It seems quite obvious that in the case of many relational properties which things have, *the fact that they have them is a mere matter of fact.*"[30] Relational properties, in other words, do not need to be accounted for; they are simply a "mere matter of fact."

As I have argued throughout this book, Deleuze and Deleuze and Guattari accept a version of the PSR, and what is integral to their version is that they do not endorse the standard line whereby, as Spinoza puts it, "For each thing there must be assigned a cause, *or* reason, as much for its existence as for its nonexistence," with this sufficient cause or reason being understood to be a determinate cause or reason. What they argue for instead is that for each and every determinate phenomenon there is an inexplicable difference that is, as Deleuze claims, the "sufficient reason of all that appears."[31] This difference is crucial for, on an initial reading of Deleuze's texts, it appears that Deleuze launches us upon the regress that Bradley sought to avoid. In *What is Philosophy?*, for example, and in the context of arguing that there are components to each and every concept, Deleuze and Guattari claim (as discussed above [see Chapter 1, §4]) that these components

> remain distinct, but something passes from one to the other, something that is undecidable between them. There is an area *ab* that belongs to both *a* and *b*, where *a* and *b* 'become' indiscernible. These zones, thresholds, or becomings, this inseparability, define the internal consistency of the concept. (WP 19–20/QP 25)

To account for the relationship between components "a" and "b," it appears Deleuze and Guattari call upon a special relation, the "area *ab*," but in doing so have they not brought along Bradley's regress argument? What accounts for this "area ab"? And so on. . . . This regress would indeed be a concern if the "area *ab*" were to be understood as a determinate, extensive relation between *a* and *b*, but Deleuze and Guattari are clear that they are speaking of an "internal consistency." It is this internal consistency, or intensive difference and disparity, that is constitutive of the identity of elements and thus for the determinate relations that presuppose them. This was also the lesson we drew from our earlier discussion of Benardete's arguments (see Chapter 2, §3). It is this understanding of difference that will enable Deleuze and Deleuze and Guattari to avoid Bradley's regress argument while also allowing them to uphold the PSR, and it will be central to their critique of representation and to their efforts to address the problem of individuation without succumbing to the transcendental illusion as we have laid it out earlier.

To understand how they begin to take on this problem of individuation, we can begin with Ideas (and yes, Ideas with a capital 'I'; and even, as Deleuze argues at one point, Ideas in the Platonic sense, as long as we do not mistake Ideas for the simplicity of the solution but understand them rather as problems[32]). In extending the claim that multiplicity is the "true substantive, substance itself," Deleuze further adds that "Everything is a multiplicity in so far as it incarnates an Idea."[33] But what does it mean for a multiplicity to incarnate an Idea? Maïmon provides Deleuze with the means to clarify this point, for it is in his discussion of Maïmon that Deleuze argues that Ideas are by their nature systematic: "Ideas [quoting Deleuze] appear in the form of a system of ideal connections – in other words, a system of differential relations between reciprocally determined genetic elements."[34] It is precisely the "system of ideal connections" that is incarnated in a spatio-temporal process. To clarify by way of example, let us take the case of the fruit fly larvae as an incarnated Idea, elaborating here upon Deleuze's own example. The "system of differential relations" in the fruit fly larvae would be the systematic and reciprocally determined relations between genetic elements, such as the bicoid protein and other elements that constitute the singularities and signs that trigger the spatio-temporal processes of the growth and development of the fruit fly larvae. Bicoid protein, in particular, is integral to the growth and development of the thorax and head of the fruit fly. When the level of bicoid protein in the developing larvae of the fruit fly reaches a critical threshold, or singularity, it elicits the response of other genes that trigger the growth of the head and thorax. If this threshold is altered – that is, if the singularity or sign is changed – then the entire machinic assemblage (multiplicity) of singularities is likewise modified and the connections, differences, and elicited responses subsequently play themselves out throughout the unfolding spatio-temporal growth and development of the fruit fly. The head and thorax of the fruit fly may become overdeveloped and too large, or may not develop at all. The developing larva is thus the spatio-temporal process that incarnates the system or multiplicity (Idea) of singularities and thresholds, the "system of ideal connections." Each of these determinate genetic elements, moreover, is itself the result of an ongoing incarnation of an Idea. Bicoid, for example, consists of a system of differential relations and singularities between reciprocally determined relations (ideal connections) of carbon, nitrogen, and other chemical elements; and these elements in turn presuppose their own Ideas. Carbon, for example, requires the threshold singularities of pressure within the core of stars in order to transform helium atoms into carbon atoms. What is key to the process whereby the Idea as a system of ideal connections becomes actualized within spatio-temporal processes of a fruit fly, bicoid protein, or carbon, for instance, is that the ideal connections come to be drawn into a consistent system that avoids the poles of the abstract machine – chaos and absolute deterritorialization on the one hand and stasis and absolute stratification on the other. If the multiplicity of ideal connections is drawn too far to chaos and deterritorialization, the result will be the death of the fruit fly, and if the developing larva never altered from its course, never mutated or changed, then similarly the fruit fly species will eventually die out due to its failure to adapt to ever-changing circumstances. That said, however, such shifts between the two poles are what makes the incarnation of the Idea possible in the first place, for it is a multiplicity or dynamic system that is incarnated. Any determinate individual, therefore, presupposes its conditions of transformation, the necessity of its becoming other; or, as Deleuze and Guattari put it in *A Thousand Plateaus*, "there is no genetics without 'genetic drift.'"[35]

To come at this point from a slightly different angle, the Idea is the multiplicity of "contemplations" Deleuze refers to in *Difference and Repetition* when he extends Hume's argument that it is not the repetition of the determinate elements themselves that brings about the expectation of B upon being given A, but rather it is something in the mind, in "contemplation," that accounts for this synthesis (what Deleuze calls "passive synthesis"). Every individuated and determinate entity or element presupposes an Idea, according to Deleuze, and hence a system of ideal connections or contemplations.

> What organism [Deleuze asks] is not made of elements and cases of repetition, of contemplated and contracted water, nitrogen, carbon, chlorides and sulphates, thereby intertwining all the habits of which it is composed? Organisms awake [Deleuze concludes] to the sublime words of the third *Ennead*: all is contemplation![36]

But there is more, for if all is contemplation this is because all is Idea *and* multiplicity in that all systems are assemblages that stave off the two limits of reality. On this point, Deleuze and Guattari admittedly echo Spinoza when, in *What is Philosophy?*, they argue that the "plane of immanence has two facets as Thought and as Nature, as *Nous* and as *Physis*" (WP 38/QP 41). The Idea is the mental pole, the pole of *Nous*, that is never fully actualized and never fully integrates elements into a systematic, self-contained unity of Thought. On the other hand, a multiplicity never fully incarnates and substantiates the Idea as Nature, never fully delivers the determinate contemplations that constitute and compose the multiplicity. *Nous* is thus the pole of unity, the formal unity and strata of the abstract machine, the unity that accounts for the identity of that which is; and multiplicity is that which differentiates and individuates one thing from another. Both poles, however, are never fully actualized and thus what we have with a multiplicity for Deleuze is a failed or fragmentary hylomorphism (recall that for Deleuze and Guattari a concept is "a fragmentary whole" [WP 16/QP 21]). We have a formal cause that never fully forms relations between elements into a systematic whole, a cosmos; nor does matter ever fully differentiate into disconnected elements – chaos.[37] What we have, Deleuze and Guattari argue, is a chaosmos.[38]

A consequence of their fragmentary hylomorphism is that the role of pre-individual singularities will loom especially large in Deleuze and Deleuze and Guattari's metaphysics. The pre-individual singularities and contemplations that compose a multiplicity are not undifferentiated. We do not have the night where all cows are black (as Hegel said of Schelling's theory). The contemplations are differentiated. The bicoid protein of the fruit fly larvae, for example, is differentiated from the other proteins and enzymes, and the "contemplated and contracted water, nitrogen, carbon, chlorides and sulphates" are likewise differentiated from one another. What is pre-individual about pre-individual singularities is that the reciprocal relations of the differentiated content, the area *ab* or plane of consistency, is what is not to be confused with the determinate individuals they make possible. The reciprocal relations of bicoid protein to the other proteins and enzymes, and the singularities and thresholds of these relations, do not resemble and are not to be identified with the thorax and head of the fruit fly. The differentiated elements themselves, moreover, presuppose their own Ideas and thus their own system of reciprocally related genetic elements, elements with their own Ideas and pre-individual singularities, and so on *ad infinitum.* This infinitely doubled series of differences was precisely what Deleuze defined as disparity, the sufficient reason of all that appears.

An Idea as a system of ideal connections, therefore, and to recall Deleuze's discussion of Maïmon, brings into play relations to other ideal connections, and so on *ad infinitum.* We do not, however, have Hegel's bad infinity, for, as should be clear, the system of ideal connections is not, *in actuality*, related to other determinate connections, but rather it presupposes an infinite series of pre-individual intensive differences, or singularities that are the condition for the possibility of the process of determinate individuation, and hence for the possibility of the bad infinite Hegel sought to circumvent. The system of ideal connections and contemplations that range between the pole of Thought (Ideas and Form) and Nature (Multiplicity and Substance) consists of a selection and filtering of components. The plane of immanence, according to Deleuze and Guattari, is precisely the partial, fragmentary whole and problem space that is then drawn into the plane of consistency, or the "area *ab*," that is the condition for the possibility of determinate individuation. The plane itself is "like a section of chaos and acts like a sieve" (WP 42/QP 44), and it is this plane that is presupposed as elements are drawn into a plane of consistency. The plane of immanence, therefore, serves as a sieve for it is only when there is a selection of components and elements, a filtering of chaos, that there can then be the possibility of the transformation that brings about a spatio-temporal process of individuation. This occurs when this "section of chaos" is drawn into a plane of consistency – into the "intension" of the problem – that allows for the contemplation or sign that effectuates what one could call a phase transition. As we saw in the case of bicoid protein in the fruit fly larvae, when the intensive, reciprocal relations of bicoid to other proteins and enzymes is drawn into a particular threshold or intensive consistency, the result is a contemplation or sign that triggers new spatio-temporal processes whereby new determinate individuals and their attendant singularities are constituted.

Let us recap the arguments to this point and relate them to the "objectivity of the problem." Stated succinctly, every individual, including all the facts and extensive properties and qualities associated with them, is an assemblage of phase transitions, a problem space, and the key to this problem space is the "learning" that entails the bringing together and conjugation of signs (genetic elements) in an ongoing response to the objectivity of the problem that is A LIFE – the transcendental lived reality. The fruit fly larva, for example, is an assemblage of such transitions, including the transition associated with the bicoid protein that signaled the growth and development of the head and thorax. These genetic elements in turn, and all the facts and properties associated with them, are likewise the actualization of a plane of consistency of other genetic elements and phase transitions, and so on. A term Deleuze will use to capture the sense of that which allows for the differentiation and individuation of elements is concrete universal. A concrete universal is neither the Idea as the Mental or Formal pole (*Nous*); nor is it the Multiplicity or Substantive pole (*Physis*). A concrete universal is precisely the plane of consistency that is inseparable from each and every determinate individual. Deleuze first brings up the concept of a concrete universal early on in an essay on Bergson, though he will return to it in one of his final essays. In this latter essay – on Spinoza, appropriately enough – Deleuze returns to the example of white light as a case in point of a concrete universal. In reference to Goethe's analysis of color, Deleuze argues that

> Colors enter into relations of complementarity and contrast, which means that each of them, at the limit, reconstitutes the whole, and that

they all merge together in whiteness following an order of composition, or stand out from it in the order of decomposition.[39]

In other words, in developing Goethe's claim that white light is the "last opaque degree" that is the minimal condition that allows for the emergence and extensive differentiation of color, Deleuze argues that the determinate, extensive, qualitative differences between colors presuppose the concrete universal that ranges between its minimal, material pole (the opaque transparency) and its maximal, formal pole (white light as the systematic convergence of all colors). Goethe's "opaque transparency," the minimal whiteness that allows for the emergence of color is the minimal material condition for the determinate fact that something is colored. Similarly, white light as the convergence of all colors is the formal condition that allows for the individuated identity of colors. White light is a concrete universal, or as Deleuze puts it in the Bergson essay, it is the "far end of the particular" or the difference that makes a difference in that "the different colors are no longer objects under a concept, but nuances or degrees of the concept itself. Degrees of difference itself, and not differences of degree."[40] Put simply, the concrete universal is the intensive, dynamic system that is the presupposed condition for the possibility of determinate, individuated differences; it is the intensive Idea (*Nous*)/Multiplicity (*Physis*) difference. To place determinate instances in an external relationship to their determinable universals, such as the determinate scarlet in relation to the determinable red, is already to assume an extensive, external relationship between a determinable (red) and its determinate instances (scarlet), or between a determinable one and a multiplicity of determinate particulars. To do this would be to commit the transcendental illusion of assuming the identity of the determinable and determinate rather than accounting for identity itself (recall our discussion of the fourfold roots of representation). For Deleuze, by contrast, the concrete universal is precisely the dynamic system and problem space that allows for the possibility of determinate, extensive relations as it triggers, though singularities and phase transitions, the spatio-temporal processes of individuation.

§5

Let us wrap up this chapter by honing in on the relationship between propositions and concepts. Stated in the starkest terms, for Deleuze and Guattari concepts are not propositions. Based on what we has been said to this point, one can quickly see why Deleuze and Guattari refuse to identify concepts with propositions and why, more importantly, they refuse to grant propositions a privileged status within their or any philosophical project. As Deleuze and Guattari argue in *What is Philosophy?*, "[a]ll concepts are connected to problems without which they would have no meaning," and it is learning, Deleuze argued, in *Difference and Repetition*, that is "the appropriate name for the subjective acts carried out when one is confronted with the objectivity of a problem (Idea)."[41] We are thus brought to the heart of Deleuze and Guattari's concerns to develop a pedagogy of the concept, and we have now developed a number of the components that are associated with this pedagogy. Let us see what we have learned.

Anyone who has spent any amount of time reading Deleuze will likely admit that they are still learning to make sense of Deleuze. This is not a confession of despair, however, for that is precisely the point for Deleuze. There is nothing but learning, nothing but continual responses to the objectivity of a problem. These responses to the problem are precisely the "contemplations," or "subjective acts" writ large that endorse Plotinus's claim that "all is contemplation." These contemplations allow for the transition from a plane of consistency to an extensive, determinate process, including one that can be represented in discursive or propositional form. In learning to drive a stick shift car, one first encounters the objectivity of the problem, the elements and components that constitute the problem space, and then one must bring the elements together such that a systematic consistency develops. This consistency is what enables the actualization of solutions as a routinized, knowledgeable skill.

The same is true relative to the pedagogy of the concept. A concept also has elements. In the case of Descartes's concept of the cogito (see example 1), Deleuze and Guattari argue that the components of this concept are doubting, thinking, and being. These elements constitute the objectivity of the problem space which, in the case of Descartes, entails drawing these elements into a particular systematic relation such that one is able to make propositional claims about the objectivity of knowledge, and do so without presupposing anything about the objective nature of reality. These claims, however, did not wipe away or exhaust the nature of the problem for it retains its irreducible status and may give rise to different propositional claims, claims that in turn may alter the conditions of the problem and lead to yet further problems and the creation of other concepts in response. This is the quick and easy summary of Deleuze and Guattari's argument regarding the creation of concepts, but what is difficult about getting a handle on the thrust of their argument is the strong tendency to associate concepts with propositions, much as there is the tendency for problems to be hidden by solutions in a "true cover up." As a result, philosophical concepts tend to be identified with discursive formations – namely, sentences – that express propositions. For Deleuze and Guattari, however, concepts are both non-discursive and non-propositional. Deleuze and Guattari could not be clearer on this point: "the concept," they argue, "is not discursive, and philosophy is not a discursive formation, because it does not link propositions together" (WP 22/QP 27).

So what, then, is the relationship between philosophy and language? Why do we write and read books, participate in conference talks, or even, Deleuze and Guattari's criticisms notwithstanding, engage in pleasant, philosophical dinner conversation?[42] What are we grappling with, if not discursive formations? As I write, am I not involved in an effort to express my thoughts in words as well and as clearly as I can? To answer the question in haste, I would say that I am attempting to learn and to think, and in the present circumstance I am doing so while confronting the objectivity of the problem of how to make sense of Deleuze and Deleuze and Guattari. The effort to do this is indeed an effort to *make* sense of *What is Philosophy?*, to discern what it means to create concepts, the nature of concepts, and the relation between philosophy, science, and art, among many other things. As an effort to make sense, this effort is a matter of learning rather than one of becoming the brilliant commentator who finds and clearly and precisely represents to others the sense that is already there.

This answer, brief as it is, is very much in line with what I have been arguing for here, and it is what we find at work in *What is Philosophy?* To create a concept is to create a multiplicity, an assemblage, and such multiplicities are the very life of thought, that which is "intrinsic to thought, a condition of possibility of thought itself" (WP 3/QP 19). To close with another example, Deleuze offers the example of a linguistic multiplicity in *Difference and Repetition*. A linguistic multiplicity, Deleuze claims, consists of the phonemes that are the differentiated elements that are drawn into a plane of immanence and consistency, through contractions and contemplations, into a "system of ideal connections . . . a system of differential relations between reciprocally determined genetic elements."[43] These phonemic elements are in turn individuated by virtue of contractions and contemplations of their own "reciprocally determined genetic elements" – namely, they are the contractions of lungs, diaphragm, larynx, tongue, mouth, and so on, that then become the determinate sounds drawn together into a "virtual system of reciprocal connections between 'phonemes'." This virtual system is the plane of consistency, or the "area *ab*" that is the Idea that is then "incarnated in the actual terms and relations of diverse languages."[44] To this mix we can add the objectivity of the problem associated with learning a language, the social interactions and institutional structures and relations that become the elements that need to be drawn into the "virtual system" that is then incarnated in the language that one has come to learn to speak, and speak within an extensive context of social–historical expectations and habits, habits that are themselves the ongoing response to the objectivity of a problem that is living a life. And so on. . . .

The "virtual system of reciprocal connections between phonemes," however, the plane of consistency, is not to be confused with the "empirical usage of a given language," and if this virtual language is to be spoken, Deleuze argues, then "it must be spoken and can be spoken only in the poetic usage of speech coextensive with virtuality."[45] Learning a language is thus much more than learning the set of rules and extensional relations between propositions and the content that renders these propositions true or false. More importantly, for Deleuze learning a language is on a par with learning improvisational jazz, which in turn is on a par with learning to live a life and think. The jazz instructor who "knows" how to play improvisational jazz does indeed possess an "orderly" content that is on display when they successfully play improvisational jazz, but they cannot pass on this "knowledge" in the form of representational content. It is rather a process, what David Sudnow calls "melodying," that is irreducible to a set of extensive rules and relations.[46] The case is the same for one who knows how to speak. One who speaks meaningfully will indeed be in possession of an "orderly" content, but this content is not to be confused with discursive formations, or with propositions and their extensional relations. The "poetic usage of speech" is the hidden power and life of speech, the dynamic, intensive differentiating process of pure immanence (A LIFE) that allows for the possibility of everyday speech which is simply the sedimented, routinized form of the "poetic usage."

With these examples, including our earlier examples from

Kafka, what we have set out to do in this chapter is to discern and draw together a number of concepts and points from Deleuze and Deleuze and Guattari regarding the necessity of the plane of immanence. Rather than set forth the clear, definitive representation of Deleuze and Guattari, however, these efforts are best understood as attempts to engender thought in response to the objectivity of a problem, the problem of life itself, or the problem of how, when, why, and under what circumstances A LIFE of pure immanence becomes the orderly, individuated phenomenon one comes to identify with a life as lived. It is this problem that is the hidden power and life of thought. To think is not to resolve problems; it is to live in perpetual and forced response to them.

Example 3

Deleuze and Guattari begin example 3 with a broad, largely rhetorical question – "Can the history of philosophy be presented from the viewpoint of the instituting of a plane of immanence?" (WP 44/QP 46) – and by the end of the example they divide the history of philosophy into three eras, each of which is to be characterized by the manner in which they both institute the plane of immanence and yet, despite this move, restore pride of place to a form of transcendence. These three eras are the "Eidetic, Critical, and Phenomenological," and because each ultimately restores transcendence they each ultimately turn away from the plane of immanence and form part of "the long history of an illusion [to wit, the transcendental illusion]" (WP 47/QP 49).

Deleuze and Guattari begin their third example with a distinction that looms large in the "Plane of Immanence" chapter – the distinction between *Nous* and *Physis*. The pre-Socratic philosophers, for instance, contended over various views regarding the ultimate nature and substance of reality. For some, what was ultimate were certain physical principles (*Physis*) – water for Thales; earth, wind, water, and fire for Empedocles; and indivisible atoms for Democritus – while for others such as Anaxagoras, and then Socrates, Plato, and the neo-Platonists such as Plotinus, it was argued that a rational or mental principle (*Nous*) is what is ultimate. The standing of immanence in these philosophies is that while all is taken to be water, for instance, or all is made possible by *Nous* for Anaxagoras, immanence itself, Deleuze and Guattari claim, "will be related to something like a 'dative,' Matter or Mind" (WP 44/QP 47). In other words, immanence is not pure immanence, A LIFE, but rather immanence to something ("like a 'dative'"), whereas for Deleuze and Guattari pure immanence is always only immanent to itself and never to something. Deleuze and Guattari are clear on this point: "Whenever immanence is interpreted as immanent 'to' something a confusion of plane and concept results, so that the concept becomes a transcendent universal and the plane becomes an attribute in the concept" (WP 44–5/QP 47). A concept is a working part of the abstract machine, to use the terminology discussed in this chapter, and as such the concept is that which resists actualizing the two poles of stratification and deterritorialization. The concept, however, is always a working part of the abstract machine, or it is a response to the objectivity of the problem (that is, plane of immanence) of staving off the two poles of the abstract machine. The tendency, however, is to confuse immanence of the concept with being an attribute of the concept, an attribute of the universal truth that is always already there for instance (see example 2). In the case of Plotinus, immanence becomes an attribute of the One, the "One beyond the One" that is the universal that becomes the object of philosophical contemplation. This is what characterizes the first era of the history of philosophy, the Eidetic, with its emphasis upon the contemplation of the universal essences or truths that immanence always already belongs to as their attribute.

Why the resistance to immanence? Why the tendency to understand immanence as immanent to something? Might a devil's advocate not argue that the reason we understand immanence as immanent to something, to a universal such as Plotinus's One or Plato's Ideas, is because they are right? Why are Deleuze and Guattari so sure that pure immanence, A LIFE, is only immanent to itself rather than *to* something? There are two related answers to this question. First, by continuing to affirm the PSR, Deleuze and Guattari argue that there must be a reason why there is something at all rather than nothing.[47] One cannot simply assume, as the Eidetic tradition does, according to Deleuze and Guattari, that there is always already a determinate something there to which immanence is immanent, whether this be the One or Ideas. To account for the determinate individuality of an already existent something, Deleuze and Guattari rely upon a Spinozistic theory of infinite substance. It is only an infinite, indeterminate substance that can account for the individuation of finite, determinate substances while the infinite substance itself is, as Spinoza understood it, that which cannot be limited by anything that is not itself. This was why Spinoza famously argued that all determination is negation, for what makes something determinate is the fact that it is not something else, a fact that limits the nature of the something. An absolutely infinite substance, however, must include all, for if there is something this substance is not then this substance becomes limited and determinate.[48] Following in Spinoza's footsteps, Deleuze and Guattari similarly argue that "Immanence is immanent only to itself and consequently captures everything, absorbs All-One, and leaves nothing remaining to which it could be immanent" (WP 45/QP 47). Immanence captures all that is determinate, all that can be understood to be "something," for all that is determinate presupposes, as its sufficient reason, an absolutely infinite substance: namely, the pure immanence of A LIFE. It is when this determinate "something" is taken to be the true substance and subject of philosophy that philosophy then succumbs to the transcendental illusion, and an illusion that has a long history.

In the Kantian (Critical) and Husserlian (Phenomenological) versions of the illusion, immanence becomes immanent to a transcendental subject. This subject, Deleuze and Guattari point out, "is transcendental rather than transcendent, precisely because it is the subject of the field of immanence of all possible experience from which nothing, the external as well as the internal, escapes" (WP 46/QP 48). As with immanence that is immanent only to itself and hence "captures everything," so too does the transcendental subject capture everything, and thus on an initial reading it appears that Kant embraces immanence. For Kant, however, transcendent Ideas become "the 'horizon' of the field immanent to the subject," and the transcendental subject itself becomes that to which immanence belongs. Understood in this way, the infinite nature of substance comes to be limited by the horizon that then becomes an attribute of the transcendental subject. The task for the critical tradition, then, as Kant set it forth, is to assure that our thoughts stay within the proper limits of this horizon.

For Husserl, the transcendent comes to be that which is "transcendent within immanence itself," within the "flux lived by subjectivity" (ibid.). But Husserl's efforts also fail to recognize immanence as only immanent to itself for here too, within the midst of "flux lived by subjectivity," this lived subjectivity "does not belong completely to the self that represents it to itself, [and thus] something transcendent is reestablished on the horizon, in the regions of nonbelonging" (WP 46/QP 48). These nonbelongings constitute the limits of transcendental subjectivity, that which transcends the subject, and this includes the "intentional objects," or noematic correlates of lived experience, as Husserl refers to them, the intersubjective world of others, and "an ideal world populated by cultural formations and the human community" (WP 47/QP 48). As Spinoza taught us, however, whenever substance is limited by something it is not – for example, the nonbelongings of transcendental subjectivity, its horizon, intentional objects, other consciousnesses, and so on – then we have, by definition for Spinoza, a substance that is not infinite, and hence we do not have true, immanent substance, a substance immanent only to itself. Deleuze and Guattari thus echo Spinoza, then, when they claim that "Transcendence enters as soon as movement of infinite speed is stopped" (WP 47/QP 49). Kant's "critical" tradition in philosophy, as well as Husserl's "phenomenological" tradition, each places limits on the immanence of substance, and consequently each makes immanence immanent to something finite and determinate; as a result, Kant and Husserl fall in line with "the long history of an illusion."

Deleuze and Guattari do not dismiss the entire history of philosophy – far from it, for they find numerous philosophers for whom immanence is given a much fuller reckoning than one finds in the three eras examined in example 3. Deleuze and Guattari single out three in particular – Sartre, Hume, and Spinoza.[49] Sartre is an important if perhaps surprising figure to single out, given his connection to the phenomenological tradition, but Deleuze and Guattari are quite straightforward in their assertion that he "restores the rights of immanence" with his "presupposition of an impersonal transcendental field" (WP 47/QP 49). The immanence of the transcendental field is no longer an immanence that belongs to something, to a transcendental ego (hence the importance of Sartre's book *Transcendence of the Ego*), but we have rather an immanence that captures everything. The same is true for "radical empiricism," Deleuze and Guattari argue, for here we have an example of a plane where "immanence is no longer immanent to something other than itself," and the plane of radical empiricism does this for "it does not present a flux of the lived that is immanent to a subject and individualized in that which belongs to a self" (WP 47/QP 49). We have instead simply a radical field of experience, a field that captures everything.[50] And then there is Spinoza, who Deleuze and Deleuze and Guattari hold in the highest esteem. Spinoza, they claim, "was the prince of philosophers ... the only philosopher never to have compromised with transcendence and to have hunted it down everywhere" (WP 48/QP 49). For Spinoza, absolutely infinite substance is the sufficient reason for all that is finite and determinate, for all that is accounted for when the "infinite is

stopped" and limited. Spinoza, Deleuze and Guattari loudly pro-
claim, "fulfilled philosophy," and he did so "because he satisfied its
prephilosophical presupposition" (WP 48/QP 50). That is, Spinoza
fulfilled the prephilosophical presupposition that it is a prephilosophical plane of immanence that every determinate philosophical
concept presupposes, and thus Spinoza set out to restore "the rights
of immanence" and, as Deleuze and Guattari see it, he succeeded.

With this general sketch of the relationship between the plane
of immanence and the history of philosophy, Deleuze and Guattari
turn in the next example (example 4) to offer a more precise
account of how a history of philosophy that restores "the rights of
immanence" should proceed.

Suggested reading for example 3
> Edmund Husserl, *Cartesian Meditations: An Introduction to Phenomenology*
> Jean-Paul Sartre, *The Transcendence of the Ego: An Existentialist Theory of Consciousness.*

Example 4

As Deleuze and Guattari make clear, the plane of immanence is
inseparable from a process of selection – "The plane of immanence
is like a section of chaos and acts like a sieve" (WP 42/QP 44) – in
that it filters the chaos into the problematic field from which a plane
of consistency – the "area *ab*" – is drawn that allows for the actualization and individuation of determinate, finite entities. When the
three eras of the history of philosophy discussed in example 3 make
immanence immanent to something, this something already presupposes that something has been actualized and individuated, and
this in turn presupposes the plane of immanence and plane of consistency. In drawing a plane of consistency in response to the problematic plane of immanence, what we have, as we have seen, is an
assemblage, such as a concept which is an assemblage for Deleuze
and Guattari, and all assemblages, to maintain their status as
working parts of the abstract machine, must stave off the two poles
of the abstract machine. What occurs in the midst of this process of
drawing a plane of consistency, however, and this is how Deleuze
and Guattari begin example 4, is that "When the plane selects what
is right due to thought . . . it relegates other determinations to the
status of mere facts, characteristics of states of affairs, or lived contents" (WP 51–2/QP 53). What is "right due to thought," Deleuze
and Guattari claim, are its "diagrammatic features," or the internal

consistency and "area *ab*" that is inseparable from learning (to continue with a central theme of this book) that cannot be reduced to a determinate set of facts, rules, and/or algorithms. What we have instead is an event, and events always elude, Deleuze and Guattari claim, the determinate states of affairs, facts, and all that can be captured by the net of determinate rules.[51] What is "right due to thought," therefore, and what philosophy does as it engages with our lives as lived and with the states of affairs associated with these lives, is "to draw out concepts from these states of affairs inasmuch as it extracts the event from them" (WP 52/QP 53). In short, philosophy sets out to extract A LIFE, an event, from our lives as lived and the states of affairs within which these lives occur.

What frequently occurs when the plane of immanence selects what is "right due to thought" and relegates the rest to being mere facts, states of affairs, or lived contents, is that thought comes to be understood in relationship to that which is finite, limited and determinate, and this entails both a positive and a negative image. In the previous example we saw that Deleuze and Guattari argued that in the history of philosophy one can find a long history of an illusion when philosophy puts a stop to infinite movement and places immanence in a relationship such that immanence is immanent to something. As with Kant's argument that the transcendental illusion is a natural and inevitable accompaniment to thought, so too for Deleuze and Guattari the illusion regarding transcendence is a likely consequence when a plane of consistency is drawn in response to a problematic plane of immanence, resulting in *both* what is "right due to thought" *and* that which is relegated to the status of being determinate facts and states of affairs. A result of this process, according to Deleuze and Guattari, is that thought itself can come to be thought of in accordance with a *determinate* image, and an image that can be both positive (what is "right due to thought") and negative (the relegated elements, or that which falls from grace with what is positive). These contrasting images of thought are quite common and can be found throughout the history of philosophy. Descartes, for example, works with an image of thought where it is error that "expresses what is in principle negative in thought," and thus it is "Error," Deleuze and Guattari claim, which "is the infinite movement that gathers together the whole of the negative" (WP 52/QP 53). As we saw in the first example, Descartes began his *Meditations* aware that there was much that he had taken to be true in his youth that he later came to realize was false. How could he be sure that what he currently took to be true was not also mistaken?

How can he avoid falling into error? Descartes's answer, and this is his positive image of thought, is that truth becomes the certainty of the subjective grasp itself – namely, the clear and distinct ideas that will result when we follow the proper method and hew close to the limits laid down by clear and distinct ideas.

Error is not the only manner in which the negative image of thought comes to be developed in the history of philosophy, or it is not the only possible image philosophers may presuppose. Deleuze and Guattari claim that there are rival determinations, "like the delirium of the Phaedrus," or the Greek "madness of the double turning away" (WP 54/QP 54): that is, the turning towards Plato's cave that the poets induce in us and the path of philosophy that leads out of the cave and towards the truth. There is also the emphasis the late seventeenth-century philosopher Bernard Fontenelle gives to "ignorance and superstition," which expresses, Deleuze and Guattari claim, "what by right is the negative of thought" (WP 52/QP 53). Then there is Kant's argument about the inevitability of the transcendental illusion. These inevitable illusions entail an image of thought that is less threatened by the error of pursuing a line of thought down the wrong path but rather, as Deleuze and Guattari put it, it is threatened by "Nordic fogs that cover everything" (WP 53/QP 53), a fog brought on by a thought that is not kept within its proper limits.

In the eighteenth century another image of thought emerges, an image that threatens the long history of illusion, the history of putting a stop to the infinite, as discussed in the previous example. This new image emerges with "the substitution of belief for knowledge – that is, a new infinite movement implying another image of thought" (WP 53/QP 54). With this new image of thought it is no longer a matter of being on the path that leads us out of the Platonic cave towards the truth but it is instead a matter of drawing the best inferences. The problem, then, becomes, Deleuze and Guattari claim, one of determining "Under what conditions is inference legitimate?" (ibid.). The radical empiricism and Humeanism of this image of thought will be one that will greatly influence Deleuze, and it is perhaps the restoration of immanence and the capacity of this image of thought to capture everything that woke Kant from his dogmatic slumber and led him to restore the limits that stop the infinite movements, the Nordic fog, that in the end restores transcendence.

The history of philosophy, therefore, is not a history of the progressive realization of truth; nor is the history of philosophy simply a catalogue of random thoughts – the collections of writings that express, as Nietzsche put it, "a type of involuntary and unself-conscious memoir" that serves as "a confession of faith on the part of its author."[52] For Deleuze and Guattari, by contrast, there is a systematic nature to philosophical thought and to the history of philosophy, but this is not a systematic process of progression to an already determined truth. The history of philosophy is rather a history of processes whereby the filtering of the plane of immanence involves "what is right due to thought" – namely, multiplicities and planes of consistency – and it "relegates other determinations to the status of mere facts, characteristics of states of affairs, or lived contents." This leads Deleuze and Guattari to claim that "The history of philosophy is comparable to the art of the portrait" (WP 55/QP 55). This comparison is appropriate, Deleuze and Guattari go on to clarify, not because philosophy is in the business "of 'making lifelike,'" that is, of repeating what a philosopher said," but rather it is involved in "separating out both the plane of immanence," the abstract machine, "and the new concepts he created," or the working parts of the machine; hence the portraits the historian of philosophy creates are "machinic portraits" (WP 55/QP 55–6). In imagining a "machinic portrait of Kant," Deleuze and Guattari propose, "attention should be given to the plane of immanence laid out as abstract machine and to created concepts as [working] parts of the machine" (WP 56/QP 57). In the case of Kant's machinic portrait, for example, we have time as the form of interiority whereby the passive self comes to acquire its determinate givenness, and then we have the relationship of the "I think" to this passive self and "the transcendental field of possible experience, immanent to the 'I' (plane of immanence)" (WP 57/QP 57). The "categories as universal concepts," "the moving wheel of the schemata," and "space as form of exteriority" combine together to provide the "working parts" of Kant's machinic portrait, and this portrait both shows how the plane of immanence gives rise to that which is "right due to thought" – to wit, the legitimate thoughts that arise within the limits of possible experience of the transcendental ego ("I think") – and determines those thoughts that are not "right due to thought" for they transcend the limits of possible experience. The key question for Deleuze and Guattari, however, is the degree to which the concepts created by the philosopher embrace the "rights of immanence" rather than putting a stop to infinite movements in a process that restores transcendence. As Deleuze and Guattari have argued, much of the history of philosophy, Kant included, does not follow Spinoza's lead and restore the rights of immanence, but instead argues for an immanence that is always immanent to something: namely, to an already determinate and individuated substance such as the concept as determinate universal. How, then, can a philosopher create concepts that do embrace the "rights of immanence"? What is involved? This becomes the guiding question of the next chapter and the topic of example 5.

Suggested reading for example 4

    Bernard le Bovier de Fontenelle, *Conversations on the Plurality of Worlds*

    David Hume, *An Enquiry Concerning Human Understanding.*

NOTES

1. G. W. F. Hegel, *Lectures on the History of Philosophy*, ed. Robert F. Brown, trans. Robert F. Brown and J. M. Stewart (Berkeley: University of California Press, 1990), p. 156. See our earlier discussion, p. ??
2. Gilles Deleuze, *Difference and Repetition*, trans. Paul Patton (New York: Columbia University Press, 1994), p. 182.
3. Recall WP 16/QP 22: "All concepts are connected to problems without which they would have no meaning and which can themselves only be isolated or understood as their solution emerges."
4. Franz Kafka, *The Trial*, trans. Willa and Edwin Muir (New York: Schocken, 1964), p. 1.
5. Ibid., p. 4.
6. Ibid.
7. Gilles Deleuze and Félix Guattari, *Kafka: Toward a Minor Literature*, trans. Dana Polan (Minneapolis: University of Minnesota Press, 1986), p. 51.
8. Ibid., p. 48.
9. Ibid.
10. See my *Philosophy at the Edge of Chaos* (Toronto: University of Toronto Press, 2006), where I develop a dynamic systems approach to the reading of Deleuze's work. We will return to this theme again in the Conclusion.
11. *Kafka*, p. 49.
12. Gilles Deleuze, *Desert Islands and Other Texts 1953–1974*, trans. Michael Taormina (New York: Semiotext(e), 2004), p. 96.
13. *Kafka*, p. 51.
14. Ibid.
15. Ibid., p. 52.
16. See *Difference and Repetition*, p. 228: "It is not surprising that, strictly speaking, difference should be 'inexplicable'. Difference is explicated,

but in systems in which it tends to be cancelled; this means only that difference is essentially implicated, that its being is implication. For difference, to be explicated is to be cancelled or to dispel the inequality which constitutes it."

17. See Gilles Deleuze and Félix Guattari, *A Thousand Plateaus: Capitalism and Schizophrenia*, trans. Brian Massumi (Minneapolis: University of Minnesota Press, 1987), p. 4: "All this, lines and measurable speeds, constitutes an assemblage. A book is an assemblage of this kind, and as such is unattributable. It is a multiplicity – but we don't know yet what the multiple entails when it is no longer attributed, that is, after it has been elevated to the status of a substantive." In other words, an assemblage is "unattributable" when it is "elevated to the status of a substantive" – that is, when it is a multiplicity.
18. *Kafka*, p. 49.
19. *Difference and Repetition*, p. 222.
20. See Kant's *Critique of Pure Reason*, trans. Norman Kemp Smith (London: Macmillan, 1929), A297/B353.
21. See *Difference and Repetition*, p. 29: "Difference is 'mediated' to the extent that it is subjected to the fourfold root of identity, opposition, analogy, and resemblance."
22. See Kant's *Critique of Pure Reason*, A433–4/B461–2.
23. See Wilfrid Sellars, *Empiricism and the Philosophy of Mind* (Cambridge, MA: Harvard University Press, [1956] 1997).
24. See John McDowell, *Mind and World* (Cambridge, MA: Harvard University Press, 1996), and especially page 42 for the "frictionless spinning in a void" reference. For his discussion of the "world-disclosing experience," see his essay "What Myth?" in *Inquiry* 50, no. 4 (August 2007), 338–51.
25. Hume, *Treatise of Human Nature*, ed. L. A. Silby-Bigge (Oxford: Clarendon Press, [1739] 1978), p. 637.
26. For a particularly good history of the emergence of analytic philosophy that explores the relationship between Russell and the idealists of his time, see Peter Hylton, *Russell, Idealism, and the Emergence of Analytic Philosophy* (Oxford: Oxford University Press, 1993).
27. Michael Della Rocca, "Taming of Philosophy," in *Philosophy and its History*, ed. Mogens Lærke, Justin E. H. Smith, and Eric Schliesser (Oxford: Oxford University Press, 2013), p. 201.
28. Ibid., p. 202.
29. Bertrand Russell, "Some Explanations in Reply to Mr. Bradley," *Mind* 19, no. 75 (1910), pp. 373–8 (emphasis mine).
30. G. E. Moore, "External and Internal Relations," in *Proceedings of the Aristotelian Society*, New Series, Vol. 20 (1919–20), p. 51, emphasis mine.
31. *Difference and Repetition*, p. 222.
32. See "Method of Dramatization," in *Desert Islands*, p. 116: "If we think

of the Plato from the later dialectic, where the Ideas are something like multiplicities that must be traversed by questions such as *how? how much? In which case?*, then yes, everything I've said has something Platonic about it. If you're thinking of the Plato who favors a simplicity of the esscncc or a ipseity of the Idea, then no."

33. *Difference and Repetition*, p. 182.
34. Ibid., pp. 173–4.
35. *A Thousand Plateaus*, p. 53.
36. *Difference and Repetition*, p. 75.
37. Recall Deleuze and Guattari's definition of chaos as the lack of connection by virtue of the infinite speeds with which things appear and vanish. The chaos needs to be filtered and slowed down in order to allow for the emergence of connections and hence for the fragmentary wholes that are assemblages and multiplicities. Reality, in short, is a chaosmos.
38. In the conclusion to *What is Philosophy?* Deleuze and Guattari stress the importance of chaosmos, referring, for instance, to concepts as a case in point of a "mental chaosmos" (WP 208/QP 196). This theme will become central to Chapter 7 and the Conclusion, but we can already see that the concept of a plane of immanence already presupposed the notion of a chaosmos.
39. Gilles Deleuze, *Essays Critical and Clinical*, trans. Daniel W. Smith and Michael A. Greco (Minneapolis: University of Minnesota Press, 1997), p. 143.
40. *Desert Islands*, p. 43.
41. *Difference and Repetition*, p. 182.
42. Referring to Deleuze and Guattari's claims that philosophy is not to be confused with conversation (see our earlier discussion, p. ??), and thus philosophy is not to be identified with "the Western democratic, popular conception of philosophy as providing pleasant or aggressive dinner conversations at Mr. Rorty's" (WP 144).
43. *Difference and Repetition*, p. 182.
44. Ibid., p. 193.
45. Ibid.
46. See David Sudnow, *Ways of the Hand* (Cambridge, MA: Harvard University Press, 1978). See my discussion in *Deleuze's Hume: Philosophy, Culture and the Scottish Enlightenment* (Edinburgh: Edinburgh University Press, 2009).
47. On this point Deleuze and Guattari are continuing the tradition of Leibniz and Heidegger, especially the Heidegger of his *Introduction to Metaphysics*, ed. Ralph Manheim (New Haven: Yale University Press, 1959).
48. See Spinoza's *Ethics* (*Collected Works of Spinoza*, vol. 1, trans. and ed. Edwin Curley [Princeton: Princeton University Press, 1985]). For the argument that all determination is negation, see letter 50.

49. If one looks through the historical manuscripts Deleuze wrote, one can find a list of examples of philosophers Deleuze believes gave greater weight to the nature of immanence, with especial emphasis placed upon Spinoza (and it is not a coincidence that Deleuze wrote two books and several essays on Spinoza).

50. With the reference to "radical empiricism," the more appropriate reference should perhaps be William James. James is certainly a philosopher Deleuze holds in high esteem, and the reference to "radical empiricism" is no doubt intended to refer us to James, but I have argued that Hume is the more important influence on these matters and the guiding thread through much of Deleuze's own work in thinking through the plane of immanence. See my *Deleuze's Hume.*

51. We will discuss this theme in greater detail in later chapters, especially Chapters 6 and 7, but Deleuze and Guattari will claim that the event is "the part that eludes its own actualization in everything that happens. The event is not a state of affairs. It is actualized in a state of affairs, in a body, in a lived [*un vécu*], but it has a shadowy and secret part that is continually subtracted from or added to its actualization . . . it neither begins nor ends but has gained or kept the infinite movement to which it gives consistency" (WP 156). And in their discussion of art, Deleuze and Guattari contrast the creation of percepts and affects with conceptual creations which involve events, and the "event itself eludes what is" (WP 177).

52. *Beyond Good and Evil,* trans. Walter Kaufmann (New York: Vintage, 1966), section 6, p. 8.

3

How to Become a Philosopher

In the previous chapter we focused upon the metaphysical implications of Deleuze's claim that learning provides us with an example of encountering the objectivity of a problem, where a problem is irreducible to, and is not exhausted by, the solutions it makes possible. Although we began with examples of learning to swim or drive a stick shift car, we soon saw that the implications for learning were extended by Deleuze well beyond the first-person point of view associated with these examples. Learning does indeed entail drawing from the problem space a sufficient degree of connections – a plane of consistency – in order to sustain the efforts involved in learning, and this learning cannot be captured by a set of rules that would predetermine and guide the process. As a metaphysical concept, what is fundamental to learning is not the end for the sake of which one might engage in the process of learning – to swim, for example – but rather it is the process of sustaining a dynamic and systemic range of connections – an assemblage or multiplicity of ideal connections, as we have seen – that avoids *both* the chaos that renders connections impossible *and* the rigidity of rules that undermines the dynamism of learning itself. This sustaining of consistent relations, a sustaining that is "self-positing" or "autopoetic," as Deleuze and Guattari put it (WP 11), maintains a dynamic equilibrium state between chaos and rigid stratification, and this is precisely the plane of consistency that staves off the two poles of the abstract machine (see Chapter 2). This dynamic state and plane of consistency are what need to be produced in any and every successful case of learning. The plane of immanence is thus the objectivity of a problem itself, the problem space that is A LIFE, and this allows for the emergence of assemblages and multiplicities, multiplicities being for Deleuze "true substantive, substance itself,"[1] and it is this substance that is the sufficient reason of all that appears.

In this chapter we will narrow our focus to the efforts of the philosopher, to what is involved in becoming a philosopher and the processes associated with creating concepts. As we have seen in previous chapters, Deleuze and Guattari argue that the specific task of philosophy is to create concepts, and "the concept," they argue, "belongs to philosophy and only to philosophy" (WP 34/QP 37). It was in the context of our effort to understand the nature of the concept that we were led to our analysis of the nature of problems and learning, and then to the wide-ranging metaphysical implications that Deleuze and Guattari draw from this. It is now time to return to one of our guiding questions: namely, what does the philosopher do when they create concepts? We can start by turning to what Deleuze and Guattari take to be two common misperceptions regarding who or what philosophers are and what it is they do.

The first and most notable misperception regarding philosophers is the assumption that what they do is to ask questions, the assumption being that such questions eventually lead to the solutions that constitute the real payoff for engaging in philosophy. This assumption, however, is precisely what Deleuze and Guattari criticize when they claim that problems are irreducible to their solutions. Problems are not simply the ghostly premonition of a solution to come; to the contrary, they have an objectivity and reality that are never exhausted by any of the solutions or concepts that come to be associated with them. It is for this reason that Deleuze and Guattari argue that "little is gained by saying that philosophy asks 'questions' because *question* is merely a word for problems that are irreducible to those of science" (WP 79/QP 76). We will explore the relationship between philosophy and science in a later chapter (Chapter 5), but for the moment we can say that philosophical questioning is not an exercise of thought that is turned towards problems that can be solved by way of a mapping and tracking of the relations between the qualities and properties of determinate facts. These determinate facts, Deleuze and Guattari argue, are just what needs to be accounted for, and this account was the primary metaphysical aim of the previous chapter. The philosopher's questions, therefore, are to be understood in relation to the problems that are the conditions presupposed by determinate facts rather than the questions being understood in terms of determinate, individuated solutions that will resolve and subsequently hide and displace the problems.

The second misperception of philosophers is the tendency to associate them with schools and established doctrines. One comes to learn the doctrines of the Platonic, Aristotelian, or Hegelian schools of thought, for example, and such a student may even proudly refer to themselves as a Platonist, Aristotelian, Hegelian (or Deleuzian!), and while the interpretations of the particular philosopher may take on a variety of forms and interesting variations, the *philosophy* the acolyte professes continues to be perceived as falling within the orbit of the philosopher in question. For Deleuze and Guattari, however, such a mindset in philosophy reflects a "bad taste," or an "art of the plebe," in that it reduces the very creative and dynamic process associated with philosophy to a number of key propositions associated with "teachers or leaders of schools" (WP 80/QP 77). The analytic tradition in philosophy (which will be discussed in Chapter 6) may appear to be an exception to this characterization of philosophy, for many analytic philosophers pride themselves on being more concerned with following the development of problems wherever they may lead than with remaining true to a particular school or teacher. Despite this tendency, the dominant trend within analytic philosophy is to follow the lead of the sciences and place their work in subservience to the solutions that are the sought-for product of their efforts. Analytic philosophy, therefore, will not give true pride of place to problems, or restore the "rights of immanence" (WP 47/QP 49) as this was discussed in the previous chapter. On Deleuze and Guattari's view of becoming a philosopher, therefore, one does not set out to ask questions that will lead to determinate solutions; nor does one become subservient to the set doctrines of a school or individual philosopher. What is necessary, instead, they argue, is to acquire a philosophical taste for problems and for the *conceptual personae* that "play a part in the very creation of the author's concepts" (WP 63/QP 62) and serve as the "powers of concepts" (WP 65/QP 64). To form a sense of this philosophical taste and the role conceptual personae play, let us turn first to Heidegger, for with Heidegger we find a similar effort to distance the philosophical task of thinking from the scientific and technological efforts to control and order the world of things, or the world of determinate beings, facts, lived states, and states of affairs, as Deleuze and Guattari would put it.

§1

The effort on the part of Heidegger to call upon philosophy to think the "extra-ordinary," rather than the ordinary, everyday world of beings, is well known and has been discussed in a number of different contexts (including serving as an explanation for Heidegger's becoming involved with the National Socialist party).[2] Our concern here is with how Heidegger's arguments are part of an effort to highlight the distinctive nature of philosophy *vis-à-vis* science. In *An Introduction to Metaphysics*, for example, Heidegger argues that "No questioning and accordingly no single scientific 'problem' can be fully intelligible if it does not include – that is, ask – the question of all questions,"[3] this question being "Why are there essents rather than nothing?"[4] But if one fully integrates the "question of all questions" into one's inquiry, then one forever risks, as Heidegger fully recognized, undoing the relationship between thought and the determinate content that gives this thought its meaning and significance. For example, in matters of religious faith what may motivate the thoughts one has of God could well be the "question of all questions." God, a person of faith will argue, is the reason why there are beings (essents) rather than nothing – "'In the beginning God created heaven and earth.'"[5] For Heidegger, however, this answer can "supply no answer to our question because they [the person of faith] are in no way related to it [that is, the "question of all questions"]."[6] If one's faith is indeed motivated by the fundamental question, then that which provides the meaning and significance for one's faith – namely, God – is itself subject to the "question of all questions" if God is taken to be a being rather than nothing. "Why is there God rather than nothing?" they might ask if they truly raise the "question of all questions." For Heidegger this is an essential truth of faith: "a faith that does not perpetually expose itself to the possibility of unfaith is not faith but merely a convenience."[7]

The same risk is in play, Heidegger argues, for the scientific mode of thinking if it does not confront the fundamental question, at which point science becomes an applied discipline with preconceived targets and goals, along with a set of established metrics and rubrics that are laid out in order to help one to achieve these goals. This was the situation Heidegger found himself in, a state of affairs where "science today is a technical, practical matter of gaining information and communicating it. No awakening of the spirit at all can proceed from it as science. Science itself needs such an awakening."[8] Such awakening will come about, in part, through a resurrection of the fundamental question, what Heidegger calls the question of Being (*Seinsfrage*), which had been forgotten with the advent of philosophy itself in ancient Greece (for more on this, see the next chapter). With this awakening science regains its spirit, and just as religious faith risks unfaith if it truly engages with the fundamental question, so too does science open itself to the undoing of its own established ways of thinking about the world.[9] For Heidegger it is philosophy that thinks in a manner that is irreducible to any set or ordering of determinate facts, and even if philosophy begins with and is always situated among such facts, its thoughtful engagement with these facts leads ultimately, if philosophy asks the "question of all questions," to an undoing of the determinate world of essents and a subsequent thinking of the extra-ordinary. Deleuze and Guattari will call upon philosophy to enact a similar relationship to established, determinate facts, and they will recognize the paradoxical implications that befall philosophy as a result: "If philosophy is paradoxical by nature, this is not because it sides with the least plausible opinion or because it maintains contradictory opinions but rather because it uses sentences of a standard language to express something that does not belong to the order of opinion or even of the proposition" (WP 80/QP 78).

We can now begin to make some preliminary claims regarding what Deleuze and Guattari think is involved in becoming a philosopher. Following the lead of Heidegger, one becomes a philosopher when one's attitude and stance towards the way of beings, the way things are, becomes problematic. In these states one is not content with what is the case but one finds instead a host of problems inseparable from what is the case. It is for this reason that Deleuze argues that the question, "what is the nature of x?" is an inadequate question in that it fails to encompass the full range of the problem and attempts to reduce the problem to a simple, determinate nature that will already presage its answer. A better question or set of questions in response to the problem space that prompts the philosophical attitude would be, Deleuze claims, "the questions who? how? how much? where and when? in which case,"[10] for with these questions we get a better sense of the "genuine spatio-temporal coordinates of the Idea," or of the problem spaces intrinsic to multiplicities that are then incarnated in spatio-temporal processes.[11] For a philosopher, therefore, the objectivity of a problem is not a state with determinate content, a state where we can locate what it is that is going on and move on from there; rather, a problem is best characterized as an event with unknown conditions and implications such that one is left, much as K. from *The Trial* was (see Chapter 2), asking the questions Deleuze lists. It is in this way that a philosopher's efforts become paradoxical, for as they express their concepts with the "sentences of a standard language," the problematic nature of these concepts problematizes the determinate meaning one might ordinarily take the sentence to have, and this leaves one wondering under what conditions the sentence has the meaning it has, or if it has any meaning at all. One often confronts such sentences with an incredulous stare. In what circumstance, when expressed by whom, how, where, when, and in which times and places does this sentence have any meaning?

As a philosopher sets to work, they do so amidst a world of things, with the standard sentences in their language along with the established customs, norms, traditions, and institutions of the society within which they live, work, and think. A traditional way in which this work has been divided is to identify three distinct tasks that engage the philosopher. According to the Stoics, who were the first to set forth this tripartite division, the philosopher is a lover and seeker of wisdom, and wisdom, as the Stoics understand it, involves the "knowledge of human and divine matters,"[12] and this knowledge in turn entails three distinct problems: namely, the problem of understanding the nature of knowledge itself, the nature of human matters, and the nature of divine matters. As Diogenes Laërtius succinctly describes the pursuit and love of wisdom (*philo sophia*), it entails logic (knowledge), ethics (human matters), and physics (divine matters).[13] In his Preface to his *Groundwork of the Metaphysics of Morals*, Kant adopts this tripartite division and argues that it "is perfectly suitable to the subject [namely, philosophy] and there is no need to improve upon it."[14] Deleuze and Guattari will likewise adopt this tripartite division – what they call "the philosophical trinity" (WP 77/QP 74) – and it is in fact central to the manner in which they set forth the role conceptual personae play in philosophy. It is to Kant's and Deleuze and Guattari's understanding of this tripartite division that we now turn.

§2

In addition to arguing that the Stoic division of philosophy into logic, ethics, and physics is "perfectly suited to the subject" of philosophy itself, Kant argues that we could "add its principle" so that we are better "able to determine correctly the necessary subdivisions."[15] In other words, we could add the principle that accounts for this tripartite division of the nature of philosophy. Kant claims this principle is the principle of rational cognition. In particular, Kant argues that all rational cognition is "either material and concerned with some object, or formal and occupied only with the form of the understanding and of reason itself and with the universal rules of thinking in general." "Formal logic," Kant continues, "is called logic," and is concerned only with "the form of the understanding and of reason itself." The rational cognition that is material addresses "determinate objects" and will in turn focus on either "the laws of nature" (divine matters, or physics) or "the laws of freedom" (human matters, or ethics).

In the *Critique of Pure Reason*, Kant will elaborate further upon this tripartite division by detailing the relationship between understanding and reason. The understanding, according to Kant, is the faculty whereby a determinate object, given to us through the intuitions of sensibility, is thought.[16] The understanding is thus the faculty that enables us to have thoughts regarding determinate objects. What the understanding does to secure the thought of a determinate object is to synthesize the unity of appearances by way of *a priori* rules – namely, the transcendental categories of the understanding.[17] Logic, for Kant, thus becomes the "science of the rules of the understanding," which can in turn be divided into general logic regarding "the absolutely necessary rules of thought without which there can be no employment whatsoever of the understanding," and logic of the "special employment of the understanding,"[18] which is the logic and rules associated with the sciences. Reason, by contrast, provides for the unity of the rules of the understanding themselves by way of principles. As Kant puts it, reason is the "faculty of the unity of the rules of understanding under principles,"[19], with these principles being referred to, a few pages later, as "transcendental ideas."[20]

It is at this point that the faculty of the imagination looms largest in Kant's project, for it is this faculty that helps Kant to address the question one might now ask regarding the nature of the appearances themselves, the appearances that are synthesized into a unity of thought by the rules of the understanding. What accounts for their determinate identity and unity? For Kant, it is the imagination that provides for this necessary unity. The imagination, he argues, "aims at nothing but necessary unity in the synthesis of what is manifold in appearance," so "experience itself . . . [is] possible only by means of this transcendental function of the imagination."[21] In short, if the understanding provides for the unity of a given object by way of the rules of the understanding, and if reason provides for the unity of the rules of the understanding, it is the imagination that gets this process off the ground and it is what accounts for the "synthesis of intuitions, conforming as it does to the categories, [which] must be the transcendental synthesis of the imagination," and this synthesis, Kant urges, "is an action of the understanding on the sensibility; and is its first application – and thereby the ground of all its other applications – to the objects of our possible intuition" (ibid.). It is the imagination, therefore, that appears to be the key, generative faculty upon which both understanding and reason depend. Without imagination, there would be no unitary, determinate something, and hence no determinate formal rules of the understanding and reason (that is, the categories and "transcendental ideas").[22]

This primacy of the imagination as it has just been sketched here, however, was called upon in order to address a problem – namely, how we account for determinate unity itself, whether this be the unity of appearances themselves, appearances that are then synthesized in accordance with the categories of the understanding, categories that are then unified in accordance with the "transcendental ideas" of reason. Early critics of Kant, however, noted that Kant had not adequately addressed this problem. Solomon Maïmon, for instance, argued that Kant left a *quid juris* question unanswered when he argued that *determinable* categories and concepts are external to the *determinate* intuitions that are unified in accordance with the rules of these categories. The unanswered *quid juris* question is how do we account for the relationship between *determinable* concepts and their *determinate* intuitions? Is the determinable being applied correctly, or what justifies its being applied to these rather than to other determinate intuitions? To resolve these questions, Maïmon argues that we need to understand the categories not as already constituted facts and identities that are then related and applied to a determinate content; rather, Maïmon begins with the concept of differentials and argues that one is able to *generate* and thereby account for the very relationship between a *determinable* concept and its *determinate* content. Maïmon thus exemplifies a turn to generative account of difference with his theory of differentials, and this will greatly influence Deleuze's own project.

With this influence in mind we can now turn to Deleuze and Guattari's version of the tripartite division of philosophy – what they call the "philosophical trinity" – to see how they extend Kant's project along lines suggested by Maïmon, and how in doing so they are led to an understanding of philosophy that is in many ways closer to the pre-Kantian tradition (namely, the Stoic tradition, but also Hume and Spinoza as well) than the tradition that has largely followed in Kant's footsteps.

§3

The most obvious way in which Deleuze (and later Deleuze and Guattari) follow Maïmon's lead is by turning to Hume. As Beiser has argued in his book, *Fate of Reason*, Hume left in his wake a skeptical dilemma that would become a major problem for the enlighten- ment philosophers: either reason leads us to skepticism and the recognition that all we know of causal relations, for instance, is merely a constant conjunction of impressions, or we must have a blind, dogmatic faith in causality, among other things, that cannot be justified by reason. Much of the German tradition of idealism, Beiser argues, can be understood as an attempt to steer a middle path between skepticism and dogmatism. As for Maïmon, Beiser argues that he "falls under the spell of Hume's skepticism, doubt- ing whether Kant ever rescues the possibility of natural science from Humean doubts."[23] In short, Maïmon concludes that there is no way, despite Kant's arguments, "of distinguishing cases where there is only a contingent constant conjunction from those where there is a universal and necessary connection," and as a result Kant "leaves the faculty of judgment without a rule for determining *when the category of causality applies to a sequence of perceptions*."[24] In other words, Kant leaves the *quid juris* question unaddressed. Since Kant is left unable to account for when a category applies to a sequence of perceptions or not, Maïmon's approach, by contrast, is to avoid the attempt altogether and argue that the categories are not rules external to the intuitions to which they apply; rather, and as Beiser shows, Maïmon returns to "the classical idea of the infinite under- standing, the *intellectus archetypus*," and it is this infinite understand- ing "which creates all objects in the very act of knowing them."[25] It is this return to the metaphysics of an infinite understanding that appeals to Deleuze and Guattari, who will also return to a Spinozist metaphysics of infinite substance (as we saw in earlier chapters) in order to account for the possibility of determinate identities.

We are now in a position to clarify the "philosophical trinity" that characterizes philosophy according to Deleuze and Guattari and see why it frames much of what they have to say about the nature of philosophy and what is involved in becoming a philosopher and creating concepts. Deleuze and Guattari state the nature of the trinity as follows:

> Philosophy presents three elements, each of which fits with the other two but must be considered for itself: the prephilosophical plane it must lay out (immanence), the persona or personae it must invent and bring to life (insistence), and the philosophical concepts it must create (consistency). Laying out, inventing, and creating constitute the philosophical trinity. . . . (WP 76–7/QP 74)

The terminology used to describe the three elements of the trinity may appear to be obscure, but we have already seen in earlier chapters how important it is to understand concepts in relation to problems, where problems are what is laid out when the plane of immanence serves as a sieve and filter of chaos. The problem space of a plane of immanence then allows for the possibility of drawing planes of consistency, and this is what one does when they create concepts. After their description of the three elements, Deleuze and Guattari provide us with a further clue to clarify the concepts that are operating in the background when they compare the three elements to reason, imagination, and understanding, with Kant's work no doubt in mind here. Hume, however, is also thrown into the mix as it is a philosophical faculty they call *taste* that co-adapts the three elements, for "none of these elements are deduced from the others" (WP 77/QP 74), and it is this taste that "regulates the creation of concepts" (ibid.):

> If the laying out of the plane is called Reason, the invention of personae Imagination, and the creation of concepts Understanding, then taste appears as the triple faculty of the still-undetermined concept, of the persona still in limbo, and of the still-transparent plane. (WP 77/QP 74–5)

Let us begin to unpack these claims. As was pointed out earlier, for Kant reason is the "faculty of the unity of the rules of understanding under principles" (A303/B358), or under "transcendental ideas," as Kant will later put it (A311/B368). In *Difference and Repetition* Deleuze intentionally adopts Plato's and Kant's concept of the Idea.[26] With respect to Kant's "transcendental ideas," what is most striking is that they constitute a problem without a determinate solution. For Kant the "concepts of reason" or "transcendental ideas" are what "enable us to conceive," just as the "concepts of the understanding" (the categories) enable us to understand. However, when it comes to the transcendental ideas, "No actual experience has ever been completely adequate to it, yet to it every actual experience belongs" (A311/B367). Stated slightly differently, and in the Deleuzian manner of earlier chapters, reason is the faculty or process that lays out a plane of immanence, the objectivity of a problem, and it is this plane that is presupposed by every plane of consistency that allows for the actualization of every determinate solution, and a solution that never exhausts the objectivity of the problem (solutions are never "completely adequate to it," to use Kant's phrasing). Deleuze thus largely adopts Kant's understanding of the transcendental idea as a problem that is irreducible to any and every solution, but there is a key difference. Whereas Kant will ground the faculty of reason, along with the understanding and imagination, in a non-empirical transcendental ego along with its noumenal counterpart in the thing-in-itself – in what Deleuze calls a "common sense" move – Deleuze insists there is a fundamental heterogeneity and divergence between the three elements of philosophy rather than a common source of unity.[27] As a result of the fundamental heterogeneity and divergence, what is needed is the faculty of taste that will co-adapt and bring the heterogeneity into consistency without presupposing a predetermining unity to guide the process.

Let us move on now to the creation of concepts, which Deleuze and Guattari associate with the faculty of the Understanding. With Kant's theory in mind, along with the arguments from previous chapters, we can see why Deleuze and Guattari would link Understanding with the creation of concepts. For Kant the understanding allows for the intuitions of the sensibility to be thought once the intuitions are synthesized in accordance with the rules (transcendental categories) of the understanding. For the creation of concepts we also have, Deleuze and Guattari argue, the need to draw the elements of the concept into a plane of consistency, into the "area *ab*" of earlier chapters, and it is this consistency that is integral to the creation of the concept, just as, to recall an earlier example, the paradoxical consistency of the behaviors of the monkey in the face of the objectivity of the problem of finding food under boxes of a particular color allowed for the possibility of a solution (namely, knowledge of where the food could be found). There are key differences between Kant and Deleuze and Guattari. For our present purposes, two differences stand out. First, for Deleuze and Guattari, the elements that are brought together into a consistent system are not finite, self-identical givens as they are for Kant, but are rather multiplicities in their own right, multiplicities with their own elements – multiplicities – and so on *ad infinitum*. This was precisely the reason why the substance associated with concepts, as with all phenomena for Deleuze, is an absolute, infinite substance. The second key difference is that whereas Kant argues that the intuitions are synthesized in accordance with the rules of the understanding, for Deleuze and Guattari there are no rules. The consistency associated with the creation of concepts is irreducible to a self-identical rule that is then applied to the elements to be synthesized. The consistency of the elements emerges in a dynamic, "autopoetic" fashion (to use Deleuze and Guattari's term [WP 11/ QP 16]), and without the guidance of a predetermining rule.

This brings us to the next and third element of philosophy, and this is precisely the element that is the central concern of the "Conceptual Personae" chapter of *What is Philosophy?* It is significant that Deleuze and Guattari identify the "invention of personae" with Imagination. With Kant the faculty of the imagination provided, as we saw, the "unity" that makes possible the "action of the understanding on the sensibility," and this transcendental synthesis of the imagination is in fact the "first application" of the understanding on the sensibility (B152). Largely the same is true with respect to conceptual personae – they provide the dynamic unity that regulates the creative process and synthesis of elements that becomes the internal consistency of the concept. The conceptual persona thus mediates between the plane of immanence – the problem space of A LIFE – and the consistency of the concept, as the following quotation makes clear:

> Is there something else, in Descartes's case, other than the created cogito and the presupposed image of thought? Actually there is something else, somewhat mysterious, that appears from time to time or that shows through and seems to have a hazy existence halfway between concept and preconceptual plane, passing from one to the other. (WP 61/QP 60)

This mysterious "something else" is the conceptual persona, whose hazy existence is not to be confused either with the concept – for example, Descartes's cogito – or with the preconceptual plane – that is, with the problem space associated with the unquestioned assumptions regarding what it means to think, to be, to doubt. To place this "something else" of conceptual personae into the context of what it means to become a philosopher, we could say that the conceptual persona facilitates the problematizing move away from the unquestioned assumptions of our lives as lived, and it facilitates the move to the plane of consistency made possible by the plane of immanence that is the result of the problematizing move. In short, a conceptual persona allows for both the move towards the problem space inseparable from the realities of our determinate lives as lived and towards the consistency and substance that is the sufficient reason for all determinate phenomena. Deleuze and Guattari thus argue that

> The destiny of the philosopher is to become his conceptual persona or personae, at the same time that these personae themselves become something other than what they are historically, mythologically, or commonly (the Socrates of Plato, the Dionysus of Nietzsche, the Idiot of Nicholas of Cusa). (WP 64/QP 63)

The conceptual personae of a philosopher, therefore, are not to be confused with what they might be commonly thought to be, whether as historical or mythological phenomena (for example, Dionysus, Zarathustra, and so on). The conceptual personae become something other, something "hazy" and "mysterious." At the same time, the personae are not simply to be thought of as spokespersons for the philosopher, representing the philosopher's views and concepts as if in a dialogue with rival positions one could take. Deleuze and Guattari are very clear in their warning of the

> danger of confusing the dialogue's characters with conceptual personae: they only nominally coincide and do not have the same role. The character of a dialogue sets out concepts . . . conceptual personae [on the other hand] carry out the movements that describe the author's plane of immanence, and they play a part in the very creation of the author's concepts. (WP 63/QP 62)

What, then, is the role of the conceptual persona? What is the status of this hazy "something else" that is to be confused neither with the preconceptual plane of an already affirmed and assumed reality – for example, mythological or historical characters – nor with the concepts the characters of a dialogue may then discuss and debate? Deleuze and Guattari provide some clues when they claim that the "conceptual persona and the plane of immanence presuppose each other. Sometimes the persona seems to precede the plane, sometimes to come after it" (WP 75/QP 73). On the one hand, the conceptual persona functions much as Nietzsche's "misty vapor" served as the condition for the creation of novelty in a historical context.[28] As Nietzsche argued, one should not remain single-mindedly focused on the past for this will undo the possibility of creativity. At the same time, one does not ignore history and act blindly and in ignorance of what has gone before. What is necessary is precisely the "misty vapor" that problematizes and renders profound what had previously been the unquestioned superficiality and simplicity of everyday realities.[29] As Deleuze and Guattari extend Nietzsche's arguments, the "hazy existence" (*existence flou* in French a likely allusion to Nietzsche's "misty vapor") or conceptual persona renders the everyday problematic as it "plunges into the chaos from which it extracts the determinations with which it produces the diagrammatic features of a plane of immanence" (WP 75/QP 73). The plane of immanence, as we saw in the previous chapter, is "like a section of chaos and acts like a sieve" (WP 42/QP 44). In itself, chaos involves the infinite speeds that do not allow for the connections and relations necessary for a determinate, individuated entity to emerge. For the process of individuation to get under way, therefore, the plane of immanence filters ("like a sieve") the chaos and "extracts the determinations" or elements that constitute the objectivity of a problem, a problem space that is then drawn into a plane of consistency that comes with the creation of concepts. Conceptual personae are these hazy elements that problematize the everyday, already given elements and serve as the condition for the creation of philosophical concepts, or they are the conditions for the possibility of becoming a philosopher. As Deleuze and Guattari put it: "the philosopher is only the envelope of his principal persona and of all the other personae who are the intercessors, the real subjects of his philosophy" (WP 64/QP 62). The conceptual personae are intercessors or mediators of the philosopher's philosophy for they mediate *between* the chaos that is drawn into a problematizing plane of immanence *and* the necessary unity and consistency that is integral to the creation of concepts. Just as the imagination serves, for Kant, a fundamental role in allowing for the possibility of thought by providing the necessary unity that the understanding puts to work upon the sensibility, so too the conceptual persona provides the "mobile territories" (WP 67/QP 66) on a plane of immanence that then becomes drawn into the consistency inseparable from the creation of concepts, and hence for the possibility of philosophical thought (as opposed to everyday, routine thought [recall our discussion of Heidegger]). It is for this reason that Deleuze and Guattari argue that the conceptual persona serves as "thought's internal conditions for its real exercise with this or that conceptual persona" (WP 69/QP 68).

Let us turn to some examples to clarify the role of conceptual personae within the work of philosophers. We have already drawn from Nietzsche's notion of the "misty vapor," but it is also Nietzsche that Deleuze and Guattari point to as the prime example of a philosopher whose thought was conditioned by conceptual personae. Nietzsche is one of but a "few philosophers," Deleuze and Guattari claim, who "worked so much with both sympathetic (Dionysus, Zarathustra) and antipathetic (Christ, the Priest, the Higher Men, and Socrates) conceptual personae" (WP 65/QP 63). The point for Deleuze and Guattari is that whether it is Dionysus in *Birth of Tragedy*, Zarathustra in *Thus Spoke Zarathustra*, or the various places where the Priest and Socrates appear, these personae become part of the conceptual apparatus that enables Nietzsche to rethink the unquestioned assumptions of everyday morality. Zarathustra does not represent Nietzsche's philosophical concepts, nor do Socrates and the Priest represent the philosophies being criticized; rather, Zarathustra and Socrates are movements of thought itself, or they "carry out the movements that describe the author's [Nietzsche's] plane of immanence" (WP 63/QP 62). That is, the conceptual personae are becomings, or what Deleuze and Guattari call "mobile territories" (WP 67/QP 66), that both plunge into the chaos in a process of deterritorialization that undermines and problematizes the obviousness of the everyday – where the sentences of standard language come to "express something that does not belong to the order of opinion or even of the proposition" (WP 80/QP 78) – and effect a process of reterritorialization that allows for the creation of a new thought and concept that enable a novel way of thinking and conceiving. As Deleuze and Guattari put it in the "Geophilosophy" chapter of *What is Philosophy?* (see the next chapter), "Philosophy is reterritorialized on the concept" (WP 101/QP 97), and this is the way in which conceptual personae "play a part in the very creation of the author's concepts" (WP 63/QP 62). As Deleuze and Guattari state this point, and in italics, "*The role of conceptual personae is to show thought's territories, its absolute deterritorializations and reterritorializations*" (WP 69/QP 67). A philosopher's conceptual personae thus chart the tendencies of a determinate thought on the problematic plane of immanence and move this thought into the chaos that deterritorializes and mystifies the everyday "order of opinion," and then the personae provide the "mobile territories" or unities (hence the comparison of the invention of personae with Kant's faculty of imagination) that allow for the possibility of the consistency necessary for creating the concept that reterritorializes the process of thought.

To restate this point, we could argue that when one becomes a philosopher one creates concepts that are not to be confused with representations of processes of becoming but they are processes of becoming themselves, or thought as becoming. As Deleuze and Guattari argued earlier in *What is Philosophy?*, whenever there is a process of becoming, the components of this process "remain distinct, but something passes from one to the other, something that is undecidable between them. There is an area *ab* that belongs to both *a* and *b*, where *a* and *b* 'become' indiscernible" (WP 19–20/QP 25 [see Chapter 1]). The "Conceptual Persona" chapter offers the following example of this process: "Becoming is not being, and Dionysus becomes philosopher at the same time that Nietzsche becomes Dionysus" (WP 65/QP 64). The relationship between the conceptual persona and the philosopher, between the "envelope . . . [and their] principal personae" (WP 65/QP 63), is thus one of becoming. As Nietzsche's thinking becomes deterritorialized, or as "Nietzsche becomes Dionysus," Nietzsche rethinks or thinks differently the given assumptions regarding the origins of Greek tragedy, and this rethinking in turn becomes reterritorialized on the concepts Nietzsche will create – for example, the concept of will to power.

Deleuze and Guattari go on to offer a number of other examples of conceptual personae and even offer what one could call a taxonomy of such personae. Some personae are prominent in their pathic features – the Madman or Idiot, for example, carries out movements in thought that deterritorializes it and leads to the discovery "in thought [of] an inability to think" (WP 70/QP 69). At the same time, the conceptual persona of the Idiot provides Nicholas of Cusa the mediator necessary for the creation of his own concepts.[30] Other personae stress "*relational features*" (WP 70–1/QP 69), such as the Friend, the Claimant, Rival, or, in the case of Kierkegaard, the Fiancée, where Regina becomes a deterritorializing force on the thoughts regarding commitment, relationship, and faithfulness that provides the force of the concept of the knight of faith.[31] Some personae are dominated by their dynamic features – "leaping like Kierkegaard, dancing like Nietzsche" (WP 71/QP 69); others are dominated by their "*juridical features*" – such as when "Leibniz turns the philosopher into the Lawyer of a god who is threatened on all sides . . . Or the strange persona of Investigator advanced by the empiricists" (WP 72/QP 70); and finally, some personae are characterized by their "*existential features*" – "Spinoza's liking for battles between spiders," for instance, reveals, Deleuze and Guattari claim,

"Possibilities of life or modes of existence [that] can be invented only on a plane of immanence that develops the power of conceptual personae" (WP 73/QP 71). To conclude this list of examples, we can take the case of Hume's concept of belief, one of many Deleuze claims Hume created.[32] What made this concept possible, Deleuze and Guattari argue, was a "different persona [that] call[s] for other concepts (belief, for example, and the Investigator)" (WP 81/QP 78). In other words, the conceptual persona of the Investigator transformed the concepts and thoughts regarding knowledge by deterritorializing and problematizing that which was taken to secure knowledge. In short, by pushing knowledge towards the plane of immanence and the problematic, it is the conceptual persona of the Investigator who plunges into the unknown conditions of the problem, following leads and calculating probabilities, and it is this in turn that leads to the creation of the concept belief and to the transformation of knowledge into one based on a theory of probabilities.

A key point the example from Hume highlights is that the conceptual persona carries out the deterritorializing movement which is "by right due to thought" (see example 4) and it, at the same time, carries out a reterritorializing movement that becomes concepts. The conceptual personae are therefore critical, according to Deleuze and Guattari, to the process of problematizing the current, standard ways of thinking while at the same time allowing for the possibility of bringing about other ways of thinking with the creation of concepts. The conceptual persona, in other words, is essential to becoming a philosopher. Nietzsche, for instance, becomes a philosopher as he becomes Dionysus and problematizes the standard conception of Dionysus, while at the same time Dionysus becomes reterritorialized as one of Nietzsche's key concepts – the Dionysian. Hume becomes a philosopher as he becomes an Investigator and problematizes a world that has suddenly become filled with doubts and suspicions, and then the Investigator becomes reterritorialized as Hume's concept of belief. What we can see as necessary in this process of becoming a philosopher is a taste for problems. The reason for this is rather straightforward: by pushing thought to the problematic, infinite substance (A LIFE) that is the sufficient reason of all determinate phenomena, including the already determinate Dionysus, Investigator, and so on, this deterritorializing thought enters a realm where no measure or rule can dictate and predetermine how to proceed. "No measure will be found in those infinite movements that make up the plane of immanence" (WP

77/QP 75). Philosophical taste thus becomes necessary, Deleuze and Guattari argue, for "No rule, and above all no discussion, will say in advance whether this is the good plane, the good persona, or the good concept" (WP 82/QP 79). We can only determine success and failure "as we go along and on the basis of their coadaptations" (ibid.) – that is, success and failure are based on how well the conceptual personae move thought towards the problematic plane of immanence and, in return, how well the concept draws the elements from the problematized plane into a plane of consistency that becomes a philosophical concept. In short, the question is whether learning has become possible. The coadaptation of the problematizing plane of immanence, conceptual personae, and the plane of consistency cannot be reduced to any of the other two, and it is therefore philosophical taste that becomes essential to becoming a philosopher, where what is exercised is a taste for problems, personae, and the "well-made concept." Deleuze and Guattari are clear on this point: "if the philosopher is he who creates concepts, it is thanks to a faculty of taste that is like an instinctive, almost animal *sapere* – a *Fiat* or *Fatum* that gives each philosopher the right of access to certain problems" (WP 78–9/QP 76).

With this last point we can now return to the question with which this chapter began – what is involved in becoming a philosopher? The short answer: taste. The faculty of taste is what enables the philosopher the "right of access to certain problems," and hence the means to create concepts, and it is described as being "like an instinctive, almost animal *sapere* – a *Fiat* or a *Fatum*" (WP 79/QP 76). Caution is called for at this point, however, for it would be too easy but misleading to assume that a philosopher's access to problems is predetermined by their instinctual nature, by fate. Nothing could be further from the truth. Deleuze and Guattari are indeed motioning towards the Stoics in their appeal to animal *sapere* and *Fatum* – in fact, we could well argue that the Stoic serves as the conceptual persona here. Seneca, for instance, says in one of his letters (Letter 5) to Lucilius: "Our [meaning Stoic] motto, as you know, is 'Live according to Nature'."[33] This is relevant here for, as Seneca argues, one becomes a philosopher when one has mastered the art of living in accordance with Nature, and it is this Nature that is our *Fatum*. René Brouwer has recently explored this theme in greater detail and has shown that the Stoics were likely the first to define wisdom as consisting of the knowledge of human and divine matters, or as fitting expertise, and therefore to become a philosopher is to attempt to acquire this fitting expertise whereby one is better able

How to Become a Philosopher

to live a life in accordance with nature. Moreover, since the Stoics have long equated god and nature, Brouwer goes on to argue that in the end a fitting expertise is what the philosopher attains if their life "somehow fits nature, which has an expert-like structure, too."[34] *Fatum* is taken by Deleuze and Guattari in this Stoic sense of living a life in accordance with nature, but where Deleuze and Guattari differ is that this nature is not a set of predetermining laws and an "expert-like structure," but it is rather A LIFE, in the sense argued for throughout this book, or a fundamental pure immanence and problem space that cannot be captured by any rules or categories but requires instead a taste for problems. This problem space or life is precisely the infinite substance that is the sufficient reason for all determinate phenomena. Philosophical taste, therefore, is, as it was for the Stoics, an affinity for living a life in accordance with one's nature, but the conceptual persona of the Stoic problematizes the standard Stoic conception of Nature or *Fatum*, and by doing this Deleuze and Guattari create and reterritorialize this process upon the concept of philosophical taste as the regulative, coadaptive process that allows for the creation of concepts; or, philosophical taste is the concept Deleuze and Guattari create in rethinking what it takes to become a philosopher who creates concepts.

The use to which Deleuze and Guattari put the Stoics brings us, as we close this chapter and anticipate the themes of the next chapter, to the importance of the history of philosophy. In becoming a conceptual persona in the hands of Deleuze and Guattari, the Stoic becomes Deleuze and Guattari while Deleuze and Guattari become Stoics, and it is in the indiscernibility of becoming between these two movements that the creation of concepts occurs. The history of philosophy, therefore, is never for Deleuze and Guattari a matter of surveying past concepts – the concepts of the Stoics, for instance – where these concepts are taken to be a *fait accompli*. Every philosophical concept, as we have been arguing, is connected to problems and substances that are never exhausted by the concepts they made possible or by the conceptual personae that move thought in the direction of these problems. Each concept, therefore, harbors a problematic nature and conceptual personae may well address these problems but also lead to the transformation of these "historical" concepts. Deleuze and Guattari thus conclude their "Conceptual Personae" chapter by pointing out that

> Even the history of philosophy is completely without interest if it does not undertake to awaken a dormant concept and to play it again on a

new stage, even if this comes at the price of turning it against itself. (WP 83/QP 81)

To "awaken a dormant concept," however, entails a taste for the problematic within the midst of the established concepts and problems. One becomes a philosopher in the midst of a sedimented history, or in a context that embodies numerous historical processes and solutions to previous problems. Becoming a philosopher, therefore, entails an affinity or taste for the problems that have not been exhausted by one's geographical, historical, and cultural context, even though one cannot begin to philosophize outside such contexts. To clarify the relationship between geography, history, culture, and the deterritorializing processes associated with becoming a philosopher, we turn then to the themes of the next chapter.

Example 5
When it comes to creating a concept, it is clear for Deleuze and Guattari that it is not sufficient to have either the plane of immanence or the plane of consistency alone in order to create a concept. It is not sufficient in learning, for example, to confront the objectivity of a problem (plane of immanence) from which one is able, in learning, to acquire the paradoxical consistency *ab* that allows for the acquisition of knowledge and with this the fact or rule that guides behavior. For Deleuze and Guattari, something else is necessary for the consistency to become actualized as knowledge, or for the plane of immanence to become a created concept. In the case of the monkey who learns to find food under boxes of a particular color, we could say it was its hunger and desire for food that provided the necessary impetus, or insistence (to gesture towards Deleuze and Guattari's term [*insistance* in French]), to push the process to the point of actualization. In the case of Descartes, for instance, Deleuze and Guattari argue that "there is something else, somewhat mysterious," and it has a "hazy existence halfway between concept and preconceptual plane, passing from one to the other" (WP 61/QP 60). This something else, on Deleuze and Guattari's reading of Descartes, "is the Idiot" (ibid.).

Why the Idiot? The Idiot, Deleuze and Guattari argue, is the conceptual persona that mediates between the objectivity of a problem (plane of immanence) and the conditions necessary to create the concept of the cogito (plane of consistency). On this point, the writings of Dostoevsky will echo those of Descartes, and it is for this reason that Deleuze and Guattari bring Descartes and Dostoevsky together into the same example. The Idiot, in short, is precisely the "something else" Deleuze and Guattari are trying to discern in Descartes's project, and by doing this they attempt to "awaken a dormant concept" (WP 83/QP 81) and enliven the creative process that prompted the creation of Descartes's concepts rather than focus upon the concept as a solution to a problem, a solution that hides, in a true cover up, the objectivity of the problem. With this in mind, what emerges as crucial about the Idiot for Deleuze and Guattari is that the idiot is a "private thinker" (WP 62/QP 60). Let us unpack this claim.

If we recall how Descartes began his *Meditations*, he was taking advantage of the luxury of time to withdraw to his study, in solitude, and give himself the opportunity to question his beliefs and raise doubts he would not otherwise have been able raise while engaged in his everyday affairs. The process of being freed from the social role associated with knowledge is integral to Descartes's concept of the cogito for this concept, as we saw (see example 1), was an attempt to conceptualize the preconceptual and avoid any "any explicit objective presupposition" (WP 26/QP 31) whereby concepts always refer to other concepts. In this context, therefore, the private thinker avoids the associations that come with what Deleuze and Guattari describe as "the public teacher (the schoolman)" who is tied to an accepted body of knowledge – an orthodoxy – and as such the public teacher "refers constantly to taught concepts (man–rational animal), whereas the private thinker forms a concept with innate forces that everyone possesses on their own account by right ('I think')" (ibid.). The private thinker is also able to avoid the sociological pressures of conformity and is therefore able to explore questions and doubts that might otherwise appear idiotic to one actively engaged in a social life. In his *Discourse on Method* Descartes recognizes this when he notes that

> conversing with those of other ages is about the same thing as traveling. It is good to know something of the customs of various peoples, so as to judge our own more soundly and so as not to think that everything that is contrary to our ways is ridiculous and against reason, as those who have seen nothing have a habit of doing.[35]

In other words, for Descartes it is important to be able to "form a more correct judgment regarding our own" manners and beliefs by being able to contrast them with those of different times or by traveling to different countries. Doing this should also instill a modicum of tolerance too, for we should come to recognize that customs, manners, and beliefs that are unlike our own are not, for that reason, to be thought of as "ridiculous and irrational." However, and this is key, Descartes warns that if "too much time is occupied in travelling, we become strangers to our native country," and hence we are unable to fit in anywhere – we become an outsider, a stranger, and if taken to an extreme we become "ridiculous and irrational," an Idiot.

We can now begin to see why Deleuze and Guattari bring Descartes and Dostoevsky together. In the latter's novel *The Idiot*, as well as in his long story *Notes from Underground*, we have the narrative of a person who, in many ways, falls through the cracks of socially accepted norms and rules. In *The Idiot*, for example, the protagonist Myshkin, having been recently released from a sanatorium, increasingly finds himself unable to adjust to life in St Petersburg due to his uncommonly gentle and virtuous nature. In *Notes from Underground*, similarly, we have the story of a reclusive man who fails (or refuses?) to live in accordance with the rigidified rules and social expectations that were pervasive in the St Petersburg of Dostoevsky's time. The underground man was indeed, as evidenced by the reaction of the other characters of the story (except perhaps Liza[36]), and perhaps by the reader as well, a "ridiculous and irrational" creature. And yet this may very well be Dostoevsky's point. If one is to live an authentic life, a life well lived, then something more is needed than to live in accordance with the rules and expectations of society – a life "by the book," one might say, or "from a book," as this is expressed in *Notes from Underground*.[37]

The Idiot, therefore, plays a similar role in both Descartes's philosophical project and in Dostoevsky's literature. The Idiot is the means, or what Deleuze and Guattari call the conceptual persona, that gives the life and insistence necessary to mediate between the plane of immanence and the plane of consistency that allows for the actualization of a concept or literary figure (see Chapter 7 for more on this theme). But there is a big difference between the two, as Deleuze and Guattari note, for whereas "The old idiot," the idiot of Descartes, "wanted indubitable truths at which he could arrive by himself," in the privacy of his study, by the fire, "the new idiot wants to turn the absurd into the highest power of thought – in other words, to create" (WP 62/QP 61). "The old idiot," Deleuze and Guattari continue, "wanted, by himself, to account for what was or was not comprehensible, what was or was not rational, what was lost or saved; but the new idiot wants the lost, the incomprehensible, and the absurd to be restored to him" (WP 63/QP 61). The idiot for Descartes is the conceptual personae that enabled Descartes to forge the concept of the cogito, a concept of self that is drawn from the preconceptual, unquestioned plane where one already knows what it is to think, be, and doubt. The idiot thus provides the insistence or life that problematizes this preconceptual plane and then draws the elements of the concept together into a plane of consistency that constitutes the working parts of an abstract machine. As Deleuze and Guattari put it, "Philosophy constantly brings conceptual personae to life; it gives life to them" (WP 62/QP 61). For Dostoevsky, by contrast, the idiot is that which gives life to the character by being inseparable from a compound of affects and percepts (again, see Chapter 7). Dostoevsky is thus not, as Descartes is, attempting to draw a plane of consistency from which a concept can be created; rather, he is attempting to produce a compound of percepts and affects that expresses a life irreducible to states of affairs and the determinate facts that constitute one's life as lived. It is from such states of affairs and determinate facts that our lives find themselves capable of being regulated, ordered, and rendered predictable such that one can live "by the book." Dostoevsky's work, however, does merge with philosophical interests and concerns, with the creation of concepts, and so we should be wary of drawing too sharp a distinction between Descartes the philosopher and Dostoevsky the literary author. Dostoevsky, in particular, was influential upon the work of Nietzsche, for example, and there are further parallels between Dostoevsky and other philosophers that are often categorized as existentialists. Kierkegaard is one such example. Kierkegaard, moreover, is also interested in understanding the nature of a life that cannot be reduced to being simply a manifestation of a set of objective, rational laws – a life lived in accordance with a rationalist book of nature, so to speak. To begin to add clarity to how Dostoevsky and Descartes are drawing upon A LIFE in order to facilitate the creative processes they themselves engaged in (creating concepts and creating literary figures), we can turn to the next example.

Suggested reading for example 5
  Nicholas of Cusa, *On Learned Ignorance*
  René Descartes, *Discourse on Method*
  Fyodor Dostoevsky, *Notes from Underground.*

Example 6

In his famous essay, "The Humanism of Existentialism," Jean-Paul Sartre accepted the label of being an existentialist and summed up the core tenet of the movement in the short, pithy phrase, "existence precedes essence."[38] The vast majority of the philosophical tradition, Sartre argued, held that essence precedes existence. Plato, for instance, argued that what was ultimately real were transcendent forms, forms (Ideas) that are always already there and serve to pass judgment on how well or poorly something that exists participates in this form or essence (see example 2). With existentialism, by contrast, existence is primary and it is only in the wake of existence that we have transcendent standards and ideals by which we judge the value and worth of existence itself. Such values, however, are always open to question for they are not primary but are grounded in the freedom of existence itself, freedom being understood here in the sense that existence is not predetermined by any essential property or form that prescribes how this existence is to be. In short, existence precedes essence.

Kierkegaard is often placed among the existentialist philosophers. Although a Christian philosopher, Kierkegaard is often referred to as the father of existentialism. It may seem to be an oxymoron to refer to Kierkegaard as a Christian existentialist (Dostoevsky can be categorized here as well), for is not God the quintessential case of a transcendent being whose nature and essence precede the existence of the natural world? The horror many have of pantheism, and the reason for the outcries that met Spinoza's *Ethics* once it was posthumously published, are precisely the result of a resistance many have to the claim that God is immanent to all that exists rather than being the transcendent being that precedes all natural existence. For Kierkegaard, however, having faith in the existence of God is not a matter of objective evidence that one can cite as proof of God's existence – there is no burning bush for Kierkegaard. Unlike Locke, Kierkegaard accepts that there is no objective, transcendent standard or basis for their belief, and thus acting in faith becomes indiscernible from madness and idiocy.[39] In Kierkegaard's reading of the story of Abraham, for example, there is nothing to assure Abraham that he is not simply mad to head up the mountain to slay his only son, Isaac. God's command to Abraham violates ethical standards, including God's own – "thou shall not kill", and almost certainly any bystander who may happen to be witnessing what Abraham is about to do would attempt to intervene. Yet, and this is Kierkegaard's point, Abraham is a "knight of faith," to use Kierkegaard's phrase, for he acts on a faith that has no objective basis whatsoever. It is for this reason that Kierkegaard's "knight of faith" is a conceptual persona and an example of how, "when we take pride in encountering the transcendent within immanence, all we do is recharge the plane of immanence with immanence itself" (WP 73/QP 71). In other words, the faith in God that the knight of faith takes on, and takes on without any objective, transcendent basis for doing so, has the ultimate effect of transforming the existence of life itself by recharging the problematic plane of infinite, immanent substance (A LIFE); that is, rather than being concerned with "the transcendent existence of God," Deleuze and Guattari argue that the knight of faith is concerned "with the infinite immanent possibilities brought by the one who believes that God exists." This belief in God's existence intensifies the existence of our life as lived by extracting the infinite movements (A LIFE) that come with belief in the existence of God. This is Kierkegaard's conversion experience, or what he calls a leap of faith.

The same is true in the case of Pascal's wager. Pascal famously proposed a scenario where one is to consider the consequences of either believing or not believing in God. If one believes in the existence of God and it turns out God exists, then one gains an infinite, eternal reward. If one does not believe in the existence of God and God exists, then the result is infinite, eternal loss and punishment. If God does not exist, then there is no difference whether one believes in God or not – in either case, the result is the same and we are left with nothing but our finite mortality. The point for Deleuze and Guattari, however, is that what results from the case of Pascal's "gambler, he who throws the dice" (WP 74/QP 72), is, as it was for Kierkegaard's knight of faith, an intensification of life itself, a "recharge of immanence" (ibid.). To state this point in a slightly different manner, despite an apparent appeal to transcendent values and a transcendent God, what Kierkegaard and Pascal give us, by virtue of their conceptual personae, is a philosophy that sets out without the "need [for] transcendent values by which they [modes of existence, or lives as lived] could be compared, selected, and judged relative to one another" (ibid.). What they give us instead is "immanent criteria" for understanding a life that is well lived, and these immanent criteria are nothing other than, Deleuze and Guattari argue, that which constitutes "the tenor of existence, the intensification of life." A life well lived, therefore, is not a life lived in accordance with a set of transcendent standards or values, but it is the living of a life that is intensified by infinite movements, a life

117

irreducible to the determinate states of affairs and lived states. It is to extract A LIFE from our lives as lived.

Deleuze and Guattari close this example by gesturing towards a new manner of restoring immanence. As we saw in an earlier example (example 3), Sartre, empiricism (that is, Hume), and Spinoza were singled out as among the few instances within the history of philosophy where the "rights of immanence" (WP 47/QP 49) were restored. In this example, Deleuze and Guattari recognize that both Pascal and Kierkegaard are "encountering the transcendent within immanence" (WP 73/QP 71), and thereby recharging immanence itself. Nonetheless, this recharging of immanence occurs by way of a belief in a transcendent God and the problems that arise with coming to believe in this God. We would have a new problem altogether, Deleuze and Guattari claim, if, rather than believing in God, the concern is to believe in the world. This belief in the world, moreover, is not simply a matter of believing that the world exists but rather "in its possibilities of movements and intensities, so as once again to give birth to new modes of existence, closer to animals and rocks. It may be," Deleuze and Guattari conclude, "that believing in this world, in this life, becomes our most difficult task, or the task of a mode of existence still to be discovered on our plane of immanence today" (WP 74–5/QP 73). In their "Geophilosophy" chapter, the belief in this world comes to be referred to as the problem of "the people to come and the new earth" (WP 109/QP 105). This is the problem of our time, a problem that calls forth "the empiricist conversion" (WP 75/QP 72) that will restore the rights of immanence and the "possibilities of movements and intensities" of "the people to come and the new earth." This problem is integral to the problem of learning and to extracting A LIFE from our lives as lived – in short, it is central to Deleuze and Guattari's meditation on a life well lived.

Suggested reading for example 6
   Blaise Pascal, *Pensées*
   Søren Kierkegaard, *Stages on Life's Way.*

NOTES

1. Gilles Deleuze, *Difference and Repetition,* trans. Paul Patton (New York: Columbia University Press, 1994), p. 122.
2. The distinction at the heart of Heidegger's effort to move away from a philosophy that concerns itself with an incessant ordering of things

is that between Being and beings, or the ontological difference as this is discussed in the literature. As for the critique of American capitalism and Russian communism, and hence a clue as to Heidegger's potential reasons for accepting National Socialism as an alternative, see *An Introduction to Metaphysics*, ed. Ralph Manheim (New Haven: Yale University Press, 1959), p. 37: "From a metaphysical point of view, Russia and America are the same; the same dreary technological frenzy, the same unrestricted organization of the average man."

3. *An Introduction to Metaphysics*, p. 6.
4. Ibid., p. 1.
5. Ibid., p. 7. Heidegger is referring to the Bible, *Genesis* 1:1.
6. Ibid.
7. Ibid.
8. Ibid., p. 49.
9. Given enough space, we could at this point launch ourselves on a comparison of Heidegger and Kuhn with respect to Kuhn's notion of incommensurability and Heidegger's development of Nietzsche's concept of the untimely. What is important to note here, however, is that while Kuhn argues that certain facts lead to a revolution in that these facts bring into question the established paradigm, for Heidegger it is not the facts themselves that are revolutionary but the "untimely" spirit of science, a spirit Heidegger equates with the fundamental question of metaphysics. For Kuhn's arguments, see *The Structure of Scientific Revolutions* (Chicago: University of Chicago Press, [1962] 2012).
10. *Desert Islands*, p. 96.
11. Dan Smith has made a similar observation in his *Essays on Deleuze* (Edinburgh: Edinburgh University Press, 2012), where he argues that the model that best exemplifies the problematic state is that of Proust's jealous lover rather than the Socratic question "what is x?" As Smith puts it: "It is not the friend, says Proust, exercising a natural desire for truth in dialogue with others, but rather the jealous lover, under the pressure of his beloved's lies, and the anguish they inflict. The jealous lover is forced to confront a problem, whose coordinates are discovered, not through Socrates' 'What is . . . ?', but by posing the types of minor questions that Plato rejected: What happened?, When?, Where?, How?, With whom?" (p. 92).
12. For an excellent account of this theme, see René Brouwer, *The Stoic Sage: The Early Stoics on Wisdom, Sagehood and Socrates* (Cambridge: Cambridge University Press, 2014). The citation is from Brouwer's book (p. 5), though it is a standard Stoic definition of wisdom.
13. Diogenes Laërtius credits Zeno of Citium with initiating this tripartite division of philosophy. See Diogenes Laërtius 7.39 (*Lives of Eminent Philosophers*, Books 6–10, trans. R. D. Hicks (Cambridge, MA: Loeb

Classical Library, Harvard University Press), pp. 149–50): "They say that philosophical theory [logos] is tripartite. For one part of it concerns nature [that is, physics], another concerns character [that is, ethics], and another concerns rational discourse [that is, logic]. Zeno of Citium first gave this division in his book *On Rational Discourse* [logos] and so did Chrysippus in book 1 of *On Rational Discourse* and book 1 of his Physics. . . ."

14. Immanuel Kant, *Groundwork of the Metaphysics of Morals,* trans. Mary Gregor (Cambridge: Cambridge University Press, 1998), p. 1.

15. Ibid.

16. See Immanuel Kant, *Critique of Pure Reason,* trans. Norman Kemp Smith (London: Macmillan, 1929), A/19/B33: "The capacity (receptivity) for receiving representations through the mode in which we are affected by objects, is entitled *sensibility.* Objects are *given* to us by means of sensibility, and it alone yields us *intuitions;* they are *thought* through the understanding, and from the understanding arise *concepts.*"

17. As Kant argues in the Preface to *Critique of Pure Reason*: "For experience is itself a species of knowledge which involves understanding; and understanding has rules which I must presuppose as being in me prior to objects being given to me, and therefore a being a priori" (Bxvii).

18. Ibid., A52/B76.

19. Ibid., A303/B358.

20. Ibid., A311/B368.

21. Ibid., B152.

22. There is tremendous literature on this theme. Heidegger, most notably, argued for the primacy of the imagination. This also became an important point of contention within the neo-Kantian schools of the early twentieth century. For Heidegger's account of Kant, see *Kant and the Problem of Metaphysics,* trans. Richard Taft (Bloomington: Indiana University Press, 1997). For the neo-Kantian tradition, see Friedman's *A Parting of the Ways: Carnap, Cassirer, and Heidegger* (Chicago: Open Court, 2000).

23. Frederick C. Beiser, *The Fate of Reason: German Philosophy from Kant to Fichte* (Cambridge, MA: Harvard University Press, 1987), p. 288.

24. Ibid., p. 290, emphasis added.

25. Ibid., p. 293.

26. For Deleuze's discussion of Kant's "transcendental ideas" as problems in *Difference and Repetition,* see p. 168: "Kant never ceased to remind us that Ideas are essentially 'problematic'. Conversely, problems are Ideas."

27. Recall our discussion in the Introduction of the contrast between the Leibnizian acceptance of the convergence of predicates in the unity of a subject, and subjects in the unity of the best of all possible worlds

– monadology – and Deleuze's claim that A LIFE entails disparity and divergent series.

28. See Friedrich Nietzsche's untimely meditation, "On the Uses and Abuses of History for Life," in *Untimely Meditations*, trans. R. J. Hollingdale (Cambridge: Cambridge University Press, 1997), p. 97: "All living things require an atmosphere around them, a mysterious misty vapour; if they are deprived of this envelope, if a religion, an art, a genius is condemned to revolve as a star without atmosphere, we should no longer be surprised if they quickly wither and grow hard and unfruitful."

29. Ibid., p. 94: "the genuine historian must possess the power to remint the universally known into something never heard of before, and to express the universal so simply and profoundly that the simplicity is lost in the profundity and the profundity in the simplicity."

30. For Nicholas of Cusa, see his "On Learned Ignorance," in *Nicholas of Cusa: Selected Spiritual Writings*, trans. H. Lawrence Bond (Mahwah, NJ: Paulist Press, 2005).

31. For Kierkegaard, see Søren Kierkegaard, *Fear and Trembling*, ed. C. Stephen Taylor (Cambridge: Cambridge University Press, 2006).

32. See the previous chapter, p. ??.

33. Seneca, *Epistles* 1–65, trans. Richard Gummere (Cambridge, MA: Loeb Classical Library, Harvard University Press, 2006), p. 23.

34. *Stoic Sage*, p. 45.

35. René Descartes, *Discourse on Method* (Indianapolis: Hackett, 1998), p. 4.

36. Spoiler alert: for those who have not read *Notes from Underground*, I will mention some plot details so those who would like to read it may want to avoid reading here. In his relationship with Liza, the Underground Man does appear to have the possibility of entering into a "normal" relationship with Liza, but it becomes one that orbits solely around writing. Liza then asks the Underground Man to write a letter for her, and when the potential romance fails, she, heartbroken, comes to him and they have sex. After the sex, the Underground Man gives her money, and thus he shoots down the possibility of any relationship. At one point, Liza responds to one of the Underground Man's speeches by saying he sounds like a book, which becomes an important theme for Dostoevsky.

37. In an important passage from *Notes from Underground*, trans. M. Ginsburg (New York: Bantam, 1992), and a passage that connects with the theme of living a life well, Liza responds to a lengthy monologue of the Underground Man about life: "'Well, one would almost think that you were speaking from a book,' she said. In her tone I could detect the mocking note" (p. 85). As the Underground Man draws his writings to a close, he responds to the mocking he suspects the reader may have indulged in against him and argues that "The truth is that I have

been more *alive* than you [that is, the reader]. That is all. But look a little closer. We do not even know where present-day reality is to be found, nor what it is called. Whenever we are left to our own devices, and deprived of our bookish rules, we at once grow confused and lose our way – we know not what to do, nor what to observe, nor what to love, nor what to hate, nor what to respect, nor what to despise" (p. 113).

38. Jean-Paul Sartre, "The Humanism of Existentialism," in *Essays in Existentialism* (Secaucus, NJ: Citadel Press, 1965), p. 35.

39. This is a reference to Moses and the burning bush. In a related manner, this becomes an important theme for Locke in his arguments against what he calls "enthusiasm." What distinguishes enthusiasm from rational knowledge is precisely the fact that there is supporting evidence and it does not violate the laws of reason. Even the Bible, Locke claims, exemplifies this standard, for what lets Moses know he is not mad, or suffering from enthusiasm, is the evidence of the burning bush. See Locke's *An Essay Concerning Human Understanding*, Chapter XIX, "Of Enthusiasm."

4

Putting Philosophy in its Place

In the previous chapter we set out to detail the dynamic process involved in becoming a philosopher. To summarize Deleuze and Guattari's arguments in the barest of terms, becoming a philosopher entails a thoughtful, questioning, problematizing attitude towards the given such that new forms of thinking or rethinking the given can emerge by way of a concept. A philosopher thus invites the incredulous stare from their contemporaries who cannot help but think that the claims being asserted are nonsensical if not outright mad. If a philosopher has a taste for problems, however, and if they are able to balance and co-adapt the conflicting, heterogeneous demands of laying out a plane of immanence, inventing conceptual personae, and creating concepts, then despite the essential flirtation with madness and delirium the created concepts will come to have a power and endurance of their own. One will have become a philosopher.

One measure of success in becoming a philosopher, therefore, is that the concepts a philosopher creates find their place in history. The concepts have sufficient power, life, and complexity to thrive, adapt, and become transformed in response to varying circumstances. This can account for why, if one looks at the historical monographs Deleuze wrote, it may appear that he was rather conservative and safe in the authors he chose to study. From his first book on Hume, followed by works on Nietzsche, Bergson, Proust, Kant, Spinoza, Kafka, and Leibniz, Deleuze's approach to the history of philosophy appears to be anything but radical. Each of these figures has a solid place within the canon. The reason for this apparent conservatism, Deleuze and Guattari argue, is that a "well-made" concept has, perhaps ironically, "irregular contours" (WP 78/QP 75), by which Deleuze and Guattari mean that it has not fully masked and brushed aside the problematic plane of immanence from which the creation of the concept was drawn. It is this inseparability of the problematic from the concept that accounts for the "irregularity" of the concept and that in turn allows for the possibility of being able "to awaken a dormant concept and to play it again on a new stage" (WP 83/QP 81). The authors Deleuze turns to, therefore, are canonical precisely because they have constructed "well-made" concepts that can be awoken and placed anew on the contemporary stage, even if doing so turns the concept against the original author, as was the case especially in Deleuze's book on Kant.[1]

The focus in the fourth chapter, "Geophilosophy," shifts to address the concrete, institutional, and historical circumstances in which a philosopher becomes a philosopher. Despite the shift of emphasis, the motif or ritornello[2] from previous chapters continues – namely, just as the thinking and learning associated with becoming a philosopher mediate, by way of conceptual personae, the problematic plane of immanence and the creation of concepts, so too in this chapter thinking is described as that which "takes place in the relationship of territory and earth" (WP 85/QP 82). In the context of the current chapter, the earth serves as the problematizing plane of immanence, or as a movement of deterritorialization (see example 6). The "earth," Deleuze and Guattari argue, "constantly carries out a movement of deterritorialization on the spot, by which it goes beyond any territory: it is deterritorializing and deterritorialized" (ibid.). The territory, by contrast, is the contrasting movement, the movement of territorialization and the creation of concepts, and "philosophy," as we saw, "is reterritorialized on the concept" (WP 101/QP 97). The mediating role of conceptual personae between planes of immanence and concepts is now presented in terms of a thinking that takes place between a deterritorializing earth and a territorializing and reterritorialized context, including the full range of historical, social, institutional, and material elements native to this context. Thinking is thus becoming, but now this is a becoming between territory and earth, and territory and earth become indiscernible in this process as thinking takes place in context: "Territory and earth are two components with two zones of indiscernibility – deterritorialization (from territory to earth) and reterritorialization (from earth to territory). We cannot say which comes first" (WP 86/QP 82).

As a preliminary conclusion, and in anticipation of arguments to come in this chapter, we can say that philosophy is indeed historical – it is always in relation to a historical context where thinking begins – but this beginning is irreducible to the historical context. Deleuze and Guattari will thus be critical of the historicist tendency in philosophy, a tendency they find exemplified by Hegel and Heidegger. Although they will, in general, agree with Hegel's and Heidegger's claims regarding the ancient Greek origins of philosophy, Deleuze and Guattari will argue that they nonetheless offer a historicism that in the end serves to limit the creative thinking that can take place *vis-à-vis* the history of philosophy. In the following chapter, therefore, the first section will examine Deleuze and Guattari's critique of historicism; in the second we will show how conceptualizing philosophy as thinking between territory and earth allows for the history of philosophy to become philosophy, or become the active, engaged process of creating concepts; and in the third section we will begin to explore the political implications of Deleuze and Guattari's approach and sketch what it is they call upon when they demand that philosophy "summon forth a new earth, a new people" (WP 99/QP 95). The final section will begin to sketch the ways in which thought becomes experimental and simultaneously deterritorializing/reterritorializing in a variety of contexts. This will prepare the way for our discussion of the chapters from Part 2 of *What is Philosophy?* where Deleuze and Guattari argue for distinct ways in which thought is engaged creatively and experimentally – as philosophical thinking which creates concepts; as scientific thinking which creates what Deleuze and Guattari call functives; and as artistic thinking where it creates percepts and affects. Our conclusion will be that philosophy, science, and art each engages in a creative deterritorializing/reterritorializing thought between earth and territory, but given the context within which one is engaged, and since philosophy, science, and art are not hermetically sealed off from one another, the results will vary and may well tend more towards art, science, or philosophy.

§1

A guiding question of the "Geophilosophy" chapter is why philosophy originated with the ancient Greeks. The obvious presupposed claim is that philosophy did indeed begin with the Greeks rather than in Egypt, India, China, or another non-Western culture. Deleuze and Guattari thus appear to begin the enquiry of this chapter with a Eurocentric bias.[3] Deleuze and Guattari would argue, however, that this is a matter of historical contingency rather than a presupposed belief in the superiority of European peoples. In particular, what is crucial, Deleuze and Guattari argue, to the emergence of philosophy is the shift from Imperial State politics to City politics. In both cases there is a process of deterritorialization/reterritorialization. For with the "*imperial spatium* of the State" (WP 86/QP 83), what is deterritorialized by the State is the "territory of local groups" which is then reterritorialized upon "the palace and its supplies" (ibid.). The "*political extensio* of the city," by contrast, involves a deterritorialization that "takes place on the spot," in that the city "turns its back on the hinterlands" and looks elsewhere to establish a network of economic connections with other city-states. This networking process is then reterritorialized "on the agora and commercial networks," and it was precisely in the agora (the marketplace) that Socrates would frequently engage in the conversations Plato would make famous. This is no accident, Deleuze and Guattari argue, for while both the State and City develop their distinctive forms of de/reterritorialization, the "cities of ancient Greece and especially Autochtonous Athens . . . develop a particular mode of deterritorialization that proceeds by immanence; they form a *milieu of immanence*" (WP 87/QP 84); and it is this milieu of immanence that was critical to the emergence of philosophy.

In the introduction to his *Philosophy of History*, and notably in the "Geographical Basis of History" section, Hegel argues that

> The sea gives us the idea of the indefinite, the unlimited, and infinite; and in feeling his own infinite in that Infinite, man is stimulated and emboldened to stretch beyond the limited: the sea invites man to conquest, and to piratical plunder, but also to honest gain and to commerce.[4]

For this reason Hegel argues that the "Mediterranean is thus the heart of the Old World, for it is that which conditioned and vitalized it,"[5] or more precisely, it launched the Greek beginnings in world history and philosophy.[6] As Deleuze and Guattari might put it, the sea provides a context that is ideal for thinking immanence, or for the deterritorializing movement of thought towards the problematizing plane of immanence and the absolutely infinite substance that is the Principle of Sufficient Reason for all determinate, limited phenomena. Thales' famous claim that "all is water," for example, thus acquires philosophical legitimacy if one understands water here to be the immanent principle or sufficient reason for all determinate phenomena.[7] On this point, then, Deleuze and Guattari seem largely to agree with Hegel with respect to both the general assumption that philosophy began with the Greeks and the important role the geopolitical context had to play in this process. As Deleuze and Guattari put it, and in striking resonance with Hegel, "Salamis is the Greek miracle where Greece escapes from the Persian empire and where the autochtonous people who lost its territory prevails on the sea, is reterritorialized on the sea," and the "fractalization of Greece" led, as a result, to seeing the sea no longer "as a limit of its territory or an obstacle to its endeavor but as a wider bath of immanence" (WP 88/QP 85).

From here, differences with Hegel begin to emerge. Put simply, Hegel's argument that the State realizes the full reconciliation of the universal and the individual is, in the end, an affirmation of transcendence over immanence. This oversimplifies the difference, however, for at bottom what leads to the affirmation of transcendence over immanence emerges as a result of the relationship Hegel establishes between thought and the plane of immanence. The earth is a movement of deterritorialization and it becomes absolute deterritorialization, Deleuze and Guattari argue, "when the earth passes into the pure plane of immanence of a Being," into the absolutely infinite substance. From the perspective of thought, however, this absolute deterritorialization is a limit to be staved off and never actualized (recall our earlier discussion of the two poles of the abstract machine that multiplicities and assemblages, as working parts of the abstract machine, resist actualizing [Chapter 2, §2]). To actualize the infinite, absolute deterritorialization would entail plunging into a chaos that prevents the connections and consistency necessary for thought (or learning) to become possible at all. If the plane of immanence is to be thought, it needs to be mediated by what Deleuze and Guattari call a relative deterritorialization. In the previous chapter we saw that this mediating role was served by conceptual personae, and it was conceptual personae that facilitated and regulated the possibility for philosophical thought – that is, the creation of concepts. In the "Geophilosophy" chapter, this theme becomes quite explicit, though now the concern is the context in which philosophy takes place. As they put it, "absolute deterritorialization can only be thought according to certain still-to-be-determined relationships with relative deterritorializations that are not only cosmic but geographical, historical, and psychosocial" (WP 88/QP 85). For Hegel this relative deterritorialization is the pure subjectivity that realizes itself in the State, and thus this is a reterritorialization that prefigures the processes of world history. History and thought are thus dominated by transcendence, and as a result, the transcendent serves as the paradigmatic exemplar that is projected upon the plane of immanence which it populates with "Figures" (WP 89/QP 86). The Greek, Roman, and German Spirit that Hegel analyzes are instances of relative deterritorialization of the absolute, but for Hegel these Figures exemplify the paradigmatic Spirit of world history itself, and this Spirit limits and prefigures the processes of history itself. For Deleuze and Guattari, however, what is distinctive about the Greek context is that it "carries the movements of relative deterritorialization to infinity, pushes them to the absolute" (WP 90/QP 86). By reterritorializing upon the "bath of immanence," the Greeks initiated a thought that broke free from the limits of the figural and paradigmatic by affirming the absolute and infinite itself. In short, with the Greeks we have a place "where one thinks no longer with figures but with concepts," for concepts presuppose, as we have seen, infinite speeds and an absolute survey (see Chapter 1).

We are now in a position to understand Deleuze and Guattari's critique of the historicism they claim limits the philosophical potential of both Hegel and Heidegger. First and foremost, although Deleuze and Guattari agree with Hegel and Heidegger that philosophy began in ancient Greece, they argue that this beginning has no necessary connection to philosophy itself. According to Deleuze and Guattari, the birth of philosophy did require "the conjunction of two very different movements of deterritorialization, the relative and the absolute" (WP 93/QP 89–90). The movement of thought as a movement of absolute deterritorialization had to be, in order to be thought, "aligned or directly connected with the relative deterritorialization of Greek society" (ibid.). What we have, then, is an encounter of two different movements and there is nothing necessary that brought this encounter about; in other words, the encounter between these two "different movements of deterritorialization" cannot be accounted for by any determinate reason of the form, x happened because of y. There is thus no PSR for philosophy itself if by that is meant a determinate reason, a reason that is distinct from and accounts for philosophy (recall our earlier discussion of the PSR from the Introduction); rather, Deleuze and Guattari argue that if "philosophy does have a principle . . . it is a synthetic and contingent principle – an encounter, a conjunction" (ibid.). To restate this point in terms we have developed throughout this book, we could say that there is no determinate reason that can account for the determinate actualization of philosophy in Greek society; nor does the actualization of philosophy in Greek society exhaust the indeterminate, problematic plane of immanence that is the sufficient reason for all determinate phenomena, including philosophy. Deleuze and Guattari state this conclusion as follows:

> The principle of reason such as it appears in philosophy is a principle of contingent reason and is put like this: there is no good reason but contingent reason: there is no universal history except of contingency. (ibid.)

From here, Deleuze and Guattari's critique of Hegel's and Heidegger's historicism follows quite readily. What Heidegger and Hegel do, Deleuze and Guattari argue, is to conceive of the origins of philosophy such that "philosophy necessarily becomes indistinguishable from its own history" (WP 95/QP 91). Heidegger, moreover, "betrays the movement of deterritorialization [of philosophy] because he fixes it once and for all between being and beings, between the Greek territory and the Western earth that the Greeks would have called Being" (ibid.) (see example 7). Both Hegel and Heidegger, as a result of establishing a necessary link between philosophy and its history, will remain, in the eyes of Deleuze and Guattari, historicist reductionists in that the history of philosophy becomes the very interiority of philosophy itself, or it is the "interiority in which the concept necessarily develops or unveils its destiny" (ibid.). As a consequence of this historicist move, when it comes to the philosophies of both Hegel and Heidegger, the "unforeseeable creation of concepts is thus poorly understood" (ibid.). Rather than reducing philosophy to the interiority of its history, therefore, Deleuze and Guattari claim a philosophy that offers a better understanding of the "unforeseeable creation of concepts" will affirm the contingency of the conjunction of history *and* philosophy, and it is the embrace of this conjunction and the contingency and problematic substance inseparable from both philosophy *and* its history, that allows for the history of philosophy to become philosophy. It is to this that we now turn.

§2

When it comes to the history of philosophy, it is all too easy and natural to interpret the writings of earlier authors as having already made an attempt to address a particular problem. The results of their effort are what we read in the manuscript before us. In many cases, the problems that motivated previous philosophers may not interest or concern us, or we may feel we have moved beyond these problems and as a result their work will be seen as a novelty that bears no relevance to our present concerns. It would probably not be an exaggeration to argue that a fair amount of the historical tradition in philosophy falls into the category of irrelevance. Analytic philosophers, for instance, largely avoid the history of philosophy altogether, focused as they are on current problems and advancing the research field *vis-à-vis* those problems.[8] What can we learn, a contemporary philosopher might ask, from the pre-Socratic philosopher Empedocles? Empedocles' philosophy of nature may seem to be a relic of an ancient time and a response to problems that no longer concern us, given the advances of modern science –to wit, Empedocles' claim that all can be accounted for in terms of the four elements of fire, air, earth, and water, and the relations and interactions of these four elements in terms of the opposing forces of love and strife. Deleuze and Guattari, however, argue that to view Empedocles as a philosopher, we ought not to be focused upon the *concepts as solutions* to a fundamental problematic but rather we should emphasize the creation of concepts in relation to the fundamental problematic and de-emphasize their role as solutions, for as solutions they never exhaust the problems that prompted them. It is for this reason that Deleuze and Guattari stress the point that the "pre-Socratics treat physical elements like concepts: they take them for themselves, independently of any reference, and seek only the good rules of neighborhood between them and in their possible components" (WP 90–91/QP 87). In other words, as concepts Empedocles' elements are not to be taken as solving particular problems by means of their *reference* to particular elements and forces, but as philosophical concepts (see Chapter 1) they are to be taken in terms of the consistency of their elements in relation to a fundamental problem or plane of immanence. If they are understood in this way, then one may engage with Empedocles' concepts as problematic substance and in response to this problem draw together the components that may re-create these concepts, or awaken them and "play [them] again on a new stage" (WP 83/QP 81).

To get a better sense of the Deleuzo-Guattarian approach to the history of philosophy as one finds it at work in *What is Philosophy?*, we can recall our earlier points concerning the paradigmatic and figural understanding of the history of philosophy. Hegel, we saw, understood the periods of world history as figural projections of a developing world Spirit. Generalizing this paradigmatic approach to the understanding of historical time (or time more generally), time is most often seen as the measure of determinate entities and their relations to each other. In his cinema books, Deleuze referred to this time as *Chronos,* or the time of the movement-image whereby time is subordinate to the movement and measurement of determinate objects and events. Among historians there has been a fair amount of debate regarding the temporal biases historians often project upon the past. Fernand Braudel, for instance, argues that the bias towards what he calls social time leads historians to focus almost exclusively on the events that occur within the timeframe of a typical human life.[9] The life of the human being therefore becomes the projected temporal image historians then apply to their study of the past. The result, Braudel argues, is that this image limits the historian's capacity to acquire a broader picture of the past for it overlooks events that may occur in long temporal cycles and hence escape the notice of one who searches for events within the limited timeframe of social time. Braudel calls this time the *longue durée,* and he offers examples such as the Kondratiev cycle to illustrate an important, though often overlooked, relationship between humans and their material world.[10] Braudel's arguments would come to have an important influence upon Deleuze and Guattari, as is especially evident in *A Thousand Plateaus,* for Deleuze and Guattari are equally concerned to highlight the paradigmatic biases of historians, philosophers, and others whose thought and work projects their favored image of thought upon phenomena. Yet even Braudel continues within a paradigmatic framework, Deleuze and Guattari might argue, for Braudel continues to project cycles of time and objective material relationships upon phenomena. Braudel breaks with the limiting paradigmatic nature of social time but continues to embrace the paradigm of the *longue durée.* Deleuze and Guattari, by contrast, call for what we might call a syntagmatic framework of historical time, and it is this framework that enables a history of philosophy to create concepts – that is, to become philosophy.

In contrasting the paradigmatic with the syntagmatic, Deleuze and Guattari bluntly link the concept with the latter rather than the former: "The concept is not paradigmatic but *syntagmatic*; not projective but *connective*; not hierarchical but *linking* (*vicinal*); not referential but *consistent*" (WP 91/QP 87, emphasis in original). If historical time is to be taken as a philosophical concept, and if it is a concept that is used to approach and think the nature of other philosophical concepts, then it is no longer a question of projecting the right timeframe or problems onto the past but instead the problem is a matter of discerning the connections to make, the elements to include, and so on. Rather than a hierarchical projection based upon a presupposed identity, what emerges, Deleuze and Guattari claim, is "the importance in philosophy of the questions 'What to put in a concept?' and 'What to put with it?'" (WP 90/QP 87). From here, what may emerge is that the elements selected and put into the concept become a plane of immanence or problem that allows for the creation of a new concept, or the re-awakening of an old concept (recall our earlier example of the concept Idea as found in Plato, Kant, and then Deleuze). By moving away from the paradigmatic understanding of historical time, the result is that the elements and problems of philosophers come to be seen not in relationship to a presupposed identity – such as the "present" and what one presumes to be the problems and concerns of the present – but rather the elements and problems assume a contemporaneity that privileges no moment or period in time. We have what Nietzsche referred to as the "misty vapor" that allows for the creation of something new, and this misty vapor is a contemporaneous time – what Deleuze calls the time of *Aion*, or the eternal – that not only is irreducible to any determinate object or event in time but is the condition for the individuation of such determinate realities.[11]

None of this is to say that we should ignore the determinate facts that a thorough historical investigation may bring to light. As we will see in the next section, an important role for philosophy is to offer a critique of the present, meaning a challenging, problematizing analysis of the assumptions that may go unquestioned or are simply assumed as givens that go without saying. A problematizing critique of the present may allow for connections and encounters to occur that might not otherwise have happened, and as a result novel approaches towards conceptualizing one's current situation may become possible. The same is the case for a problematizing investigation and critique of the context in which past authors lived and wrote. This problematizing critique may reveal opportunities passed up or ignored due to the unquestioned biases and assumptions of that period. Whether one is undergoing a critique of the past or the present, the challenges are largely the same. How do we discern the guiding presuppositions and opinions of a given time period, whether this be the time in which we may happen to be living and writing or that of our historical predecessors? One of Hegel's important assumptions was that it is easier to reveal the assumptions of the time period that is not ours precisely because we can reflect upon the period and view it objectively (in what Hegel calls reflective history[12]), whereas one cannot step outside of one's own time period and is therefore disadvantaged in one's ability to recognize, and much less question, the assumptions and biases of one's own time.

This assumption that the biases of the past are more readily accessible than those of the present is overstated, if not outright false, and it reinforces the tendency to assume that the past is in some sense complete whereas the present is a work in progress where the outcome remains unknown or may even be in doubt. It is this assumption that Deleuze and Guattari challenge with a syntagmatic view of time that argues that every determinate reality, whether states of affairs and opinions of the present or the facts of ancient Greece, are each to be understood in relation to the processes of individuation that made them possible, and these processes, as we have seen, entail a problematic multiplicity and plane of immanence that is not exhausted by any determinate fact or state of affairs, or even by the totality of facts and states of affairs. As a result, not only are the present facts and states of affairs inseparable from a problematic nature that renders them provisional, but also the same is true for the states of affairs and facts of the past. The problematic nature or substance that is the PSR of all that appears is thus the reason for all phenomena, regardless of whether past or future. In fact, Deleuze will speak of the pure past as precisely that which is never to be confused with any determinate present – whether the present of our time or the past that was once present – and it is this pure past that we now understand as the problematic substance. A syntagmatic view of time, therefore, is a flat view of time and it does not relegate one time – the present – as being more real than any other. It is the problematic substance that is real, the "true substantive, substance itself."

The task of making sense of the past and present, therefore, consists of addressing the problematic nature presupposed by the determinate facts that are the subject of historical inquiry and investigation. This task is neither a positivist lining up of indubitable facts, nor a matter of spinning elaborate fictions that weave together the facts in a manner of one's choosing. From Deleuze and Guattari's perspective, the task is double: on the one hand, it is a matter of detailing the processes of individuation of determinate events; on the other hand, since these determinate events do not exhaust the problematic substance, there is thus the task of a problematizing history to move from the determinate to the indeterminate, to the hazy, misty vapor of becoming. Both tasks are essential, Deleuze and Guattari argue. "Without history," they claim, "becoming would remain indeterminate and unconditioned, but becoming is not historical" (WP 96/QP 92).[13] In other words, to open access to becoming, to allow for the affinity and philosophical taste that can allow for the creation of concepts, philosophy needs its history to provide it with the determinate conditions from which the creative, experimental process of thought proceeds. Philosophy, however, is not to be reduced to its history (to historicism).

We are now in a better position to understand both what it means to become a philosopher and what, for Deleuze and Guattari, is involved when the philosopher creates concepts. Put simply, a philosopher begins in the midst of an already established context replete with numerous historical debates, problems, and a panoply of concepts. This determinate history is in fact one key issue that does differentiate the contemporary philosopher from the ancient Greek philosophers. As Deleuze and Guattari argue,

> We today possess concepts, but the Greeks did not yet possess them; they possessed the plane that we no longer possess. That is why Plato's Greeks contemplate the concept as something that is still very far away and beyond, whereas we possess the concept – we possess it in the mind innately; all that is needed is to reflect. (WP 101/QP 97)

The key challenge for a contemporary philosopher, therefore, is to move beyond the already created concept, to a thought reterritorialized on the concept, and move to the plane, to the problematic substance, so that we can again avail ourselves of access to problems and the corresponding taste that facilitates the creation of concepts and the revitalization of thought that attends this process. It is here that the history of philosophy as problematizing practice – that is, the double task of history as discussed above – becomes critical. By beginning one's philosophical practice already immersed in a context with an established historical tradition and canon of problems and concepts to learn and master, the deterritorializing movement (the earth) associated with the determinate has the tendency to be overlooked in favor of establishing more encompassing extensional relations between already existent concepts, determinate facts, and states of affairs – in short, philosophy has largely aligned itself with the sciences (we will discuss this further in the next chapter). A problematizing history of philosophy, however, can upset the contemporary sense of already possessing concepts and reveal the problematic substance inseparable from these concepts, and the questions this may give rise to – who? where? how many? in what circumstances?, and so on – and with this we may begin the learning that we have seen is critical to the creation of the concept, what Deleuze and Guattari call the "pedagogy of the concept" (see Introduction and Chapter 1). Moreover, not only is doing a history of philosophy integral to becoming a philosopher, but it also provides a critical resource for a critique of contemporary life and society, and hence it simultaneously takes on a political component as well. It is to the political implications of the history of philosophy, and philosophical practice more generally, that we now turn.

§3

True to the arguments of the chapter as laid out to this point, "geophilosophy" is an appropriate term to describe the political project of philosophy. As we have argued, the history of philosophy should involve a double task – an analysis of the movement from the problematic to actualized states of affairs (reterritorialization) and the contrasting movement to the problematic plane of immanence (deterritorialization). History comes to be used by Deleuze and Guattari as shorthand for the first movement and geography for the second. "Geography," Deleuze and Guattari argue, "wrests history from the cult of necessity in order to stress the irreducibility of contingency. It wrests it from the cult of origins in order to affirm the power of a 'milieu'" (WP 96/QP 91–2). Geophilosophy thus engages in history but a history freed "from the cult of necessity," and affirms instead "a principle of contingent reason" (WP 93/QP 90). A geophilosophy of the present will likewise be open to a deterritorializing movement that is not to be confused or identified with any determinate fact or state of affairs in the present, whether this be contemporary capitalism, the nature of democratic institutions, and so on. Geophilosophy thus has a utopian agenda. Deleuze and Guattari are clear on this point:

> Actually, utopia is what links philosophy with its own epoch, with European capitalism, but also already with the Greek city. In each case it is with utopia that philosophy becomes political and takes the criticism of its own time to its highest point. Utopia does not split off from infinite movement: etymologically it stands for absolute deterritorialization but always at the critical point at which it is connected with the present relative milieu, and especially with the forces stifled by this milieu. (WP 99–100/QP 95–6)[14]

135

What emerges as the slogan for Deleuze and Guattari's utopian project is "*to summon forth a new earth, a new people*" (WP 99/QP 95). What is the nature of this summons? Is it a form of prophecy, a calling forth of a savior – the new earth and new people – who will rescue us from our current plight? The short answer is no. Philosophy does not have a future if by this is meant an anticipated future with determinate content. The new earth and new people that are called for are lacking in determinate content but not lacking in reality – it is precisely the contemporaneous present, the syntagmatic time, that is being summoned. This time is summoned through a critique of and resistance to determinate, chronological time, including the time of the past and present. With the coming of the new earth and new people what comes is not the people or earth we were waiting for; rather, what comes is the undoing or deterritorialization of the earth and people such as they are. This deterritorialization is not absolute, however, for as we have seen the absolute deterritorialization is a limit to be staved off if consistency, concepts, and actualized solutions to problems (that is, learning) are to remain a possibility. This is why Deleuze and Guattari argue that "Absolute deterritorialization does not take place without reterritorialization," and the new earth and new people are this relative reterritorialization: "Revolution is absolute deterritorialization even to the point where this calls for a new earth, a new people" (WP 101/QP 97).

The most pressing concern of a critique of the present for Deleuze and Guattari, which should come as no surprise to those familiar with their earlier joint-authored works, is a critique of capitalism. Inseparable from this critique is a historical analysis, but a historical analysis that brings forth the problematic conditions that have not been exhausted by the historical formations being studied. The historical study of ancient Greek philosophy, therefore, is not tasked with preserving and laying out the philosophies of the period but with intimating the problems that remain, problems that are contemporaneous to the thinking of one who is becoming a philosopher. In turning to a study of the origins of capitalism, it is also not a matter of uncovering the necessities associated with its emergence but rather the contingencies of the encounters that made it possible. In the case of capitalism, Deleuze and Guattari argue that it is the result of the conjunction of "naked labor and pure wealth" (WP 97/QP 93), meaning the deterritorialization of the worker and land, both of which come to be reterritorialized upon the immanence of capital. This conjunction of immanence with respect to capitalism repeats what occurred with the emergence of Greek philosophy, about which Deleuze and Guattari note: "there is the contingent recommencement of a same contingent process, in different conditions" (WP 98/QP 94)

The geophilosophy of the process of capitalism, at least as Deleuze and Guattari engage in it, is certainly not one of being an apologetics of capitalism, despite what some have argued.[15] In particular, the deterritorializing movement of a problematizing history would undermine the tendency of capitalism to seek its limits within *determinate* markets. Capitalism, in short, seeks not a deterritorializing movement towards the earth but an axiomatics that regulates and grids exchanges in accordance with a quantitative metrics that is geared towards staving off what Deleuze and Guattari see as the absolute limit or deterritorialization that would undermine the possibility for the extensive relations upon which capitalism is built. This is the sense in which

> Philosophy takes the relative deterritorialization of capital to the absolute; it makes it pass over the plane of immanence as movement of the infinite and suppresses it as internal limit, turns it back against itself so as to summon forth a new earth, a new people. (WP 99/QP 95)

In other words, philosophy undermines and deterritorializes the finite nature of the "internal limit" capitalism itself requires.[16] This is the utopian critique that pushes capitalism to the infinite movements of the earth, to a point where no extensive limit or set of determinate, extensive, regulated markets can function. By summoning forth "a new earth, a new people," philosophy in short is summoning the breakdown of capitalism itself, and what follows in the wake of this breakdown, the relative deterritorializations to come, remains indeterminate and unknown, and yet without the utopian critique they are much less likely to arise.

One symptom for Deleuze and Guattari of both the dominance of the contemporary mode of production associated with capitalism, and hence what we should expect as long as the system continues to function, is the form of the concept itself. Within the capitalist system, with its reliance upon internal, finite limits and determinate markets, the concept comes to be understood in terms of its extensional propositions and relations, and philosophers themselves are expected to contribute to the stock of propositions. Publish or perish, an academic is told, for a philosopher must not only have something to say, but also they must have many things to say and say them frequently, unceasingly. The churning out of propositions must continue unabated. This endless cycle of the production of concepts is of a piece with the capitalist need to continually produce and grow, to continually expand the diversity and extensity of markets. The continual need to discuss, communicate, blog, and make one's case is thus symptomatic of the continuing function of the system. As the capitalist system begins to break down, or as the critique begins to take hold, one of the expected results, Deleuze and Guattari argue, will be the ascendency of "the nonpropositional form of the concept in which communication, exchange, consensus, and opinion vanish entirely" (WP 99/QP 95). They repeat this call a few pages later: "We do not lack communication. On the contrary, we have too much of it. We lack creation. We lack resistance to the present" (WP 108/QP 104). Inseparable from this non-propositional form of the concept that is able to criticize the present without succumbing to opinion and the demands to communicate and discuss incessantly is an experimental thinking. It is this experimental thinking that is crucial to Deleuze and Guattari's understanding of philosophy, and to how philosophy differs from art and science.

§4

As we have seen throughout this book, becoming a philosopher entails, according to Deleuze and Guattari, an encounter or series of encounters with the problematic nature of substance. This encounter is best characterized as one of learning, and hence becoming a philosopher entails learning, and it is the process of learning that is inseparable from the creation of concepts that is the distinctive task of philosophy as Deleuze and Guattari understand it. We have thus been pursuing a clarification of the pedagogy of the concept that Deleuze and Guattari propose as an alternative to the extensional (that is, propositional and scientific) and idealist theories of the concept. As we have come to clarify this pedagogy of the concept, we have found that what is key to philosophy is an affinity between the philosopher and the problematic substance that provokes their attempts to think. This affinity emerges as a philosophical taste that facilitates the co-adaptation of the filtering of chaos that produces the problematic plane of immanence, and the conceptual personae that provide the double movement of de/reterritorialization (the "mobile territory" [WP 67/QP 66]) that allows for the consistency necessary for the creation of concepts. This creation of concepts, however, does not occur in a vacuum but in a historical context, in a particular time and place, and as a result the philosopher also has a utopian affinity for the problematic substance that is not to be confused with any of the determinate facts, theories, states of affairs, concepts, and so on, of their time or of the time of their predecessors; rather, they develop a philosophical taste for the syntagmatic, contemporaneous time that is never exhausted by such determinate matters. It is this syntagmatic time that underlies the creation of concepts. With this understanding of time in place, along with the other elements and processes necessary for the creation of concepts, Deleuze and Guattari come to a provisional conclusion regarding the creation of concepts:

> And this is really what the creation of concepts means: to connect internal, inseparable components to the point of closure or saturation so that we can no longer add or withdraw a component without changing the nature of the concept; to connect the concept with another, in such a way that the nature of other connections will change. (WP 90/QP 87)

To state this differently, and in terms used earlier, and to which we will return later (see Conclusion), a concept is a dynamic system of components that is to be understood and defined not in terms of the extensive relations between the components but rather in terms of an intensive "system of ideal connections," as Deleuze put it in *Difference and Repetition*;[17] these are connections that are held together in a dynamic, systemic manner – "to the point of closure or saturation" (see Chapter 7 for more on the theme of saturation, as well as our earlier discussion of fruit flies as an example of the incarnation of the "system of ideal connections," in Chapter 2, §4). In the cited passage Deleuze and Guattari are also highlighting another point Deleuze makes in *Difference and Repetition* when he argues that an intensive relation or quantity cannot be divided or added to without changing its nature, whereas this is not the case with extensive quantities.[18] For example, as an extensive quantity, one can divide a gallon of hot water (200°F) in half, or divide the bicoid protein in the developing larvae of a fruit fly into three equal portions, and the nature of what you have is still the same – you have two half-gallons of the same hot water (at 200°F) and three equal portions of bicoid protein. An intensive quantity or relation, however, cannot be added to or divided without changing the nature of the substance. Water that is 100°F is not the same as water that is 200°F, and in the developing fruit fly there are intensive thresholds where, if there is too much or too little bicoid, the fruit fly will not develop a head and thorax sufficient for its survival – the nature of the fruit fly will thus be changed. Similarly for the concept, the point of saturation is that point of dynamic or operational closure at which adding more elements to the concept changes its very nature. Deleuze points out, for example, that by adding a temporal element to Descartes's concept of the cogito, Kant fundamentally transformed the nature of that concept (see example 1). Similarly, the intensive, dynamic set of relations between concepts themselves can be changed if one adds a new concept to the mix. By adding the concept of the synthetic *a priori* to the conceptual toolbox of philosophy, Kant transformed the relationships between the other concepts of philosophy, both those that proceeded Kant as well as those to follow (this is thus an example of the syntagmatic temporal nature of creating concepts).

We can now gain a better sense of how philosophical thought, or thinking more generally, becomes experimental thinking. Deleuze and Guattari are explicit that this is the nature of thinking: "To think is to experiment, but experimentation is always that which is in the process of coming about – the new, remarkable, and interesting that replace the appearance of truth and are more demanding than it is" (WP 111/QP 106). As we have seen, in the becoming of *b* from *a*, there is the "area *ab* that belongs to both *a* and *b*, where *a* and *b* 'become' indiscernible" (WP 20/QP 25). What takes place in thinking as experimenting, therefore, is that one brings together elements into a dynamic relation with one another such that they facilitate the becoming of a concept, or the emergence of a "new, remarkable, and interesting" thought. The dynamic area that becomes indiscernible, however, does not broadcast or predetermine what will become, or even if anything new or interesting will come to be. This was why thinking and creating concepts, or philosophy as utopian project, is not a form of prophecy if prophecy is taken to be a call for a determinate savior, for a "new earth, a new people" we would recognize as precisely what was called for when they do appear. Nothing may appear at all; or, as this theme was explored in an earlier chapter, learning may fail to occur and either the thought falls apart into inconsistency and chaos or one reverts to already established habits, to repeating the tropes of one's historical tradition.

To experiment is also not to be concerned with truth, with the correct relationship between concepts and already determined and determinate facts and states of affairs, relationships that are taken to be articulable in some way, whether by way of language, mathematics, set theory, or some other accepted convention whereby the determinate facts are accurately represented in the form of true propositions. The reason thinking is experimenting, for Deleuze and Guattari, is because the determinate, individuated fact or state of affairs is not assured or predetermined. The determinate, to put it bluntly, is metaphysically indeterminate and it is the indeterminate relations of the elements brought together that allow for the becoming of that which is determinate. To think is therefore to encounter the objectivity of a problem, the metaphysically indeterminate, and if the thought is successful, the result is not a true proposition but instead a new, determinate way of thought that only later becomes part of the game of giving and asking for reasons.[19]

We are now in a position to set the stage for the second part of *What is Philosophy?*, where the focus for Deleuze and Guattari shifts from laying out the nature of philosophy to that of differentiating between philosophy, science, and art. Some have found the differences Deleuze and Guattari chart between philosophy, science, and art to be artificial and too coarsely drawn. Do not mathematicians and scientists also create concepts, or seek to draw a number of elements together into a plane of consistency that enables them to develop the equations and problems that facilitate a successful research outcome? Are not scientists at least as concerned with experiments and experimental approaches to their subject matter as philosophers are, if not more so? And should not philosophy be informed by science and take science as an ally or as engaged in a largely shared and overlapping enterprise rather than being artificially isolated from it in the manner Deleuze and Guattari appear to advocate? What of the relation between art and philosophy and science? Many of the great philosophers and scientists drew profound inspiration from the arts. By relegating art into a distinct realm, are Deleuze and Guattari dismissing such relationships and/ or ignoring the facts that appear to belie their claims regarding the distinct realms of philosophy, science, and art? And what, finally, of politics? Why is politics not included among the fundamental forms of thought?[20] These and other critical questions have been, and no doubt will continue to be, raised regarding the tripartite division Deleuze and Guattari put forth in *What is Philosophy?*

To begin to address these concerns, what needs to be stressed is that there is indeed overlap and a shared engagement among philosophy, science, and art. Each is concerned with learning to think, or with thinking as experimentation. What is different between philosophy, science, and art is the manner in which they engage in thought, the way they carry out and develop their experimental effort to think. In short, philosophy, science, and art are each creative efforts, and efforts that are, as experimental, not guaranteed success but, if successful, will alter and transform how we think. We can thus learn to think, and think differently, with philosophy, science, and art. The differences between the learning processes associated with each of the three enterprises of thought will be the focus of part 2 of *What is Philosophy?*, and it is to this that we now turn.

Example 7

In their "Geophilosophy" chapter, as we have seen, Deleuze and Guattari argue that "there is no good reason but contingent reason" and that "there is no universal history except of contingency" (WP 93/QP 90). It is for this reason that Deleuze and Guattari claim it is "pointless to seek . . . an analytic and necessary principle that would link philosophy to Greece" (WP 94/QP 90), and yet this is precisely what Hegel and Heidegger do. By arguing for a necessary link between the origins of philosophy and ancient Greece, philosophy becomes, as Deleuze and Guattari read Hegel and Heidegger, "*indistinguishable from its own history*" (WP 95/QP 91). In other words, rather than understanding philosophy as the conjunction of contingent encounters on a plane of immanence which result in the creation of concepts, philosophy instead comes to be seen as the historical development of the already determined and predetermining event that is Greece. Philosophy's determinate "point of departure" thus comes to be seen as internal to the nature of philosophy itself rather than the indeterminate, indiscernible plane of immanence being understood, as Deleuze and Guattari do, as the condition for the creation of determinate and determinable concepts – concepts as the reterritorialization of thought.

For Hegel it is quite clear that Greece marks a pivotal beginning for both world history and philosophy. In the Introduction to his *Philosophy of History*, Hegel is quite forthright in his assertion that

> The History of the World begins with its general aim – the realization of the Idea of Spirit – only in an implicit form that is, as Nature; a hidden, most profoundly hidden, unconscious instinct; and the whole process of History . . . is directed to rendering this unconscious impulse a conscious one.[21]

The key to the historical process whereby the unconscious instinct becomes a conscious impulse occurs when freedom, which is the Idea of Spirit itself, becomes the conscious content of our volitions, the known Idea that guides our actions. It is precisely here that Greece becomes essential to the "History of the World" for "It is here first that advancing Spirit makes itself the content of its volition and its knowledge."[22] But matters are more complicated than this, as Hegel well knows. For instance, the Egyptians, Hegel points out, were aware of Spirit, and thus Spirit "presented itself to their consciousness," but it did so "in the form of a problem."[23] That is, although aware of Spirit, its determinate content remains veiled and mysterious, as exemplified, for Hegel, by the inscription at the sanctuary of the Goddess Neith – "I am that which is, that which was, and that which will be; no one has lifted my veil."[24] The Greeks, by contrast, offer a determinate solution to the problem of Spirit, and the inscription at the Temple of Apollo is its most obvious statement: "Apollo is its solution; his utterance is: 'Man, know thyself.'"[25] The freedom of the individual, and the freedom that flows from knowledge of thyself in relation to Nature, become, therefore, the point where Spirit first "makes itself the content of its volition and knowledge."

Matters do not end here, however; in fact, they are just beginning. Greece is simply the point of origin of world history and philosophy. The reason for this is that the determinate content of individual freedom remains largely unknown, and the process of world history is simply the process whereby the Idea of Spirit becomes fully determinate, actualized, and conscious of itself. "The State," Hegel claims, "is the Idea of Spirit in the external manifestation of human Will and its Freedom."[26] It is the State form, therefore, that is crucial for Hegel, or more precisely it is the recognition of individual freedom as embodied in the external manifestation of a state that is grounded in and defends universal laws. If this is the full external manifestation of Spirit, then the Greeks are the first step in the process of realizing this State by virtue of the fact that historical transition itself became possible as one state came to replace another. This is why Hegel claims that

> The Persians are the first Historical People; Persia was the first Empire that passed away. While China and India remain stationary, and perpetuate a natural vegetative existence to the present time, this land has been subject to those developments and revolution, which alone manifest a historical condition.[27]

China and India remain stuck in an abstract conception of Spirit, and moreover they present a social situation that has avoided the process of historical progress that occurs through opposition and the overcoming of this opposition. The Persians are thus the first historical people, for it is their opposition to the Greeks and their passing away with the rise of Greece that give rise to historical process, and hence the possibility of the progressive determination of the content of the Idea of Spirit. With this in mind, Hegel offers a brief summary of the history of the world, leading to the Germans:

> But Egypt became a province of the great Persian kingdom, and the historical transition takes place when the Persian world comes in contact with the Greek. Here, for the first time, an historical transition meets us, viz. in the fall of an empire. China and India, as already mentioned, have remained – Persia has not. The transition to Greece is, indeed, internal; but here it shows itself also externally, as a transmission of sovereignty – an occurrence which from this time forward is ever and anon repeated. For the Greeks surrender the scepter of dominion and of civilization to the Romans, and the Romans are subdued by the Germans.[28]

As for philosophy, it too begins with the Greeks for, just as the Idea of Spirit as freedom comes to be further and further manifested in the external world as the determinate content of conscious volitions, philosophy also progressively thinks the nature of freedom but as that which is eternally present throughout this process. Whereas history attempts to understand how world events reflect the progressive determination of the Idea of Spirit (a projective history, as Deleuze and Guattari put it), "philosophy," Hegel argues, "as occupying itself with the True, has to do with the eternally present. Nothing in the past is lost for it, for the Idea is ever present. . . ."[29] And yet the relationship between this Idea of Spirit and the objective, external manifestation of this Idea remains undetermined at philosophy's "point of departure," and thus, as Deleuze and Guattari argue, on Hegel's view, "Greek thought is not conscious of the relationship to the subject that it presupposes without yet being able to reflect" (WP 94/QP 90). In other words, just as the Egyptians presupposed a Spirit that remained indeterminate and therefore a problem, so too do the Greeks presuppose a Spirit that is likewise largely undetermined and thus philosophy is in need of the historical process in order to increasingly recognize the determinate solution to the Egyptian problem. Deleuze and Guattari thus argue that on Hegel's view of the history of philosophy, "it is not clear what distinguishes the antephilosophical stage of the Orient and the philosophical stage of Greece" (ibid.). Both are confronted with the problematic, indeterminate nature of substance. At philosophy's point of departure, therefore, philosophy initiates the process of determining the indeterminate though determinable nature of Spirit, and yet this is precisely the process of the History of the World itself as Hegel understands it; thus Deleuze and Guattari conclude that, for Hegel, philosophy "necessarily becomes indistinguishable from its own history" (WP 95/QP 91).

According to Deleuze and Guattari, Heidegger takes a different, though fundamentally equivalent, approach to the relationship between philosophy and its origins in ancient Greece. Unlike Hegel, Heidegger does not restrict philosophy to the developing relationship between the Idea of Spirit and its realization in the world – between subject and object, in other words – and instead "situates the concept in the difference between Being and beings rather than in that between subject and object" (WP 94/QP 90). In other words, rather than placing the historical development of the Idea of Spirit – that is, the Concept – at the heart of philosophy itself, Heidegger places the turning away from Being towards beings as the pivotal move that characterizes the history of philosophy. In short, rather than identifying philosophy with the historical process of the Idea of freedom becoming increasingly determinate, Heidegger identifies philosophy with the turning away from the indeterminate (Being) and towards the determinate (beings).

Despite Heidegger's shifting of the nature of philosophy from the relationship between subject and object to Being and beings, Deleuze and Guattari argue that Heidegger continues to fix "the movement of deterritorialization" of philosophy "between being and beings, between the Greek territory and the Western earth" (WP 95/ QP 91). We can see this, for instance, in Heidegger's analysis of the Anaximander fragment. The English translation of the fragment reads as follows: "Whence things have their origin, there they must also pass away according to necessity; for they must pay penalty and be judged for their injustice, according to the ordinance of time."[30] To summarize Heidegger's reading of this fragment, the things that are originating are beings, and what passes away with this origination is Being, or "the presencing of what is present."[31] What is special about the Greeks, therefore, according to Heidegger, is that

> What is Greek is the dawn of that destiny in which Being illuminates itself in beings and so propounds a certain essence of man; that essence unfolds as something fateful, preserved in Being and dispensed by Being, without ever being separated from Being.[32]

What begins, as Heidegger puts it a couple of pages later, is the "epoch of Being" from which "comes the epochal essence of its destining, in which world history properly consists. When Being keeps to itself in its destining, world suddenly and unexpectedly comes to pass."[33] Philosophy proper, therefore, is for Heidegger the thinking of the presencing of what is present rather than the thinking of what is already present. When the latter occurs, Heidegger claims we have "the collapse of thinking into the sciences and into faith [that] is the baneful destiny of Being."[34] And it is precisely this destining that begins with the Greeks, where "the history of Being begins with the oblivion of Being . . . [and where] its distinction from beings – keeps to itself."[35] The destiny of Being and the history of philosophy is precisely the oblivion of Being, the forgetfulness of the distinction between Being as the "presencing of what is present" and the beings that are present and the subject of the sciences. This oblivion is marked by the event of Greek philosophy, or as Heidegger puts it, it is "the richest and most prodigious event: in it the history of the Western world comes to be borne out. It is the event of metaphysics. What now is stands in the shadow of the already foregone destiny of Being's oblivion."[36] In other words, the event of Greek philosophy, the event of metaphysics, is the event that continues to characterize the nature of philosophy – it is the "foregone destiny of Being's oblivion." By understanding the history of philosophy in this way, however, Deleuze and Guattari maintain that Heidegger excludes the contingency of encounters on the plane of immanence and the concepts that may result from such encounters, and instead Heidegger calls for the fateful destiny of all concepts in relation to the oblivion of Being whereby philosophy becomes "indistinguishable from its own history."

Suggested readings for example 7
    G. W. F. Hegel, *Lectures on the History of Philosophy*
    Martin Heidegger, *Early Greek Thinking.*

Example 8

The lesson to draw from the previous example, according to Deleuze and Guattari, is that the philosophical task of creating concepts is not to be linked by necessity to the historical moment or point of origin of this task but rather to the contingencies of encounters on a plane of immanence. As we have seen, however (see Introduction and Chapter 1), the Greeks are given a special place in Deleuze and Guattari's account of the nature of philosophy. Deleuze and Guattari admit that "The birth of philosophy required an encounter between the Greek milieu and the plane of immanence of

146

thought. It required the conjunction of two very different movements of deterritorialization, the relative and the absolute," and yet this conjunction and encounter of two "very different movements of deterritorialization" are to be accounted for not by a necessary reason that links the two together into an indissoluble unity but by a contingent reason that initiated philosophy but does not continue to predetermine the path or nature of philosophy itself.

This example adds further clarity to the distinction between necessary and contingent encounters that is pivotal to Deleuze and Guattari's understanding of the history of philosophy. As they begin the example, Deleuze and Guattari admit that "we moderns possess the concept but have lost sight of the plane of immanence," or "what the Greeks possessed Autochtonously" (WP 104/QP 100). Stated differently, for the Greeks the concept is what awaits being thought, what already exists and precedes the act of thought itself (see example 2).[37] We moderns, by contrast, possess the concept as essential to the nature of thought itself, and it is on precisely this point that we begin to see the contrast between Hegel/Heidegger and Deleuze and Guattari most clearly. For both Hegel and Heidegger (see example 7), the advent of the Greeks is integral to the nature of philosophical thought itself. For Hegel the history of philosophy is the history of the progressive determination of the content of the Idea of Spirit, content that first entered the scene with the Greeks; and for Heidegger the content of philosophical thought is the result of a turning away from the thought of presencing and Being and towards beings, a turning away that originated with the Greeks. For Deleuze and Guattari, however, what the Greeks possessed Autochtonously was not a determinate content essential to thought itself (Hegel); nor was it a thought beyond all determinate thought, a thought of Being in contrast to the thought of beings (Heidegger). To the contrary, the Greeks possessed a thought in movement, a thought of infinite speed, or a thought of "an area *ab* that belongs to both *a* and *b*, where *a* and *b* 'become' indiscernible" (WP 20/QP 25) – that is, the Greeks possessed the plane of immanence.

Despite the Greeks possessing the plane of immanence Autochtonously, the tendency of thought – one of the illusions of transcendence (see Chapter 2) – is to place the plane of immanence into a necessary, identifiable relationship where immanence is immanent to something, whether this be a determinate and determinable concept or the plane of immanence that has come to be identified as the foundation for the history of philosophy itself. Deleuze and Guattari associate the first with the French and the second with the Germans. As Deleuze and Guattari put it with respect to the French, they identify thought with concepts and hence set out to support "concepts through a simple order of reflexive knowledge, an order of reasons, an 'epistemology'" (WP 104/ QP 100). Most notably for the French, Deleuze and Guattari claim, they "are like landowners whose source of income is the cogito [see example 1]. They are always reterritorialized on consciousness" (ibid.). Thought itself, Deleuze and Guattari argue, involves both an absolute deterritorialization (the movement towards chaos) and a relative deterritorialization (the drawing of a plane of consistency [see Chapters 3 and 4]) that allow for the possibility of creating the concepts which reterritorialize thought – "Philosophy is reterritorialized on the concept." For Deleuze and Guattari, therefore, a concept "is not an object but a territory" (WP 101/QP 97). By identifying thought with the reterritorialization of the absolute, the French set out from the basis of the cogito, or consciousness, to take an "inventory of habitable, civilizable, knowable or known lands" (WP 104/QP 100) – that is, territories. In other words, the French begin from the perspective where philosophy comes to be necessarily linked to that which is always already known to thought, the concept of the cogito (consciousness), and from there they set out to determine the relationships between this concept and further territories that are or can be known. The French thus set out to build a deductive system of relationships between concepts, between known and knowable territories.

The Germans, by contrast, set out to identify philosophy not with the relative reterritorialization of thought on the determinate and determinable concept but on the absolute deterritorialization of the plane of immanence. As Deleuze and Guattari put it, Germany "wants to reconquer the Greek plane of immanence" (ibid.), but they do so by identifying the plane of immanence as that which is to be necessarily linked to philosophy itself. The result is that rather than identifying philosophy with the effort to lay out a deductive system of relationships between concepts – an "epistemology" – they identify the plane of immanence as the ground to be cleared, the place where one may lay a foundation for the determinate concepts of philosophy itself. The result, then, is that while the Greeks possessed the plane of immanence Autochtonously,

> German philosophy would have [it] through conquest and foundation, so that it would make immanence immanent *to* something, to its own

Act of philosophizing, to its own philosophizing subjectivity (the cogito therefore takes on a different meaning since it conquers and lays down the ground). (WP 104–5/QP 100–1)

The Germans thus set out to conquer the plane of immanence and clear the grounds for a foundation that will support the totality of that which may come to be built upon this foundation (by the French). In what Deleuze and Guattari refer to as the "trinity [of] Founding-Building-Inhabiting," they claim that "the French build and the Germans lay foundations, but," they add, "the English inhabit" (WP 105/QP 101). In short, the French build a deductive system that identifies philosophy with concepts; the Germans found and institute an "organic totality" that encompasses all that may come to be built; and the English avoid either of these alternatives by identifying philosophy with the movement of thought itself, or they are, Deleuze and Guattari claim, "those nomads who treat the plane of immanence as a movable and moving ground, a field of radical experience" (ibid.).

The English empiricists will thus emerge again as a critical exception to the tradition in philosophy where immanence is taken to be immanent to something. The English, in other words, do much, then, to restore the rights of immanence. In this context, rather than identify philosophy with the plane of immanence as the organic totality or foundation for all that comes to be known, or with the deductive relationship between that which is or can be determinately known, the English identify philosophy with the acquisition of beliefs as the result of habit. Instead of stressing the conditions for knowledge itself, whether by way of concepts or by way of the ground or foundation for all knowledge, the English (namely, Hume, the Scotsman) place the emphasis upon the formation of habits that vary and move as the associations and strengths of these habits themselves change. It is for this reason that Deleuze and Guattari characterize the English as nomads who "are happy to pitch their tents from island to island and over the sea" (WP 105/QP 101); that is, they are happy to understand philosophy as the process of habit formations that change and are variable, subject to the contingent encounters and conjunctions on "a field of radical experience" (ibid.). The English empiricists, and Hume in particular, thus restore the rights of immanence not by reducing it to the predetermining identity and necessity of a reterritorialized concept (cogito/consciousness) or to a totalizing foundation (Hegel's Idea of Spirit), but by placing the movement of habit itself, and the

149

contingency of that which emerges by way of habit, at the center of thought and philosophy.

What is crucial to the process of habit formation, according to Deleuze and Guattari – but this is a point that Deleuze recognized early on and throughout his career,[38] is that it does not assume the identity of that which comes to be thought (or believed) but it is habit itself that is the very process that accounts for the identity and individuation of this thought (belief). This occurs when elements are brought together and "contemplated," or "habits are taken on," Deleuze and Guattari claim, "by contemplating and by contracting that which is contemplated" (WP 105/QP 101). The elements of thought are thus contemplated, condensed, and brought together "at once" (at infinite speed [see Chapter 1]) into an "area *ab*" where they become indiscernible, and it is precisely this indiscernibility and contemplation that account for the emergence of the individuated identity. For Hume, therefore, the emergence of the belief in causation is to be accounted for by the formation of a habit, and Deleuze and Guattari extend this process well beyond the beliefs we may hold. "Habit is creative," Deleuze and Guattari claim, and they then immediately add, as if to drive home the point that they are extending Hume's arguments, that "the plant contemplates water, earth, nitrogen, carbon, chlorides, and sulphates, and it contracts them in order to acquire its own concept and fill itself with it (enjoyment)" (ibid.). The English thus give to us what Deleuze and Guattari call an "empirical neo-Platonism" in that all becomes a contemplation; however, rather than this contemplation being of a concept that is not possessed but is always already there prior to thought (see example 2), a Humean neo-Platonism is the very process that gives rise to the habits that are inseparable from the very being of things – "We are all contemplations, and therefore habits. *I* is a habit" (ibid.). These habits, moreover, "are developed and given up," Deleuze and Guattari claim, "on the plane of immanence of radical experience: they are 'conventions,'" and this is why, they conclude, "English philosophy is a free and wild creation of concepts" (ibid.). If the French and Germans give us the necessity of deductive systems or totalizing foundations, the English give us the contingency of conventions, of habit, and it is this move that avoids the historicizing necessity that befalls Hegel and Heidegger.

Suggested reading for example 8
David Hume, *A Treatise of Human Nature*

Example 9

Deleuze and Guattari close the "Geophilosophy" chapter with an example that focuses on the concept of the event. This concept looms large in Deleuze's own works and the importance of this concept continues in *What is Philosophy?* For Deleuze and Guattari a concept is described as being "incorporeal, even though it is incarnated or effectuated in bodies . . . The concept speaks the event, not the essence or the thing" (WP 21/QP 26). What becomes critical to understanding the event, and likewise the concept (or philosophy) that speaks the event, is to discern the relationship between the event and the historical states of affairs and things – including plants (recall example 8) – in which events and concepts (as multiplicities [recall our earlier discussion]) may be "incarnated or effectuated." By drawing from the work of Charles Péguy, Deleuze and Guattari distinguish "two ways of considering the event" (WP 111/QP 106): first, there is the event as embodied and incarnated in states of affairs and things – "its effectuation in history, its conditioning and deterioration in history" (ibid.) – and second, there is the process of "reassembling the event, installing oneself in it as in a becoming, a becoming young again and aging in it, both at the same time, going through all its components or singularities" (WP 111/QP 106–7). It is the second understanding of the event that interests Deleuze and Guattari, and it is precisely this event that philosophy speaks as it creates concepts; or it is this event that the concept of the plant speaks as it embodies the condensation, contraction, and reassembling of the components ("water, earth, nitrogen, carbon, chlorides, and sulphates").

To help elucidate the distinction between the two ways in which the event may be considered, Deleuze and Guattari claim that while "nothing changes or seems to change in history . . . everything changes, and we change, in the event" (WP 111/QP 107). Deleuze and Guattari then cite Péguy from his book *Clio*: "There was nothing. Then a problem to which we saw no end, a problem without solution . . . suddenly no longer exists and we wonder what we were talking about" (ibid.[39]). With our discussion of the importance of the concept of learning to Deleuze and Guattari's effort to develop a pedagogy of the concept in *What is Philosophy?* – and more importantly, to offer a meditation on a life well lived – we can restate Péguy's point. Since learning is understood by Deleuze and Guattari to be the appropriate term for encountering the objectivity of a problem, then what follows for them is that a key aspect of this encounter is that the problem itself cannot be stated in terms of the

151

elements one encounters. To learn to swim, for example, it is not sufficient simply to identify the various elements and components associated with swimming. To learn to swim one must conjugate and condense these varied elements into a plane of consistency (the "area *ab*") that is not to be confused with the elements that are conjugated and condensed (for example, *a* and *b*). Péguy's quotation highlights this contrast: when one is looking to the elements and components themselves in order to learn, then one encounters a "problem without end," for each of these determinate elements presupposes a differential of further determinate elements, and so on *in infinitum* (see our discussion of "disparity" in Chapter 1). When one learns and contracts a habit, however, one does so by way of a contemplation that is indeterminate and indiscernible, and this is precisely the event that we install ourselves in, "as in a becoming," when learning. When installed in the event of learning in this way, the determinate elements and components disappear – they become indiscernible – and we "wonder what we were talking about" before when the elements were the pressing issue. This is also the sense in which historically nothing changes – the elements and components are unchanged – but in the event "everything changes, and we change, in the event."

This brings us to a related distinction that follows from Péguy's distinction between the two types of event. There is the historical event, the event that achieves its effectuation and dissolution in states of affairs and things, and then there is the event that is not to be confused with historical time, or with an eternal time that transcends the historical. For Péguy the time associated with this latter event "is the Aternal [*Internel*]" (WP 111/QP 107). Deleuze and Guattari then note that this understanding of the Aternal bears striking similarities to Nietzsche's notion of the untimely, to "the unhistorical vapor that has nothing to do with the eternal, the becoming without which nothing would come about in history but that does not merge with history" (see example 7 and Chapter 4), and to Foucault's notion of the actual. Bringing Nietzsche and Foucault into this example enables Deleuze and Guattari to provide an important clarification of the relationship between problems and concepts, for despite the claim by Deleuze and Guattari that Péguy, Nietzsche, and Foucault are each concerned with a time that is not to be confused with actualized states of affairs, Péguy lays stress upon the Aternal, with its affinity to the eternal and atemporal; Nietzsche will stress the untimely as the condition inseparable from the timely and historical itself; and Foucault will prefer the term actual and hence presuppose an understanding of time that is apparently at odds with both Péguy and Nietzsche.

With respect to Foucault, Deleuze and Guattari argue that what is important is not the actual *per se* – that is, the actually present – but rather "what we become, what we are in the process of becoming" (WP 112/QP 107). In his work Foucault sets out to do more than a history of what was once believed, an inventory of thoughts once thought. Foucault refers to this as a history of ideas. Although Foucault certainly scrutinized and paid careful attention to the archival record of what happened, his greater interest is to do a history of thought. As Foucault describes the difference, a "history of ideas involves the analysis of a notion from its birth, through its development, and in the setting of other ideas, which constitute its context."[40] This is a history of ideas that sees thought as an event in the first sense Péguy distinguishes. This is the history of the effectuation of thought within a context and the subsequent transformation of this thought and its effects upon other thoughts. A history of thought, by contrast, entails for Foucault "the analysis of the way an unproblematic field of experience becomes a problem, raises discussions and debate, incites new reactions, and induces crisis in the previously silent behaviors, practices, and institutions."[41] Foucault's project, therefore, is not one of clarifying what is the case in the present, or of attaining clarity on what was the case in the past, but it is instead the effort to problematize the "unproblematic field of experience" and, in doing so, to induce the crises that may well transform the practices and institutions that were previously unproblematic. It is this difference between what we are, what is the case, and what we become or are in the process of becoming as a result of the problematizing of the unproblematic field of experience that Foucault refers to as the actual.

Returning to the differences and similarities between Péguy, Nietzsche, and Foucault, we can see that it is not for them a matter of using different words to describe the same concept of time, a time that is not to be confused with historical events, for instance. According to Deleuze and Guattari, "The Aternal, the Untimely, the Actual are examples of concepts in philosophy; exemplary concepts" (WP 113/QP 108). As is the nature of concepts for Deleuze and Guattari, they are always connected to problems without which they would be entirely lacking in significance.[42] Problems, moreover, are always problems of conjunction, problems of learning, and thus they are to be understood in terms of the effort to draw elements together into an indiscernible plane of consistency that enables the contemplation that transforms the problem into a possible solution. With this in mind, Deleuze and Guattari note that while there are certainly similarities between Péguy, Nietzsche, and Foucault with respect to their understanding of time, the concepts they create involve different components and different problems, and hence one should not be surprised by the differing terms they chose. For Deleuze and Guattari, this is the problem of "the Temporally eternal in Péguy, the Eternity of becoming according to Nietzsche, and the Outside-interior with Foucault" (WP 113/ QP 108). Stated differently, Péguy, Nietzsche, and Foucault each create concepts in connection to a problem, and in doing this they encounter A LIFE that is irreducible to the lived states and histories of our lives – in short, they offer a meditation on a life well lived, or, they are doing philosophy.

Suggested reading for example 9
    Charles Péguy, *Temporal and Eternal*
    Michel Foucault, *The Archaeology of Knowledge.*

NOTES

1. In discussing his approach to how he approaches the history of philosophy, Deleuze claims that he imagines himself "approaching the author from behind, and making him a child, who would indeed be his and would, nevertheless, be monstrous. That the child would be his was very important because the author had to say, in effect, everything I made him say" ("I Have Nothing to Admit," *Semiotext(e)* 2 no. 3, trans. Janis Forman, 1977).

2. Deleuze and Guattari use the French term *ritournelle*, which Brian Massumi translates as "refrain" in his translation of *A Thousand Plateaus*. We will discuss this concept further in the Conclusion.

3. This has been a common criticism of Deleuze and Guattari. David Martin-Jones, for instance, argues in *Deleuze and World Cinemas* (London: Continuum, 2011) that there is a Eurocentric bias in the films that form the basis for Deleuze's two cinema books. One could argue, similarly, that Deleuze's historical manuscripts are also Eurocentric.

4. G. W. F. Hegel, *Lectures on the Philosophy of History*, trans. J. Sibree (New York: Dover Philosophical Classics, 2004), p. 90.

5. Ibid., p. 87.

6. In the first section of his chapter on the Greek Spirit, Hegel argues again that the fact that the Greek peoples were spread in "various forms through the sea – a multitude of islands, and a continent itself

which exhibits insular features" (ibid., p. 225) was critical to the emergence of the Greek Spirit. In particular, the fragmenting of Greek territories into "insular," isolated cities led to the prominence of the individual over the universal. On Hegel's reading of the progression of history, the Greek spirit of individualism helped to launch history from the grips of a pure universality without tension or opposition. By over-stressing individuality, however, the Greek culture was only the first step on the road to the State, where Hegel argues we have the final reconciliation of the universal and the individual.

7. For more on Thales see Kirk and Raven's classic *The Presocratic Philosophers: A Critical History with a Selection of Texts* (Cambridge: Cambridge University Press, 1984).

8. It should be stressed that this is only "largely" true and that there are some notable exceptions. Michael Friedman, for instance, has written a number of historical monographs on the rise of analytic philosophy. See also Michael Della Rocca's "Taming of Philosophy," in *Philosophy and its History*, ed. Mogens Lærke, Justin E. H. Smith, and Eric Schliesser (Oxford: Oxford University Press, 2013).

9. See Fernand Braudel, *On History*, trans. Sarah Matthews (Chicago: University of Chicago Press, 1982), p. 26.

10. A Kondratiev cycle is one such extended timeframe. A Kondratiev cycle, otherwise known as a Kondratiev long wave cycle, is a roughly 40–60–year economic cycle that begins with a period of high growth in the economy followed by slow growth, a slowing that leads eventually to a new cycle. For more, see Vincent Barnett, *Kondratiev and the Dynamics of Economic Development* (London: Macmillan, 1998). There have been a number of works to follow through on Braudel's suggestions to take into account longer timeframes than historians traditionally considered. Immanuel Wallerstein, the late founder and director of the Braudel Institute, wrote a number of books analyzing the rise and progression of capitalism through the developing world-system, as he puts it (see *The Modern World System, 3 Volumes.* New York: Academic Press, 1974). William McNeill's book *Plagues and Peoples* (New York: Anchor, 1977) explores the long-term relationship between European civilization and the plague. When the plague gradually subsided in the seventeenth and eighteenth centuries, the result was a population explosion and the intensification of warfare in Europe. This is another example of taking Braudel's concerns to heart.

11. For Nietzsche's discussion of the misty vapor, see *Untimely Meditations*, trans. R. J. Hollingdale (Cambridge: Cambridge University Press, 1997), p. 97 (cited and discussed as well in the previous chapter, fn. 22).

12. *Lectures on the Philosophy of History*, p. 1.

13. Deleuze and Guattari repeat this point towards the end of the chapter: "What history grasps of the event is its effectuation in states of affairs

or in lived experience, but the event in its becoming, in its specific consistency, in its self-positing as concept, escapes History . . . Without history experimentation would remain indeterminate and unconditioned, but experimentation is not historical" (WP 110–11/QP 106).

14. Paul Patton has provided a thorough discussion of the utopian political project in Deleuze and Deleuze and Guattari, and he has connected this project to the work of other political thinkers such as John Rawls. See his *Deleuzian Concepts: Philosophy, Colonization, Politics* (Palo Alto: Stanford University Press, 2010).

15. Luc Boltanski and Eve Chiapello, for instance, have argued that Deleuze's philosophy converges all too nicely with neo-liberal arguments that defend capitalist markets as non-hierarchical, self-organizing systems. See Luc Boltanski and Eve Chiapello, *The New Spirit of Capitalism*, trans. Gregory Elliot (London: Verso, 2007). For a defense of Deleuze in light of these critiques, see my essay, "Whistle While You Work: Deleuze and the Spirit of Capitalism," in *Deleuze and Ethics* (Edinburgh: Edinburgh University Press, 2011), pp. 5–20.

16. See Gilles Deleuze and Félix Guattari, *Anti-Oedipus: Capitalism and Schizophrenia*, trans. Mark Seem and Robert Hurley (Minneapolis: University of Minnesota Press, 1977), p. 34: "What we are really trying to say is that capitalism, through its process of production, produces an awesome schizophrenic accumulation of energy or charge, against which it brings all its vast powers of repression to bear, but which nonetheless continues to act as capitalism's limit. For capitalism constantly counteracts, constantly inhibits this tendency while at the same time allowing it free rein; it continually seeks to avoid reaching its limit while simultaneously tending toward that limit."

17. Gilles Deleuze, *Difference and Repetition*, trans. Paul Patton (New York: Columbia University Press, 1994), p. 173.

18. Ibid., p. 237: "An intensive quantity may be divided, but not without changing its nature. In a sense, it is therefore indivisible, but only because no part exists prior to the division and no part retains the same nature after division."

19. This is a reference to the philosophies of Wilfrid Sellars and Robert Brandom. See Sellars's *Empiricism and the Philosophy of Mind* (Cambridge, MA: Harvard University Press, [1956] 1997), and Brandom's *Articulating Reasons: An Introduction to Inferentialism* (Cambridge, MA: Harvard University Press, 2001).

20. This was Badiou's criticism. See Badiou's *Deleuze: The Clamor of Being*, trans. Louise Burchill (Minneapolis: University of Minnesota Press, 2000), pp. 90–1. Here Badiou argues that in arguing for "absolute beginnings" he may be, as Deleuze argued, falling "back into transcendence and into the equivocity of analogy. But," Badiou counters, "all in all, if the only way to think a political revolution, an amorous encounter, an invention of the sciences, or a creation of art as distinct

infinities ... is by sacrificing immanence ... and the univocity of Being, then I would sacrifice them."

21. *Lectures on the Philosophy of History*, p. 25.
22. Ibid., p. 223.
23. Ibid., p. 220.
24. Ibid.
25. Ibid.
26. Ibid., p. 47.
27. Ibid., p. 173
28. Ibid., p. 221.
29. Ibid., p. 79.
30. Martin Heidegger, *Early Greek Thinking* (San Francisco: Harper), p. 13.
31. Ibid., p. 39: "But since the dawn of thinking 'Being' names the presencing of what is present, in the sense of the gathering which clears and shelters, which in turn is thought and designated as the Logos."
32. Ibid., p. 25.
33. Ibid., p. 27.
34. Ibid., p. 40.
35. Ibid., p. 50.
36. Ibid., p. 51.
37. "We today possess concepts, but the Greeks did not yet possess them; they possessed the plane that we no longer possess. That is why Plato's Greeks *contemplate* the concept as something that is still very far away and beyond, whereas we possess the concept – we possess it in the mind innately; all that is needed is to *reflect*" (WP 101/QP 97).
38. See my *Deleuze's Hume: Philosophy, Culture and the Scottish Enlightenment* (Edinburgh: Edinburgh University Press, 2009), where I argue for the significance of Hume's thought for Deleuze's project throughout Deleuze's career.
39. Citing *Clio* (Paris: Gallimard, 1931), pp. 266–9.
40. Michel Foucault, *Fearless Speech* (New York: Semiotext(e), 2001), p. 42.
41. Ibid.
42. See WP 16/QP 22: "All concepts are connected to problems without which they would have no meaning and which can themselves only be isolated or understood as their solution emerges."

5

Philosophy and Science

One of the more controversial moves in *What is Philosophy?* is the sharp distinction Deleuze and Guattari make between philosophy, science, and art, and especially the distinction between philosophy and science. For example, Deleuze and Guattari argue that philosophy and science each "approaches chaos in a completely different, almost opposite way" (WP 118/QP 112). On the one hand, "philosophy wants to know how to retain infinite speeds," the infinite speeds of chaos (see Chapter 1) while, on the other, science "relinquishes the infinite, infinite speed" (ibid.). The sharp contrast between philosophy and science that Deleuze and Guattari set forth in their book can be understood, as we will see in this chapter, in terms of this contrasting relationship to the infinite speeds of chaos. Despite this difference, however, philosophy and science share many features. Both philosophy and science, Deleuze and Guattari argue, engage in "thought experiment," and this experimentation entails, for both philosophy and science, a creativity in the face of problems; in fact, both philosophy and science require "a 'higher' taste" (WP 133/QP 127) that is able to co-adapt the elements that are "in the process of being determined" (ibid.). Just as becoming a philosopher (see Chapter 3) entailed a philosophical faculty of taste to co-adapt the laying out of a plane of immanence, the invention of conceptual personae, and the creation of concepts, similarly for science the "higher" taste co-adapts the tasks of "choosing the good independent variables, installing the effective partial observer on a particular route, and constructing the best coordinates of an equation or function" (ibid.). More to the point, the deployment of taste to co-adapt the elements that are "in the process of being determined" occurs for both philosophy and science in response to problems. In other words, both philosophy and science confront the objectivity of a problem, or, as Deleuze and Guattari put it, "philosophy and science (like art itself . . .) include an *I do not know* that has become positive and creative, the condition of creation itself, and that consists in determining by what one does not know" (WP 128/QP 122).

The difference between philosophy and science, therefore, is not to be found in the fact that both deploy a faculty of taste in their efforts to address the objectivity of a problem – that is, both philosophy and science are attempts at learning. The difference between them, rather, is to be found in that which is created as a consequence of this encounter and confrontation with chaos. As Deleuze and Guattari put it, "Science is haunted not by its own unity but by the plane of reference constituted by all the limits or orders through which it confronts chaos" (WP 119/QP 113). Philosophy, by contrast, confronts chaos and affirms its infinite speeds when it creates concepts on a plane of immanence, whereas science confronts chaos and relinquishes infinite speeds by installing the limits that define a plane of reference that in turn enables the creation of functions. Understanding and exploring this contrast will be the task of the current chapter.

§1

Since chaos is central to Deleuze and Guattari's understanding of the relationship between philosophy, science, and art, and since part 2 of *What is Philosophy?* is dedicated to laying out the differences and relationships between philosophy, science, logic, and art, it should, then, be no surprise that early in part 2 they begin with a definition of chaos:

> Chaos is defined not so much by its disorder as by the infinite speed with which every form taking shape in it vanishes. It is a void that is not nothingness but a virtual, containing all possible particles and drawing out all possible forms, which spring up only to disappear immediately, without consistency or reference, without consequence. (WP 118/QP 111)

The infinite speeds of chaos, therefore, are not infinite in the sense of a measurable speed taken to the infinite. If infinite speeds were to be understood in this way, then we would have an instance of the bad infinite (see Chapter 1). What we have instead is a failure to establish the connections, conjunctions, and consistency necessary for the possibility of individuation, and hence for the measurable time of individuated entities and processes (see our earlier discussion of paradigmatic history and the movement-image [Chapter 4]). In a footnote to the passage cited above, Deleuze and Guattari clarify their point by offering an example of a superfused liquid, as discussed in Ilya Prigogine and Isabelle Stengers's book *Entre le temps et l'éternité*. A superfused (or supersaturated) liquid is a liquid in a far-from-equilibrium state that is "at a temperature below its crystallization temperature" (WP 225/QP 111), and in this liquid there are, Prigogine and Stengers claim, "small germs of crystals [that] form, but these germs appear and then dissolve without involving any consequences."[1] What happens, then, when this superfused liquid comes to the singular point or threshold where it crystallizes is that the germs (elements) enter into relations with each other, and in doing so they now acquire a consistency or reference to other elements; this in turn allows for the possibility of the crystallization process itself whereby an individual crystal appears.[2]

We can now restate some of our earlier arguments in light of this example. The objectivity of a problem is precisely what occurs when the superfused liquid has entered a state where genetic elements may begin to be drawn into relations of consistency with one another. This is the problematic state, the plane of immanence, from which consistent relations are drawn in the process of individuation (crystallization). To state this process in terms of learning, the risk is that the elements might not get drawn into a plane of consistency and we could be left with elements that "appear and then dissolve without involving any consequences." If one is unable to draw the elements associated with learning to swim into consistent relations with one another, then the elements will dissolve and fail to establish the connections necessary to acquiring the skill and knowledge associated with swimming. When it comes to creating concepts, Deleuze and Guattari argue that philosophical concepts involve a plane of immanence that "acts like a sieve" (WP 42/QP 44) by filtering the chaos without relinquishing the infinite speeds of chaos. The infinite speeds are retained in an absolute survey or self-positing (see Chapter 1) whereby the elements are brought into consistent relation with one another at once, at infinite speed, meaning that there are no points of survey or observation that transcend the elements, no function external to the elements that draws them together, but instead there is an "autopoetic," self-organizing emergence where the consistency appears at once, at infinite speed, and is inseparable from each of the elements. This is the significance of Deleuze and Guattari's claim that the components of a concept are "inseparable," a claim they repeat on numerous occasions throughout *What is Philosophy?* The elements are inseparable for the reason that their consistency arises at once, and it is the emergence of this inseparable consistency of elements (the "area *ab*") that entails infinite speed and movement. Again, this is not an infinite speed as a measurable, chronological speed taken to the infinite (recall our earlier discussion of Hegel and the bad infinite in Chapter 1), but it is the speed necessary for the possibility of there being measurable, individuated elements and the speeds that track their movements. In creating concepts, therefore, even if one selects finite, already individuated components, what occurs more importantly in creating concepts is the infinite movement that allows for the internal consistency of the components to emerge. These infinite movements define the plane of immanence upon which concepts are created.

The response of science to chaos is quite different. Rather than affirm the infinite movements of the plane of immanence, science "is like a freeze-frame . . . a fantastic *slowing down*, and it is by slowing down that matter, as well as the scientific thought able to penetrate it with propositions, is actualized" (WP 118/QP 112). Referring to our example of the superfused liquid, in the hands of science the chaos that is the infinite speed with which the crystal germs dissolve without consequence comes to be understood as the limits and borders that define the point where crystallization begins.[3] The result of this move, Deleuze and Guattari argue, is that "Science is haunted not by its own unity but by the plane of reference constituted by all the limits or borders through which it confronts chaos" (WP 119/QP 113). That is, although science sets up a plane of reference where the determinate limits and borders are mapped onto a system of coordinates, this system presupposes the limits and borders that are in turn only possible when the chaos is slowed down and rendered into a cooperative freeze-frame of reality. This chaos, however, forever challenges and threatens the stability of scientific propositions even while it repeatedly prompts the creative efforts of scientists to offer functions "as propositions in discursive systems" (WP 117/QP 111).

An initial and all-important consequence of confronting chaos through the delineation of borders and limits is that variation comes to be understood in terms of its relationship to the limit that provides for its frame of reference, or its range of variation. As

Deleuze and Guattari argue, the "fantastic slowing down" of chaos entails setting "a limit in chaos to which all speeds are subject, so that they form a variable determined as abscissa" (WP 118/QP 112), and the abscissae provide the system of coordinates upon a plane of reference that is made possible by the limit. Limits and borders thus "give the plane its references . . . [and as] for the system of coordinates [the abscissae], they populate or fill out the plane of reference itself" (WP 119–20/QP 113). The speed of light, for example, sets a limit and reference to which all other speeds can be compared as variations on this limit. Similarly for temperature, on the simplistic view that temperature measures the motion of atoms, there is an upper limit as this motion approaches the speed of light and a lower limit as motion is reduced to 0 – what is called absolute zero or 0° Kelvin. In *Difference and Repetition*, however, Deleuze warns against this understanding of temperature and argues that this is an example of the transcendental illusion of presupposing the extensive, quantitative measurement of identifiable atoms in motion when it is precisely this identity that needs to be explained, and explained, as Deleuze does, in terms of intensive difference (disparity).[4]

We can find support for these claims, and for Deleuze and Guattari's more general claims regarding the importance of limits for science in establishing a plane of reference, by turning to the work of Mark Wilson. In his essay, "This Thing Called Pain," Wilson challenges the prevalent view that temperature is the measure of mean kinetic energy, with temperature understood simply as the index for mean kinetic energy. Wilson argues that this view is "generally false"[5] and yet widely espoused largely due to the influence of Ernest Nagel's philosophy of science. As Wilson elaborates, the mathematics regarding temperature and mean kinetic energy only work with a classical ideal gas at equilibrium, but not in most other dynamic contexts or with substances that are not gases in the ideal state.[6] Wilson concludes that "there seems to be no 'structural' formula of the expected type which will tell us what temperature should be in all substances."[7] The more general lesson to be drawn from the example of temperature, and a lesson that becomes the dominant theme of Wilson's more recent work, especially his monumental book *Wandering Significance*, is that a theory's practical application is justified not because of its relationship to a body of natural law that would justify its use, but rather because of "an appeal to a restricted set of considerations relating to 'temperature's operational success.'"[8] In other words, it is because we "obtain approximately similar readings from such a wide variety of distinct devices, for example, gas thermometers, liquid in glass thermometers, thermocouples, so-called 'sonic' thermometers, etc." that we are then justified in moving to a theory that is freed from its "operational underpinnings."[9] It is precisely this latter move that Kelvin makes. As Wilson puts it, the operational successes along with the "nineteenth century flourishing of thermodynamic thinking allowed Lord Kelvin to articulate an 'absolute' approach to temperature that freed it from the shackles of instrumentation."[10] The mistake, or the Deleuzian transcendental illusion, is to assume that the operational success is accounted for by virtue of a univocal, "absolute approach."

As Wilson argues in his "This Thing Called Pain" essay and in numerous other places, it is crucial to recognize that the operational success of measuring temperature, for instance, presupposes "a range of appropriate conditions," such as an environment that is not full of shock waves in the case of a mercury thermometer, or temperatures that are neither extremely high or low. In short, these ranges provide the limits within which the variations of temperature – the variables – can be accurately measured. Outside these ranges another set of parameters comes into play, parameters that may well be incompatible with the first set. Wilson refers to these differing ranges and sets of parameters as "theory façades," or as a "set of evaluative patches linked together in a Riemannian surface-like way"[11] that precludes the possibility of a "universal detection device," by which Wilson means a device that "can detect the presence or absence of P in any object whatsoever in any context."[12] As Deleuze and Guattari state much this same point, science "is haunted not by its own unity but by the plane reference constituted by all the limits or borders through which it confronts chaos" (WP 119/QP 113). Wilson provides numerous examples, and in dizzying detail, to support his thesis that scientific practice requires these limits or borders – or "sheets of doctrine," as he puts it – as part of its effort to provide adequate theoretical directives, and yet these "sheets of doctrine . . . do not truly cohere into unified doctrine in their own rights, but can merely appear as if they do if the qualities of their adjoining edges are not scrutinized scrupulously."[13] What may work well with one "sheet of doctrine" and set of parameters – at one limit and border – may begin to fail at a more detailed and enhanced level of description. As Wilson puts this in *Wandering Significance*, as our everyday descriptive terms become pressed to higher standards of accuracy or performance, as commonly occurs within industry or science, a finer and more perplexing grain of conflicting opinion begins to display itself within our applications of "hardness," "force" and even "red."[14]

Put in terms Deleuze and Guattari would use, the effort to produce accurate descriptions of phenomena encounters, with the increasing demands of a more detailed and nuanced analysis, the problematic infinite substance or disparity that is, as Deleuze puts it, and as has been repeated here many times, "the sufficient reason of all phenomena, the condition of that which appears."[15] For Deleuze and Guattari, therefore, science is "inspired less by the concern for unification in an ordered actual system than by a desire not to distance itself too much from chaos" (WP 156/QP 147). But by not distancing itself too much from chaos, the result is the failure of descriptive terms as these terms get pushed towards increasing particularity of detail. What happens as a result of these failures, Wilson argues, is that, in our efforts to maintain "inferential headway" in the face of the difficulties that arise as the level of particularity increases, we often find it easier "to decompose the system's overall behavior into descriptive fragments where the intractable complexities of the full problem become locally reduced to more tractable terms."[16] That is, a set of limits and borders become necessary in order to define, as Deleuze and Guattari understand it, a plane of reference in which we can then place the variables and variations into relation with each other and to the limits and parameters that define the plane of reference.

The point that Deleuze and Guattari stress, and one in line with Wilson's own project, is that the parameters and limits – the sheets of doctrine – do not simply reflect an incapacity of human observers (see §3 below) to unify their observations under a complete and comprehensive theory, but rather these sheets of doctrine and the need for parameters and limits reflect the disparity and problematic substance that is the sufficient reason of all phenomena. As the sufficient reason of all phenomena, therefore, disparity and the plane of immanence guarantee that no matter how detailed and nuanced the theoretical and mathematical description might be, there are underlying differences that will for ever subvert them as the level of description hews close to chaos. In other words, disparity may be the sufficient reason for all phenomena, but it is also the reason our mathematical equations and theories which track phenomena will forever flirt with, and be challenged by, the intensive differences that fail to be explicated and hence modeled by their equations. Wilson makes a very similar point in the early pages of *Wandering Significance*, and one quite in line with the Deleuzian metaphysics offered here. Wilson argues that,

> The main consideration that drives the argument of the book is the thesis that the often quirky behaviors of ordinary descriptive predicates derive, not merely from controllable human inattention or carelessness, but from a basic unwillingness of the physical universe to sit still while we frame its descriptive picture.[17]

As Wilson draws *Wandering Significance* to a close, he will restate his thesis, but this time he will draw upon the example of learning, and in doing so his argument will reinforce one of the central claims of this book – to wit, that philosophy, science, and art are each to be understood as instances of learning, or as encounters with the objectivity of a problem. Wilson begins with his main contention that "a complex set of skills can be adequately appreciated in pieces, without our needing to be able to imitate the overall bundle in question,"[18] and to illustrate he gives the example of a music instructor casting doubt upon his student's ability to learn Persian music. "There are things that every Persian on the street understands instinctively which you will never understand,"[19] the instructor tells his student. Since the student was not born and raised in a Persian context, the instructor concludes that the student can never fully learn and come to know Persian music as a native knows it. The student responds by accepting that they "don't really expect to understand it that way [but they are] just trying to figure out how it is put together."[20] The instructor accepts that "that is something you can probably learn, but it's not really very important." Stated in the terms Deleuze and Guattari develop, and as has been developed throughout these chapters, the student is confronting the objectivity of the problem of learning Persian music, and that student's subsequent effort is to connect the elements of this music, "to figure out how it is put together." The instructor assumes, however, that there is a unitary essence or nature of Persian music that the student is missing, and thus figuring out how this music is put together is not, in the end, "really very important." Wilson, by contrast, and on this point he is in agreement with Deleuze and Guattari, argues that the

> instructor underestimated what we might potentially learn about his [Persian] music, but he may very will be right: *if our understanding becomes too dispersed*, it might not seem very important . . . [but that]

doesn't mean that we can't, with a lot of hard work, gain a pretty solid understanding of why Achilles once wept to hear those strains.[21]

If we fail to draw the elements into a plane of consistency, if our "understanding becomes too dispersed," then indeed we may fail to learn anything significant about Persian music, but learning does indeed entail the effort to figure out how to put things together, to conjugate the elements, and thus the student is on to something, Wilson argues. Similarly for science, as it confronts chaos it establishes a number of limits and borders – façades or sheets of theory – that are inseparable from the effort of science to learn how nature is put together. This effort, moreover, is in turn inseparable from its history – and it is to this topic that we now turn.

§2

Continuing with Wilson's arguments for a moment, a central tenet of his philosophy of science is that the reference of predicates to the various natural properties – for example, "is hard," "is red," and so on – is to be understood in the context of a set of parameters (a plane of reference) that renders the application of the predicate to a new, unanticipated phenomenon possible. If the new, unanticipated phenomenon does not fall within the current plane of reference, however, the tendency nonetheless is to continue to apply the predicate as if there were a continuous, rather than discontinuous, transition from one plane of reference to another – hence the title of Wilson's book, *Wandering Significance*.[22] The differing sheets and façades of theory, however, are not continuous with one another – they do not form a unitary whole – but rather they constitute a multiplicity of heterogeneous, often incompatible façades. The continued use of a predicate across incompatible façades provides for the illusion of continuity when in fact there is none. It is for this reason that Wilson claims "Human beings, unlike thermometers, are self-correcting measurement devices with memories ... [and thus they are] affected by the *history* of [their] earlier classifications."[23] Stated in Deleuzian terms, the current use of a predicate to refer to a set of extensive, qualitative properties reflects a history of prior efforts to track and refer to extensive properties and qualities, but these properties mask an underlying disparity and multiplicity that is the sufficient reason for these extensive properties and qualities. This sufficient reason, as we have seen, guarantees the failure of the continuous, homogenous use of predicates and accounts for the emergence of discontinuous, contingent events that fail to be referred to by existing predicates. According to Deleuze and Guattari, the history of science is testament to this process.

What is at work in the history of science, Deleuze and Guattari argue, is an ongoing series of encounters with chaos, encounters that result in the drawing of a plane of reference where a system of coordinates becomes possible relative to the limits, borders, and parameters of this system. The relationship between chaos and the plane of reference becomes, as a result of this move, a relationship between the potentials of the system and its actualized states of affairs. Deleuze and Guattari are clear on this point: "a state of affairs does not actualize a chaotic virtual without taking from it a *potential* that is distributed in the system of coordinates. From the virtual that it actualizes it draws a potential that it appropriates" (WP 122/QP 116). In other words, to each determinate coordinate and variable there is an undetermined potential, and it is this potential that becomes, in the hands of science, the dependent variable in relation to the independent variable. If we take the determinate facts regarding a person's income, we can then investigate whether there is a functional relationship between this independent variable and the level of education (dependent variable). Is there a functional relationship between dependent and independent variables? This relationship between variables and the limits and boundaries that make these relationships possible on the plane of reference is what Deleuze and Guattari define as a *functive*: "The first functives are therefore the limit and the variable, and reference is a relationship between values of the variable or, more profoundly, the relationship of the variable . . . with the limit" (WP 118–19/QP 112). These relationships, however, are inseparable from the intensive difference and disparity that is their sufficient reason, and as a result these relationships continually become other – that is, the established relations continually bifurcate when, for example, and as Wilson argued, the level of detail becomes more nuanced. It is this process that becomes particularly clear when one examines the history of science. As Deleuze and Guattari put it:

> It is as if the bifurcation were searching the infinite chaos of the virtual for new forms to actualize by carrying out a sort of potentialization of matter: carbon introduces a bifurcation into Mendeleyev's table, which, through its plastic properties, produces the state of organic matter . . . This [bifurcation] is because reference, implying a renunciation of the infinite, can only connect up chains of functives that necessarily break at some point. (WP 123–4/QP 117)

The renunciation of the infinite occurs, as we have seen, by way of the limits and borders that define the plane of reference that allows for a system of coordinates, and the functives to carry out the "potentialization" of the virtual chaos by placing it into relation with a determinate, independent variable. Nevertheless, functives, the "chains of functives," "necessarily break at some point" because the determinate relations are inseparable from the problematic, deterritorializing substance that acts as a sieve, a filter of chaos; thus, as the referential relations push and hew closer to this substance, they break and fail to track the paths the functives lay out for them (as Wilson argues). In the history of science, for instance, Deleuze and Guattari provide some "basic examples" of these breaks, "the fractional number [which] breaks with the whole number, irrational with rational numbers, Riemannian with Euclidean geometry" (WP 124/QP 117–18). To return to the terminology of an earlier chapter (see Chapter 3), these bifurcations and breaks deterritorialize determinate and determinable facts as well as the functives that map their relationships. Irrational numbers, for example, deterritorialize rational numbers; Riemannian geometry deterritorializes Euclidean geometry. With this deterritorializing process there is also the process of reterritorialization where, for example, "the whole number appears as a particular case of the fractional number" (ibid.), Euclidean geometry appears as a particular case of Riemannian geometry, Newtonian physics becomes a particular case of Einstein's theories, and so on. Deleuze and Guattari conclude that this "amounts to saying with Kuhn that science is paradigmatic, whereas philosophy is syntagmatic" (ibid. [see Chapter 4 on syntagmatic/paradigmatic distinction]). In other words, during periods of revolution, problems emerge that, as Kuhn argued, are incommensurable with the established paradigm, or with already determined functives and chains of functives. It is at this point that the efforts of scientists are more akin to those of philosophers in that the task now is to draw together, through a higher taste for problems, the various elements into a plane of reference that is capable of being actualized as a determinate functive or set of functives. As a science, however, these functives are placed in relation to a limit and border (paradigm) that is precisely the plane of reference for these functives. Science is thus paradigmatic.

As Kuhn himself was quick to point out, however, the history of science is not one of continuous progress. When one paradigm replaces another – for example, Einstein replaces Newton, thermodynamics replaces caloric theory, which in turn replaced phlogiston theory – Kuhn argued that not all that was accounted for by the replaced theory finds its way into the new theory. This is referred to as "Kuhn loss."[24] To restate Kuhn's point in Deleuze and Guattari's terms, the reterritorialization of science within and by a dominant paradigm continues to be haunted by the disparity and problematic substance that was the sufficient reason for the initial deterritorialization of the earlier paradigm. As a result, whatever paradigm comes to the fore will continue to be haunted by problems that remain unaddressed and yet are immanent to the paradigm itself. Every paradigm, in short, is incomplete and partial. Gödel will provide related formal arguments with his incompleteness theorem (see the next chapter), and although his arguments will address logical systems, Deleuze and Guattari would generalize this to include all systems as they appear on the plane of reference. The concept that is integral to supporting this claim is that of a partial observer, to which we now turn.

§3

Earlier in Chapter 3 we saw that Deleuze and Guattari compared their understanding of the conceptual persona with Kant's arguments for the role of the imagination in providing the necessary unity for the "action of the understanding on the sensibility."[25] For Deleuze and Guattari, similarly, the conceptual persona provides the "mobile territory" that mediates between the plane of immanence – a plane of immanence that is "like a section of chaos and acts like a sieve" (WP 42/QP 44) – and the concepts that philosophy creates. Deleuze and Guattari note that a similar process is at work in science. Instead of the conceptual personae mediating between the plane of immanence and concepts, partial observers mediate between the plane of reference and functives. Whereas the conceptual persona provides the necessary unity within the plane of immanence so that a concept can be created, the partial observer provides the unity in a system of coordinates on the plane of reference that allows for the creation of a functive that maps the relations between these coordinates. As Deleuze and Guattari put it, "We saw earlier the philosophical role of conceptual personae in relation to fragmentary concepts on a plane of immanence, but now science brings to light partial observers in relation to functions within systems of reference" (WP 128–9/QP 122). The reason why partial observers are partial, moreover, is that one cannot begin with a given state of affairs and "calculate the future and the past"

169

(WP 129/QP 123). The reason for this is rather straightforward, for, as we have seen, science draws up limits and borders in its encounter with chaos, and it is this that defines the plane of reference whereby states of affairs come to be mapped and represented within discursive systems by way of scientific functions and propositions. These states of affairs, however, are already the result of a filtering and selection of chaos – in the case of science a filtering that relinquishes the infinite speeds of chaos – and it is just this process that the observer takes on: "Wherever purely functional properties of recognition or selection appear, without direct action, there are observers" (WP 130/QP 124). An observer, therefore, is by definition partial for Deleuze and Guattari.

There is a second and equally important sense in which the partial observer is partial, and that is to be partial in the subjective sense of the term. As we might say a mother is partial towards her children, implying a motivation that guides her preferential selection in favor of her children rather than someone else's children, so too the partial observer is partial in their selecting and filtering of elements. There is thus a basic truth at work in animism, for

> [e]ven animism [Deleuze and Guattari argue], when it multiplies little immanent souls in organs and functions, is not so far removed from biological science as it is said to be, on condition that these immanent souls are withdrawn from any active or efficient role so as to become solely sources of molecular perception and affection. (WP 130/QP 124)

To come at this point from a slightly different angle, the partial observer is not a cause of action but a source of "contemplations," as Deleuze uses this term in *Difference and Repetition* when he extends Hume's argument (see Chapter 2, §5, and examples 3 and 8). As Deleuze notes, it is not the repetition of the determinate elements that brings about the expectation of B upon being given A, or the synthesis of A and B, but it is something in the mind, in "contemplation," that accounts for this synthesis (what Deleuze calls "passive synthesis"). Every individuated and determinate entity or element thus presupposes a mediating unity – or Idea, as Deleuze appropriates the concept (see Chapter 1 and example 2). The conceptual personae and partial observers provide this mediating unity and they, along with the contemplations of passive synthesis and the animism of immanent souls, do not presuppose the identity of an active, partial subject, but such souls, partial subjects, and contemplations are precisely the condition for the identification of such an active subject. This is true, for Deleuze, of all determinate, active, spatio-temporal phenomena.

> What organism [Deleuze asks] is not made of elements and cases of repetition, of contemplated and contracted water, nitrogen, carbon, chlorides and sulphates, thereby intertwining all the habits of which it is composed? Organisms awake [Deleuze concludes] to the sublime words of the third *Ennead*: all is contemplation![26]

Earlier, we saw the importance of Deleuze's arguments that all is multiplicity, or that multiplicity is the "true substantive, substance itself."[27] This provided the basis for the metaphysics of difference that had been crucial to Deleuze's ongoing project to develop a philosophy of difference that enables us to think difference as the condition for the possibility of identity rather than thinking of difference in terms of identity. By taking on Plotinus's "sublime words" that "all is contemplation!" Deleuze and Guattari are continuing to work within the conceptual space of Deleuze's theory of multiplicities. In particular, a contemplation is the condition for the individuation of a determinate identity, whether this be the identification of B on being given A, the individuation of a plant by way of its "contemplated and contracted water, nitrogen, carbon, chlorides and sulfates," and so on. The partial observer is a contemplation in just this sense, but there is an important difference between the partial observer and the conceptual persona. Whereas the conceptual persona initiates the creation of concepts by drawing from the infinite speeds of the plane of immanence the necessary unity and consistency – the "mobile territories" – for the creation of concepts, the contemplation of partial observers occurs within an already delimited space – that is, within the parameters and borders of the plane of reference. Rather than presuppose contemplation as the process of individuation that is the condition for the possibility of a determinate identity, the contemplation of the partial observer already takes place within the determinate limits laid down by the plane of reference and it serves as the qualitative, sensory, and *nonsubjective* evidence for the identifiable variables on the plane of reference. As Deleuze and Guattari argue,

> Rather than oppose sensory knowledge and scientific knowledge, we should identify the sensibilia that populate systems of coordinates and are peculiar to science. This is what Russell did when he evoked those qualities devoid of all subjectivity, sense data distinct from all sensation, sites established in states of affairs, empty perspectives belonging to things themselves, contracted bits of space-time that correspond to the whole or to parts of a function. (WP 131/QP 125)

171

As we argued above in Chapter 2, one way to understand contemporary analytic philosophy is to see it as consciously modeling its efforts after the methods and problems of science. A key move in the history of the development of this effort was the rejection of Bradley's absolute idealism, and along with this was the rejection of Bradley's reliance upon the Principle of Sufficient Reason. Rather than accept, as Bradley did, that every determinate fact and relation requires a sufficient reason for why it is rather than is not – a position that pushed Bradley to the monism of absolute idealism – Russell and Moore reject the PSR and accept that certain facts are simply the case and are in no need of explanation. The "sensibilia that populate [the] systems of coordinates" peculiar to science are precisely these inexplicable facts, and yet Deleuze and Guattari argue, following through on Deleuze's claim that difference or disparity is the sufficient reason of "all phenomena, the condition of that which appears," that the contemplative role of partial observers is the condition of possibility for these sensibilia. These partial observers are in turn made possible by the slowing down of the infinite speeds of chaos and the resulting limits and borders that allow for the drawing of a plane of reference. Moreover, the instruments that measure and detect these sensibilia on a plane of reference – whether "the photographic plate, camera, or mirror that captures what no one is there to see" (WP 131/QP 125) – "presuppose," Deleuze and Guattari argue, "the ideal partial observer situated at a good vantage point in things: the nonsubjective observer is precisely the sensory that qualifies (sometimes in a thousand ways) a scientifically determined state of affairs, thing, or body" (ibid.). In other words, the partial observer is the condition for the possibility of determinate, scientific facts, and for the scientific propositions and functives that represent these facts. To see how this works, and to return as well to the theme of how to relate philosophy and science, let us turn to an extended example – namely, let us briefly examine the arguments in James Ladyman and Don Ross's book, *Every Thing Must Go.*

§4

The primary objective of *Every Thing Must Go* is to steer a successful path between the Scylla and Charybdis of two dominant positions. On the one hand, there is Humean antirealism (best exemplified for Ladyman and Ross in the work of Bas van Fraassen), which holds that all we can know of reality as it is in itself is what appears by way of the evidence given to our senses and then through the systematic representations of this evidence (the sensibilia). On the other hand, there is traditional scientific realism, or the view that there is a fundamental, mind-independent reality, and it is science that provides us with the truths regarding the nature of this reality. Ladyman and Ross's project is one of attempting to achieve a rapprochement between antirealism and realism, or it is an effort of "consilience," to cite a term they use repeatedly throughout the book. The conceptual workhorse of this effort is the concept of "real patterns," which they get from Daniel Dennett's classic 1991 *Journal of Philosophy* essay of the same name. Ladyman and Ross are quite forthright in affirming the importance of this concept. As they say, "to put matters as simply and crudely as possible, it's real patterns all the way down. This slogan could summarize the whole conclusion of this book. . . ."[28]

With this concept in hand, Ladyman and Ross will tackle the subject of scientific realism and argue that with their version of realism, what they call "ontic structural realism," they can avoid some of the very compelling arguments against traditional views of scientific realism, arguments that could be seen as motivating van Fraassen's antirealist verificationism. At the same time, however, Ladyman and Ross argue that van Fraassen's antirealism is inadequate if one is "to circumscribe the observable in a principled way . . . [and as a result] it is necessary to endorse some modal facts that are theory-independent."[29] In their efforts at consilience between realism and antirealism, the concept of real patterns plays a crucial role by enabling one to maintain a realist position that is immune to its most common criticisms while at the same time giving due emphasis to a verificationism that allows for modal facts - namely, real patterns – and hence the importance of their claim that it is real patterns all the way down.

Realism
With respect to science, realism is most commonly used in order to account for the success and failure of scientific theories and research. The reason why the theory of the ether failed is that there is no ether, and, conversely, the reason why Pasteur's theory of microorganisms succeeded was that there really are microorganisms. More generally, the scientific realist will argue that the reason why we know more about the natural universe today than we did in Newton's or Aristotle's day is that we are being ineluctably drawn by the real towards the true opinion of reality itself.

173

There are problems, however, with this understanding of realism. There are several criticisms that have been made of the traditional conception of scientific realism, or what has also been called naive realism, but "the most compelling form of argument against standard scientific realism," Ladyman and Ross argue, hinges on the understanding of theory change.[30] Put simply, if a theory at one point relies upon there being a particular entity such as ether, phlogiston, and so on, then the advent of a new theory that dismisses such entities will entail a change in the ontology of what is real: ether is no longer taken to be a real substance, nor is phlogiston. The resulting problem for the scientific realist is that, as Ladyman and Ross put it, we have very solid "grounds not for mere agnosticism but for the positive belief that many central theoretical terms of our best contemporary science will be regarded as non-referring by future science."[31] Ladyman and Ross's way around this problem is to reject the notion that the reality referred to by "our best contemporary science" consists of self-individuating elements and objects such as ether, phlogiston, electrons, and so on, but rather it refers to a structural pattern of relationships – namely, real patterns. Ladyman and Ross state their solution as follows:

> Our solution to this problem is to give up the attempt to learn about the nature of unobservable entities from science. The metaphysical import of successful scientific theories consists in their giving correct descriptions of the structure of the world.[32]

This does not mean that science is to be restricted solely to what is actually observable, or to what has actually been observed. This is van Fraassen's solution, and a solution Ladyman and Ross find inadequate in accounting for the fact that the observable entails modal possibilities, a modal structure; it is this modal structure of the world that our best science (mathematics) represents. For example, in the search for exoplanets astronomers use instrumentation to detect subtle changes in the brightness of a star - a slight dimming - with the theory being that this darkening is the result of a planet that passes between the observational perspective and the star. Astronomers will also use other instruments to detect slight wobbles that are the result of the gravitational pull of planets. In both cases we could say that the observation of the exoplanet is dependent upon a particular theory, and upon our detecting the sensibilia associated with this theory. For Ladyman and Ross, however, a stronger modal claim is implied: namely, what our scientific theories represent is not simply what is actually observed but what might possibly be observed. In other words, they represent a structure of modal relations that can be tracked and which allows for the possibility of verification. Given better instrumentation, or a long-distance voyage, one could actually see the exoplanet. Now what is primary here for Ladyman and Ross are not the entities that are observed or observable (for example, exoplanets), but the modal structure of the phenomena themselves. It is this modal structure (pattern) that ultimately enables Ladyman and Ross to address the problem of theory change. Although the theory of the ether might have been abandoned, the theory that replaces it continues to project forward the structural relations between phenomena – that is, the sensibilia as made possible by partial observers. For Ladyman and Ross, therefore, what is fundamental are the structural relations themselves, and relations without relata; or it is the real patterns without a fundamental layer of entities upon which these patterns supervene. In short, it is real patterns all the way down:

> there are mind-independent phenomena (both possible and actual), but these relations are not supervenient on the properties of unobservable objects and the external relations between them. Rather, this structure is ontologically basic.[33]

This largely summarizes Ladyman and Ross's arguments for their version of realism. To return to the themes of this chapter, it is worth noting that Ladyman and Ross claim that their approach is amenable to a Platonic reading. As they put it, "To say that all there is are relations and no relata, is therefore to follow Plato and say that the world of appearances is illusory."[34] In other words, for Ladyman and Ross, the world of objects, the world of things, is illusory for they are merely the emergent phenomena associated with relations – or with processes of individuation, as Deleuze and Guattari argue. Deleuze, in fact, makes this exact point in response to a question raised by Alexis Philonenko during the question-and-answer session of Deleuze's dissertation defense (published as "Method of Dramatization"). Philonenko asked Deleuze whether, in comparing his own project to that of Maïmon, Deleuze was likewise leaving an important role for illusion to play in his project. Deleuze responds:

> It seems to me we have the means to penetrate the sub-representational, to reach all the way to the roots of spatio-temporal dynamisms, and all the way to the Ideas actualized in them: the elements and ideal events, the relations and singularities are perfectly determinable.[35]

The comparison with Plato should be apparent with Deleuze's use of the term Ideas (see example 2). Similarly, for Ladyman and Ross, the "world-structure" or the universal real pattern, as they will also discuss this, corresponds to the Platonic Idea. The world of objects as self-individuated elements, as relata, is thus the illusory manifestation of this Idea, much as they are for Deleuze (recall our earlier discussion of Deleuze's version of Kant's transcendental illusion). It is for this reason that Deleuze responds to Philonenko's question by locating the illusory on the side of the constituted rather than on the side of the constitutive conditions: "The illusion only comes afterward, from the direction of constituted extensions and the qualities that fill these extensions."[36] But there is a further question: what does it mean for these relations and singularities to be perfectly determinable? For Ladyman and Ross it means to be represented by our best science. "The 'world-structure,' Ladyman and Ross argue, "just is and exists independently of us and we represent it mathematico-physically via our theories."[37] For Deleuze and Guattari, however, this mathematico-physical representation is made possible by the limits and borders that define the plane of reference, and thus it is not Ideas that are represented but states of affairs – that is, states of affairs as the structured, organized relations between bodies and things. In short, what is fundamental for Deleuze in Ideas is not a plane of reference or system of coordinates that can be represented by a discursive system – by our best mathematico-physical theories – but rather what is fundamental are multiplicities that are the true substance, the sufficient reason of all that appears – that is, for all states of affairs. Deleuze is explicit on this notion of Ideas, and he credits it to Plato:

> If we think of the Plato from the later dialectic, where the Ideas are something like multiplicities that must be traversed by questions such as how? how much? in which case?, then yes, everything I've said has something Platonic about it. If you're thinking of the Plato who favors a simplicity of the essence or a ipseity of the Idea, then no.[38]

It is possible a case could be made that Ladyman and Ross understand the "world-structure" as "something like multiplicities" and not as "a simplicity of the essence," but once this Idea is represented by a discursive, mathematico-physical system we no longer have the dynamisms of multiplicities – we no longer have the infinite speeds of the plane of immanence but we have instead limited, constrained dynamisms (see example 10).

Verificationism

On the one hand, it might seem that verificationism of any sort would undermine the type of realism Ladyman and Ross affirm. If the "world-structure" just is and exists "independently of us," where independently of us is taken to mean independent of any givenness or accessibility to a perceiving subject, then tying real patterns to verification would seem to undermine their position. Ladyman and Ross are aware of these potential difficulties and attempt to head them off by emphasizing that they endorse what they call a Peircean verificationism, by which they mean that, for a pattern to be real,

> it must be such that a community of inquirers who wished to maximize their stock of true beliefs would continue to be motivated to track the pattern notwithstanding any shifts in practical, commercial, or ideological preferences that are not justified by new evidence bearing on the epistemic redundancy or non-redundancy of the pattern.[39]

Ladyman and Ross will later follow Dennett and argue that

> there are (presumably) real patterns in lifeless parts of the universe that no actual observer will ever reach, and further real patterns whose data points are before our eyes right now, but which no computer we can instantiate or design will ever marshal the energy to compact.[40]

To resolve the apparent inconsistency between the claim that a real pattern is real only if it motivates a community of inquirers to continue to track it and the subsequent claim that there are untrackable patterns, Ladyman and Ross will make a distinction between the universal real pattern, the Platonic Idea, which is real independent of what we take it to be, even though it is inseparable from the tracking of fundamental physics, and the real patterns of different ontic scales - what they will call the *scale relativity of ontology*, or rainforest realism. In short, Ladyman and Ross invoke the boundaries and limits that define the plane of reference for Deleuze and Guattari. In this case, it is the universal real pattern that establishes the basic limits and borders that define the plane of reference wherein the variables that are relative to this universal real pattern come to be defined in what Ladyman and Ross call "scale relativity of ontology." For example, my ability to track a song across a variety of instrumental and vocal performances – *My Way*, as sung by Sid Vicious or Frank Sinatra, for instance – entails tracking the song at a scale that need not consider the physics of sound waves, though the latter, and especially the fundamental physics associated with it (that is, the universal real pattern), sets the ultimate constraints and limits upon which the relative ontologies depend. To give another example, economies and institutions can be tracked as real patterns at their relative scale and independently of the biology and psychology of the individuals involved, which would involve yet another scale.

The question to address now is what it means to track a real pattern. The answer to this question gets to the heart of Ladyman and Ross's understanding of verificationism. The first important component of their answer is the concept of "compressibility." A basic component of real patterns for Ladyman and Ross (following Dennett), and hence of reality since it is real patterns all the way down, is that they entail the compression of a larger data set, a compression that allows for the tracking and projectibility of the pattern. My ability to recognize the song as sung by Sid Vicious or Frank Sinatra is an example of tracking a real pattern that compresses the data such that it can be tracked repeatedly and in different contexts and circumstances. Compressibility, however, does not mean that any particular or even possible person needs to be capable of compressing the data into a trackable pattern. Ladyman and Ross are clear on this point:

> As scientific realists we understand the foregoing as referring to compressibility by any physically possible observer/computer – that is to say, given our verificationism, compressible *period*, rather than compressibility *by people*.[41]

That said, some trackable patterns are real and others are not. I can follow the patterns of the stock charts; I may look for patterns in the stars and create elaborate astrological charts; or I may seek to resurrect the ancient Roman practice of reading entrails. In each of these cases, one may seek a pattern in order to project future possibilities - when to buy or sell; whether another person is compatible; or when to initiate a military campaign. But Ladyman and Ross would claim that we are right not to admit these patterns, even if they are there, for they are not ultimately real. What differentiates real from unreal patterns, according to Ladyman and Ross, is "that a pattern, to be real, must be projectible from a perspective that physics tells us could be physically occupied."[42] In other words, if a pattern is projectible in terms of our best contemporary science – namely, our best 'mathematico-physical' representations of the world-structure, then it is real; if not, it is not. In other words, Ladyman and Ross adopt a paradigmatic view of science (see Chapter 4) whereby a pattern is real if it is a projection of the universal world structure as represented by our best scientific theories. Since the reading of entrails has long ceased being tracked by our best science, it has likewise long ceased to be considered a real pattern.[43]

Bringing this example to a close, it is clear that, to a point, Deleuze and Guattari agree with Ladyman and Ross's characterization of science – namely, science, and in particular fundamental physics, attempts to set forth and map the functions that represent the relations of the system of coordinates that is made possible by the parameters and limits that define the plane of reference. For Ladyman and Ross, these limits were established by the universal world structure, and the various sciences that address other scaled levels of reality are to be understood relative to the limitations of this ultimate set of parameters. For Deleuze and Guattari, by contrast, the processes of individuation, the metaphysics of multiplicity, entail a problematic plane of immanence, or A LIFE. For Deleuze and Guattari, it is multiplicity that is real, the "true substantive, substance itself," and yet multiplicity deterritorializes the stable, determinate relations and patterns that are the subject of fundamental physics. The real patterns that Ladyman and Ross take to be ultimately real are, for Deleuze and Guattari, to be understood as reterritorializations of multiplicity, whereas, for Deleuze and Guattari, it is precisely the deterritorializing nature of multiplicity (the problematic substance) that is real. A multiplicity is inseparable from a real pattern but it is not reducible to it. As a result, insofar as philosophy encounters and affirms the problematic nature of multiplicity, then philosophy will have a role that is not that of underlaborer to science; and insofar as science develops its best theories and practices in order to account for the real, trackable patterns of sensibilia, then science will continue to have its important role to fill. But as we will now see as we turn to the next chapter, philosophy loses its key contribution to thought – namely, to meditate on a life well lived – when it accepts its role as under-laborer to science, and science itself loses its creative potential, its need for and reliance upon "a higher 'taste' as problematic faculty" (WP 133/QP 127), if it fails to appreciate the nature of problematic substance.

Example 10

As we have seen in Chapter 5, crucial to science's confrontation with chaos is the process of relinquishing the infinite in order to constitute the plane of reference upon which variables and their corresponding functions can then be created. In highlighting the

179

difference between philosophy and science, Deleuze and Guattari will point to the fact that philosophy affirms the infinite speed of chaos that is then drawn into a plane of consistency in creating concepts while science relinquishes the infinite and sets limits and parameters that define the plane of reference (see Chapter 5). Underlying this difference for Deleuze and Guattari is, as we have seen, a Spinozist metaphysics and affirmation of an absolutely infinite and limitless substance, the substance that is limited – the "freeze-frame" (WP 118/QP 112) – so as to make the plane of reference and hence science possible. Echoing Spinoza, Deleuze and Guattari argue that despite the need for limits in the case of science, "Every limit is illusory and every determination is negation" (WP 120/QP 113).[44] Despite their illusory nature, Deleuze and Guattari argue that the "theory of science and functions depends upon this [that is, these limits]" (ibid.). Moving on to mathematics, Cantor is often credited, Deleuze and Guattari claim, with having "reintroduced infinity into mathematics" (WP 120/QP 114). This is misleading, however, Deleuze and Guattari claim, for Cantor has not affirmed an absolutely infinite substance but has rather set out to "inscribe the limit within the infinite itself" (ibid.). Cantor thus makes possible the discursive, representational function of sets on the plane of reference, but at the cost of relinquishing the infinite.

Cantor is very much aware of the long history of philosophers who reject the infinite, and he places his own thought in contrast to this tradition. Aristotle, for example, rejects the infinite, Cantor claims, because "if the infinite existed then it would absorb the finite and destroy it."[45] Even Spinoza, Cantor claims, sets forth a notion of the infinite that absorbs and destroys, on Cantor's reading, the finite: "the true infinite or Absolute, which is in God, permits no determination whatsoever."[46] In short, as traditionally understood, the infinite and the finite are mutually exclusive, for if the infinite were to be thought in terms of the finite or determinate, then the infinite "would absorb the finite and destroy it." For Cantor, by contrast, if the infinite itself were to be

> thought of as determinate and completed, a finite number can very well be adjoined and united to it without thereby effecting the cancellation of the latter; rather, the infinite number is modified by such an adjunction of a finite number to it.[47]

As Cantor will clarify, if ω is a "determinate and completed" infinite number, then if we add a finite integer to it, $\omega + 1$ for instance, then the result for Cantor is "$\omega + 1 = (\omega + 1)$, where $(\omega + 1)$ is a number entirely distinct from ω."[48] By contrast, if we add an infinite number ω to a finite integer, the result is an infinite number, and thus $1 + \omega = \omega$. This is the sense in which the infinite absorbs the finite and destroys it. With respect to infinite numbers, therefore, Cantor concludes that the "commutative law in general has no validity," and as a result Cantor, with the help of "determinate and completed" infinite numbers, is able to reintroduce the infinite into mathematics in a way that does not absorb or destroy the finite. But how does Cantor get to this conclusion?

A key step in the process for Cantor is first to distinguish between what he sees as the proper and improper infinite. The improper infinite, Cantor claims, is what we have when we assume there is an infinite that "grows beyond all bounds or diminishes to any desired minuteness, but always remains finite. I call this infinite the improper infinite."[49] To imagine the infinite as that which results when we assume that, for every finite number, we can always add a greater number or find a smaller number, we nonetheless still have the infinite understood as something that "always remains finite." Cantor's critique of the improper infinite recalls Hegel's critique of the bad infinite (see Chapter 2). For both Hegel and Cantor, an infinite number that is thought to be that which is always beyond the finite remains essentially tied to the finite and is not therefore the proper infinite. The proper infinite, by contrast, is for Cantor "a thoroughly determinate infinite" rather than a "variable infinite" that continuously grows beyond or diminishes relative to any given finite number.[50] These "new determinate-infinite numbers will be defined," Cantor argues, "with the help of two principles of generation."[51] The first principle of generation gives us the "sequence (I) of positive integers 1, 2, 3, ..., ν ... [and it] has its ground of origin in the repeated positing and uniting of underlying unities."[52] Essential to the first principle of generation, therefore, is the idea that the "formation of the finite real integers thus rests upon the principle of adding a unity to an already formed and existing number."[53] This principle will become foundational for set theory.[54] As for the second principle of generation, Cantor argues that we can think of "a new number which we shall call ω and which shall be the expression for the fact that the entire aggregate (I) is given in its natural succession according to a law."[55] That is, the sequence (I) of positive integers, ν, is a well-ordered sequence and thus a countable sequence when each integer is in a determinate relationship to other sequences (hence "according to a law"). From here, Cantor continues,

181

We may even imagine the newly created number ω as a limit which the numbers ν approach, provided that we understand nothing more thereby than that ω is the first integer which follows all numbers ν: that is, it is to be called greater than each of the numbers ν.[56]

As this second principle of generation is commonly discussed in the literature, and as Deleuze and Guattari discuss it in example 10, the "entire aggregate" ν is infinite

if it presents a term-by-term correspondence with one of its parts or subsets, the set and the subset having the same power or the same number of elements that can be designated by 'aleph o', as with the set of whole numbers. (WP 120/QP 114)

If we take, for example, the set of whole numbers, or the "sequence (I) of positive integers, ν," 1, 2, 3, 4, 5, . . . this sequence can be placed in term-by-term correspondence with all of its subsets – for instance, the subset of even numbers 2, 4, 6, 8, 10 – and in doing this we end up with an equivalent number of elements – an infinite set. If we take the set of all subsets, however, or what is called the power set, then we end up with, as Deleuze and Guattari point out, a "set [that] is necessarily larger than the original set" (ibid.), or we have the transfinite integer ω. This is the sense in which we have a number ω, a number that expresses the power set, that is "greater than each of the numbers ν." Cantor subsequently defines the second principle of generation as follows:

I call it the *second principle of generation* of integers, and define it more exactly thus: if any definite succession of defined integers is put forward of which no greater exists, a new number is created by means of this second principle of generation, *which is thought of as the limit of those numbers*; that is, it is defined as the next number greater than all of them.[57]

As we can now see, Cantor does address the traditional concern regarding infinite numbers. The number ω is indeed for Cantor "a thoroughly determinate infinite," and moreover we can begin with this thoroughly determinate infinite number – begin with the second sequence (II) that starts with ω – and add a finite number to ω and the result will be a different number. If we add an infinite number to the first sequence, ν, however, then we simply end up with an infinite number – that is, ν+ω=ω. To avoid Aristotle's concern that the infinite simply absorbs and destroys the finite, however, Cantor had to inscribe the limit of ν into the very nature of the transfinite number, for the number ω, as we saw, "is thought of

182

as the limit of those numbers." Deleuze and Guattari are thus quite right in asserting that what Cantor's "theory of sets does is inscribe the limit within the infinite itself" (WP 120/QP 114).

As we have seen in previous chapters and examples, for Deleuze and Guattari it is *not* the infinite speeds of multiplicities and concepts that are illusory, but rather it is the finite, limited, and constituted that is illusory. Multiplicity is the "true substantive, substance itself." Unlike Cantor, for Deleuze and Guattari unities and limits are not that which needs to be presupposed in order to draw a plane of reference; to the contrary, unities and limits are precisely that which needs to be accounted for, and it is precisely multiplicity that is the substance and sufficient reason of these limits and that offers this account. In particular, limits and unities are that which emerges as the infinite speeds of chaos and the plane of immanence come to be slowed down into a "freeze-frame" that makes possible a plane of reference. The chaos that is filtered by the plane of immanence, however, is not an undifferentiated abyss which destroys difference and absorbs it into a homogenous identity; to the contrary, chaos is fully differentiated and it contains "all possible particles and draw[s] out all possible forms, which spring up only to disappear immediately, without consistency or reference, without consequence. Chaos is an infinite speed of birth and disappearance" (WP 118/QP 111–12). It is the plane of immanence that acts like a sieve and filters the chaos such that a consistency of infinite speeds and hence processes of individuation (that is, learning) can get under way. Science goes one step further and relinquishes the infinite speeds altogether so that functional relationships between variables on a plane of reference can be constituted. For Deleuze and Guattari, therefore, they argue, as does Cantor, that the infinite is not incompatible with the finite and determinate, but unlike Cantor they argue that this compatibility is not founded upon an always presupposed unity and limit but rather on a multiplicity and plane of immanence that need to be drawn into planes of consistency in order to allow for the processes of individuation (learning) that give rise to determinate, finite entities. This point becomes especially clear in example 12, but before turning to this example let us first return to the theme of a life well lived and to the role philosophy plays in challenging opinion. The challenging of opinion, Deleuze and Guattari argue, is integral to a life well lived and is, as we will see in the next chapter and example, a central task of philosophy.

Suggested reading for example 10
   Spinoza, Letter on the Infinite (Letter 12)

NOTES

1. Ilya Prigogine and Isabelle Stengers, *Entre le temps et l'éternité* (Paris: Fayard, 1988), pp. 162–3.
2. Gilbert Simondon's development of the philosophical implications of crystallization in understanding the processes of individuation was to have a tremendous influence on Deleuze. See Gilbert Simondon, *L'Individuation: À la lumière des notions de forme et d'information* (Grenoble: Millon, 2013).
3. In reference to Hegel, Deleuze and Guattari note that the variables that most interest Hegel are not those that "can be changed (2/3 and 4/6) or are left undetermined (a = 2b)" but those that involve a higher power ($y^{2/x} = P$). In this way a relation comes to be determined as a differential relation, dy/dx, and "the only determination of the value of the variables is that of disappearing or being born, even thought it is wrested from infinite speeds" (WP 122/QP 115). In other words, rather than embracing the infinite movements and speeds of the plane of immanence, science embraces the limit-point where the virtual plane of immanence becomes actualized or becomes transformed – that is, its points of "disappearing or being born." As we have seen in our discussion in an earlier chapter (Chapter 2), Deleuze and Guattari embrace a notion of infinite substance, and it is this move that is unique to philosophy.
4. See Gilles Deleuze, *Difference and Repetition*, trans. Paul Patton (New York: Columbia University Press, 1994), pp. 223–4.
5. Mark Wilson, "This Thing Called Pain," *Pacific Philosophical Quarterly* 66, no. 3–4, p. 228. Wilson refers to Nagel's *Structure of Science* (pp. 338–45), as well as Nagel's Feynman Lectures, as the *locus classicus* for the argument that temperature is to be equated with mean kinetic energy.
6. In support of this claim, Wilson cites Ralph Baierlein, *Atoms and Information Theory*: "a direct proportionality between temperature and mean energy is quite a special case" (cited ibid.). At low temperatures, for instance, the equations become nonlinear.
7. Ibid.
8. Ibid., p. 243.
9. Ibid., p. 244.
10. Mark Wilson, *Wandering Significance: An Essay on Conceptual Behavior* (Oxford: Oxford University Press, 2008), p. 348.
11. Ibid., p. 350.
12. Ibid., p. 576.
13. Ibid., p. 273.

14. Ibid., p. 7.
15. *Difference and Repetition*, p. 222.
16. Mark Wilson, "Theory Façades," *Proceedings of the Aristotelian Society*, New Series, vol. 104 (2004), pp. 273–4.
17. *Wandering Significance*, p. 11.
18. Ibid., p. 660. Wilson has Quine and Davidson's commitment to holism particularly in mind – what amounts to, as one might put it, a metaphysical faith.
19. Ibid.
20. Ibid.
21. Ibid., p. 661. Emphasis mine.
22. Wilson offers the example of the Druids, who, upon seeing a plane in the sky for the first time, apply the predicate "is a bird" to it (Mark Wilson, "Predicate Meets Property," *Philosophical Review* XCI, no. 4 (October 1982), pp. 549–50).
23. *Wandering Significance*, p. 576.
24. The term "Kuhn loss" is credited to H. R. Post, in his essay, "Correspondence, Invariance, and Heuristics: In Praise of Conservative Induction," *Studies in History and Philosophy of Science Part A* 2 (1971), p. 229, n. 38.
25. Kant, *Critique of Pure Reason*, trans. Norman Kemp Smith (London: Macmillan, 1929), B152.
26. *Difference and Repetition*, p. 75; see also WP 105/QP 101.
27. *Difference and Repetition*, p. 182.
28. Ladyman and Ross, *Every Thing Must Go* (Oxford: Oxford University Press, 2007), p. 228.
29. Ibid., p. 107.
30. Ibid., p. 83.
31. Ibid.
32. Ibid., p. 92.
33. Ibid., p. 128.
34. Ibid., p. 152.
35. Gilles Deleuze, *Desert Islands and Other Texts 1953–1974*, trans. Michael Taormina (New York: Semiotext(e), 2004), p. 115.
36. Ibid.
37. *Every Thing Must Go*, p. 158.
38. *Desert Islands*, p. 116.
39. Ibid., p. 36. This is a controversial position, and one which Deleuze and Guattari would not endorse, following Nietzsche, among others, who criticizes the ascetic ideal of a value-free science.
40. Ibid., p. 203.
41. Ibid., p. 221.
42. Ibid., p. 236.
43. The same is true for astrological charts. As for stock charts, to the extent that they track the behavioral patterns of buyers and sellers

of stocks, there is a sense in which they do latch on, in accordance with Ladyman and Ross's scale relativity ontology, to real patterns as opposed to unreal patterns. See the next paragraph.

44. For Spinoza's claim that all determination is negation, see Letter 50.
45. Georg Cantor, "Foundations of a General Theory of Manifolds: A Mathematico-Philosophical Investigation into the Theory of the Infinite," in *From Kant to Hilbert: A Source Book in the Foundations of Mathematics*, vol. II, ed. W. B. Ewald (Oxford: Oxford University Press, 1996), p. 890.
46. Ibid., p. 891.
47. Ibid., p. 890.
48. Ibid., p. 892.
49. Ibid., p. 882.
50. Ibid.
51. Ibid., p. 883.
52. Ibid., p. 907.
53. Ibid.
54. In Paul Halmos's influential book, *Naive Set Theory* (Princeton: Van Nostrand, 1991), for example, Halmos generates the natural numbers by virtue of the unities of sets, beginning with the null set (see p. 44).
55. "Foundations of a General Theory of Manifolds," p. 907.
56. Ibid.
57. Ibid., pp. 907–8 (emphasis added).

6

Philosophy and Logic

In the previous chapter we explored Deleuze and Guattari's arguments regarding the nature of science and the manner in which science responds to chaos by relinquishing the infinite in order to lay out a plane of reference so that functional relationships between variables may be established. The plane of reference itself is made possible by the fundamental limits, boundaries, and parameters that define this plane. In Ladyman and Ross's work, we saw that the basic parameter that defines the plane of reference upon which representational claims regarding reality can be made is the "universal world structure." This structure provides the foundational legitimacy and basis for the ontological scale relativity of the various sciences and for the patterns they track – for example, economics, music theory, biology, and so on. These sciences acquire their legitimacy to the extent that they provide a successful tracking of phenomena (sensibilia) and do so in a way that is consistent with the fundamental parameters laid down by the "universal world structure"; and it this "universal world structure" that is the subject of our best contemporary science – to wit, fundamental physics, according to Ladyman and Ross. This is the sense, then, in which science, according to Deleuze and Guattari, sets out to establish "a necessary reason" (WP 126/QP 119) that constitutes the functional relation between independent and dependent variables. If the patterned relations of economics or other scale-relative ontologies are not supervenient upon the patterns associated with the "universal world structure," then Ladyman and Ross argue that they become referentially void. The patterns associated with the reading of entrails fail to supervene upon more fundamental patterns and

187

hence entrail patterns are no longer thought to refer to anything substantively real, and hence functional relations to and predictions regarding future possibilities are in turn nullified. To be real, therefore, is, for Ladyman and Ross, to be reducible to a pattern of the "universal world structure."

One of the fundamental tasks for philosophy, as we have seen repeatedly throughout this book, is to create concepts as a result of the encounter with the objectivity of a problem – or as a consequence of learning. This understanding of philosophy reflects an affirmation, on the part of Deleuze and Deleuze and Guattari, of a version of the Principle of Sufficient Reason (see the Introduction). This sufficient reason, however, is not the "necessary reason" science seeks to establish, for it is not a determinate reason or fact that provides the counterfactual explanations of phenomena, the determinate reasons without which a given phenomenon would not be. This was the reason why Deleuze argued that although disparity (difference-in-itself) is the sufficient reason for "all that appears," it is inexplicable, meaning that it is not to be confused with the determinate, identifiable phenomenon associated with extensive properties, qualities, and states of affairs. The actualization and individuation of determinate states of affairs mask and cancel this difference and disparity, mask the inexplicable difference that is the sufficient reason of "all that appears."[1] In their affirmation of the PSR, therefore, Deleuze and Guattari pursue not the necessary reason of phenomena (sensibilia), but rather the contingent reason that is irreducible to any determinate fact or set of facts, and hence to any functives and necessary reasons that may be built upon these facts.

Turning now to the rise of analytic philosophy in the early twentieth century, it is important to note that a primary motivation among the philosophers who helped to shepherd analytic philosophy to its current position of dominance within Anglo-American philosophy was to develop a philosophy that could serve and further the interests of science. Integral to the efforts of the early proponents of this approach – namely, Bertrand Russell and G. E. Moore (see Chapter 2, §3) – was the rejection of the PSR. The reasoning behind this move is straightforward. Since a fundamental task of science is to provide the necessary reasons that constitute the functional relations between variables, a key assumption is that such relations are real and constitute the proper subject of scientific enquiry. In his relentless pursuit of the PSR of all phenomena, however, Bradley came to the conclusion that relations are not real (again, see

Chapter 2) and that what is truly real is the Absolute, the Absolute being a single reality that is irreducible to determinate relations. To avoid Bradley's conclusion, and in order to affirm the reality of relations, Russell and Moore will reject both Bradley's absolute idealism and his use of the PSR. Rather than demand that everything must have a reason for why it is or is not, Russell and Moore will argue that there are certain facts that are simply true, without reason or explanation.

Deleuze and Guattari will also reject Bradley's conclusion concerning relations, but only because Bradley assumes that the PSR requires that one discover a *determinate* reason or fact that accounts for the reality of a given relation, whereas Deleuze and Guattari argue that the sufficient reason – disparity – is absolutely indeterminate and inexplicable. A consequence of this move is that for Deleuze and Guattari philosophy will create concepts, whereas for Russell and Moore it will set out to develop a logic of relations. Deleuze and Guattari argue, however, that "logic is reductionist," and this is so "not accidentally but essentially and necessarily: following the route marked out by Frege and Russell, it wants to turn the concept into a function" (WP 135/QP 128). As will be argued for in this chapter, the philosophy that sets out "to turn the concept into a function" ultimately attempts to ground philosophy in determinate states of affairs. This philosophical approach tends towards the reductionist and the continual reaffirmation of common sense and the status quo, while the philosophical task of creating concepts will challenge common sense and provoke the thinking necessary for the creation of concepts, as well as a rethinking of our world and our place in it. In short, philosophy will prompt a meditation on our life as lived, a meditation that is, on the reading of Deleuze and Guattari offered here, inseparable from a life well lived.

§1

A key move in analytic philosophy in its effort to adopt the methods and aspirations of the sciences is to provide for an analysis of the proposition. More precisely, whereas science uses the tools of mathematico-physical theory in order to state propositions that accurately track phenomena (sensibilia),[2] the effort of Anglo-American philosophy is to discern and clarify the nature of propositions by turning to the discursive practices themselves, most notably natural language but also the languages of mathematics, set theory, and logic. The result of this move is that a "new, specifically logical type of function must be invented" – to wit, the propositional function, which assumes the role of the concept in analytic philosophy. In the propositional function "x is human" (WP 135/QP 128), for instance, where x is the independent variable and "is human" is the argument, the propositional function or concept is incomplete until the value of the independent variable is added to the propositional function. When this is done, the value of the propositional function (concept) is a truth value.[3] Frege offers the example of "the capital of x" as an example of the "expression of a function," and "if we take the German Empire as the argument, we get Berlin as the value of the function," or the value that renders the propositional function or concept true.[4] Frege is clear on this point: "Indeed, we may say at once: a concept is a function whose value is always a truth value."[5] To give another example, if we take the propositional function, $f(a)$ (x is a), where "a" is the argument "is human," this function or concept remains incomplete until a value is introduced into the place of the independent variable. From the "relation of the propositional function to the independent variable or argument," we thus arrive, Deleuze and Guattari argue, in summarizing the Fregean position, at "the proposition's reference, or the function's truth value ('true' or 'false') for the argument: John is a man, but Bill is a cat" (WP 136/QP 128). If I take my friend Pete as the value of the independent variable x for the function $f(a)$ (x is a), where "a" is the argument "is human," then we can restate the propositional function as follows: there is an x, and x is human, and if Pete is the value of the independent variable x, then we have a true propositional function and concept, and thus the truth value is the referent of a propositional function.

With the reconceptualization of the philosophical concept in terms of propositional functions, we can restate the scientific maxim Ladyman and Ross give us when they argue that to be real is to be reducible to a pattern of the "universal world structure." It is Quine who provides us with this well-known restatement: "to be is to be the value of a variable."[6] What is significant about Quine's maxim is that it enables us to avoid commitments to unwanted ontologies. For instance, if one were to state the proposition that "Sagittarius is a centaur," then some would argue that there must be something one is referring to for there must be something that is being stated if, as is the case for most, one most readily understands what is being said. The question is what the nature of the something that is being stated is.[7] To restate the proposition as a propositional function, however – $f(c)$ (x is c), where x is the independent variable and c is the argument "is a centaur" – we can see that there is no value that we can plug into the independent variable that will give us a true proposition. If we say that there is a prime number greater than a million, or a particle (for example, the Higgs boson) that accounts for certain physical processes, then we are committing ourselves, albeit with qualifications in the case of the Higgs boson particle, to the belief that there is a value for the independent variable, even if we do not know this value at the time we state our belief. What becomes of the concept once it comes to be identified with a propositional function is that it becomes nothing less than the set of values that result in true propositions when they are taken as the value of the independent variable – hence Quine's maxim: "to be is to be the value of a variable." This is precisely how Deleuze and Guattari characterize this move:

> Thus the concept itself is the function for the set of objects that consti-
> tute its extension. In this sense every complete concept is a set and has
> a determinate number; the concept's objects are the elements of the
> set. (WP 136/QP 129)

As Deleuze and Guattari go on to point out, however, a number of problems result when we begin to consider the conditions of reference itself, or the manner "into which a variable enters in a true proposition" (ibid). "Such conditions of reference," as is well known within the analytic tradition, "constitute not the concept's comprehension [that is, its extension] but its intension" (ibid.). Hesperus is the evening star and Phosphorus is the morning star, or "the victor at Jena" and "defeated at Waterloo" are famous examples where very different intensions may result in two true propositional functions that are rendered true when one and the same value is substituted for the independent variable. In the case of Hesperus and Phosphorus, one may not realize that one and the same value makes both propositional functions (concepts) true. Hesperus, as the first visible star in the evening, and Phosphorus, the last visible star in the morning, may be presented in different ways, or they entail different intensions, but it is the same object, Venus, that is the value that renders both propositional functions true. In what has come to be called Frege's puzzle, after the person who gave us this example, the puzzle is to account for the fact that while we can readily accept as tautological the proposition "Hesperus is Hesperus," the same is not true for "Hesperus is Phosphorus." The question, as Deleuze and Guattari understand it, is one of knowing how, through these intensional presentations, we arrive at a univocal determination of objects or elements of the concept, of propositional variables, and of arguments of the function from the point of view of exoreference . . . This is the problem of proper names. (WP 136/QP 129)

From Frege's puzzle, therefore, we come to the problem of proper names.

Saul Kripke has been one of the most influential philosophers to address the problem of proper names. In his essay, "Puzzle about Belief," for instance, Kripke challenges John Stuart Mill's claim that if the name has the same referent, then one should be able to substitute names and express the same proposition. According to Kripke, "If Mill is completely right, not only should 'Cicero was lazy' have the same truth value as 'Tully was lazy', but the two sentences should express the same proposition, have the same content."[8] As Kripke argues, however, echoing the conclusion Frege comes to from his own example of Hesperus and Phosphorus, Mill's conclusion is not so obvious. Whereas one may find the sentences "Hesperus is Hesperus" and "Cicero is Cicero" to be tautologies, in that one can carry out a substitution of like for like without changing the nature of the propositions, the sentences "Hesperus is Phosphorus" and "Cicero is Tully" may well come as a surprise, such that one might not have thought one was substituting like for like and thereby expressing the same proposition. As Kripke goes on to show by way of other examples, this same problem can arise even if the same name is used. For instance, Kripke notes that Peter may assent to the sentence "Paderewski had musical talent" but at the same time be skeptical about the musical abilities of politicians, and thus assent to the sentence, "Paderewski has no musical talent."[9] If Peter is unaware that Paderewski the Polish pianist is identical to Paderewski who was the Polish Prime Minister for most of 1919, then it may well come as a surprise to Peter that "Paderewski is Paderewski."

One explanation and potential solution for the puzzles that Kripke lists is to argue that the sentences of natural language are not as finely grained as they need to be to express the full range of propositions. One could thus adopt Russell's proposed solution, whereby if one is surprised and finds the sentence "Paderewski is Paderewski" to be significant rather than tautological, then this would be because there is a difference in the complex structure associated with the names. According to Russell's theory of names as descriptions, one comes to learn that the complex set of descriptions that one once thought named two different people are in fact the complex set of descriptions for one person. It is therefore the set of descriptions, according to Russell, that fixes and determines the reference of a proper name such as Paderewski. Russell's proposed solution to the problem of proper names has received extensive treatment in the literature,[10] and it has been criticized as being inadequate to the task, most notably by Kripke, who proposes a causal theory of reference to address the problems he claims remain with Russell's theory.[11]

Without delving too deeply into the immense literature that has been spawned by Frege's and Russell's projects (which would entail recounting much of the history of analytic philosophy to the present day), and the various proposed solutions to the problems and puzzles regarding proper names, along with the many responses to these solutions, Deleuze and Guattari argue that there is another equally important problem that arises and follows naturally from the effort to "turn the concept into a function." This problem arises in the context of Gödel's incompleteness theorems. As Deleuze and Guattari sketch the implications of Gödel's theorems, it is the logical consequence of the fact, as Deleuze and Guattari put it, that "Sentences have no self-reference, as the paradox 'I lie' shows" (WP 137/QP 130). What sentences do have, Deleuze and Guattari argue, is both "an exoreference of the proposition ... and an endoreference," so that a sentence, including a performative such as "I swear," "I love you," and so on, entails both an endoreference wherein the sentence refers to the conditions of its utterance, as in "a witness in court, a child blamed for something, a lover declaring himself, etc." (ibid.), and an exoreference where the sentence refers to other sentences, and it is this relation between propositions that constitutes the consistency of the proposition. It is at this point that Gödel's theorems come into play, for the two key implications of Gödel's theorems, Deleuze and Guattari note, is that "the proof of the consistency of arithmetic cannot be represented," and "the system necessarily comes up against true statements that are nevertheless not demonstrable, are undecidable" (ibid.). In short, no consistent system can prove or demonstrate the consistency of the elements of the system itself – there is therefore no endoconsistency. At the same time, as Deleuze and Guattari note, for Gödel there are also statements in a consistent system that the system itself cannot prove – there is no complete exoconsistency. From the perspective of Deleuze and Guattari, both the problem of proper names and Gödel's incompleteness theorems share a common

underlying assumption – namely, they both presuppose a propositional function that in turn presupposes the determinate identity,
independence, and separability of elements, whether this be independent variables in the case of proper names or the elements that
constitute the endo-/exoconsistency of a system for Gödel. Deleuze
and Guattari are clear on this point:

> In short, in becoming propositional, the concept loses all the char-
> acteristics it possessed as philosophical concept: its self-reference, its
> endoconsistency and its exoconsistency. This is because a regime of
> independence (of variables, axioms, and undecidable propositions)
> has replaced that of inseparability. (WP 137–8/QP 130)

A philosophy that attempts to turn the concept into a propositional function, with the help of a logic of relations and/or set
theoretic analyses along the way, will inevitably, and necessarily (as
Deleuze and Guattari say in the opening lines of their "Prospects
and Concepts" chapter), be reductionist in that the philosophical
concept will be reduced to the status of determinate states of affairs
and to the values of independent variables. A question that remains
open, however, and one that Deleuze and Guattari explore, is
whether a transcendental logic is possible: that is, a logic that does
not presuppose any determinate facts or relations to which the philosophical concept is to be reduced, but rather a logic that provides
the reasons for the very individuation and emergence of determinate facts and relations. It is to this question that we now turn.

§2

A continual theme or ritornello that runs throughout Deleuze and
Deleuze and Guattari's work is their claim that the effort to think
difference and becoming in terms of the identity of determinate
states of affairs is an effort that is destined to fail. As difference
becomes explicated in extensive properties and qualities, the difference, disparity, and problematic substance that are the sufficient
reason for these properties become cancelled in what Deleuze calls
a "true cover up."[12] The effort to turn philosophical concepts into
propositional functions is simply the latest in a string of natural tendencies to mistake (that is, Deleuze's version of the transcendental
illusion) the constituted identities for being the constitutive conditions. This is why Deleuze and Guattari argue that logic is "reductionist not accidentally but essentially and necessarily," for although
Frege's and Russell's propositional logic will recognize the distinc-

tion between the extensional reference of a proposition and the intensional conditions of this reference, the intensional conditions are nonetheless understood to be reducible to a structure or composition of separable components (that is, a set of descriptions), and it is widely thought by many in the analytic tradition that an analysis and greater discernment of the structural relations between these components will clarify the conditions of reference for propositions. Deleuze and Guattari argue, however, that this approach will fail to offer an adequate account of the constitutive conditions for reference since it continues to attempt to think the constitutive process of intensional conditions in terms of separable, already determinate conditions rather than in terms of "the inseparability of intensional components (zone of indiscernibility)" (WP 138/QP 131). Instead of thinking of the constitutive conditions for reference *B* in terms of distinct and separable components *A*, *A**, *A***, and so on, Deleuze and Guattari (to draw again from Chapter 1) argue that the constitutive conditions are to be thought of in terms of the "zone of indiscernibility" *AA*A*** (WP 20/QP 25: "the area *ab*").

When one does this, however, Deleuze and Guattari argue that this involves an effort of thought that engages with the constitutive conditions of reference in a way that constitutes and produces the very objects being referred to rather than simply identifying and recognizing an object *as* the already constituted referent they seek. For Deleuze and Guattari, both science (see Chapter 5) and the adoption of a historical perspective (see Chapter 4) do move some way in this direction:

> Acts of reference are finite movements of thought by which *science constitutes or modifies states of affairs and bodies*. Historical man may also be said to *carry out such modifications*, but under conditions of the lived, where functives are replaced by perceptions, affections, and actions. (WP 138/QP 131; emphasis added)

Logic, by contrast, insofar as the reference of a propositional function or concept is a "simple truth value," can only apply its acts of reference "to already constituted states of affairs or bodies, in established scientific propositions or in factual propositions (Napoleon is the one who was defeated at Waterloo) or in simple opinions ('X thinks that . . . ')" (ibid.). It is for this reason that logic always only thrives on the most mundane of examples – for example, "Scott is the author of *Waverley*," "the cat is on the mat," and so on[13] – for logic attends to the recognition of the truth of already constituted states of affairs, and "Of all the finite movements of thought, the form of recognition," Deleuze and Guattari argue, "is certainly the one that goes the least far and is the most impoverished and puerile" (WP 139/QP 132). The primary reason for Deleuze and Guattari's particularly harsh characterization is that they believe analytic philosophy begins and ends with the recognition of the truth of already constituted states of affairs rather than allow itself an encounter with the objectivity of a problem. Philosophy in *this* form of logic is thus not a case of learning but rather it takes the already constituted states of affairs as the answer to their questions, the solution to their problems, and the working assumption is that a further, more detailed analysis will provide more complete answers to their questions regarding the conditions of reference. The objectivity of the problem, however, is distinct from its solutions, and it is for this reason that Deleuze and Guattari argue that "a problem has nothing to do with a question, which is only a suspended proposition, the bloodless double of an affirmative proposition that is supposed to serve as its answer ('Who is the Author of *Waverley*?' 'Is Scott the author of *Waverley*?')" (WP 139/QP 132).

The task of philosophy, therefore, is not to assume the already constituted as that which awaits a rigorous logical analysis that will enable us to provide a more detailed account of the conditions of reference; nor is the task of philosophy to provide the historical and scientific conditions for the actualization of the constituted. This is the sense in which the scientific and historical pursuits carry out their efforts "under conditions of the lived" (WP 138/QP 131), for all they do, in effect, is attempt to understand the conditions of the constituted (the lived) in terms of the already constituted, an understanding that may indeed modify our lives as lived along the way, but this is a task that is not to be confused with philosophy. The task of philosophy, instead, is to begin with already constituted states of affairs, propositions, everyday language, our lives as lived, and so on, and move towards the problematic conditions that remain inseparable (zone of indiscernibility) from them. The conceptual persona, as we saw in Chapter 3, mediates this process by moving both towards the problematic substance and plane of immanence, the pole of absolute deterritorialization, *and* towards the pole of stratification and reterritorialization. It was this mediating process, we saw, that facilitated, with the help of the faculty of taste, the creation of philosophical concepts. With this process in mind, we can see why Deleuze and Guattari argue that the task of philosophy is one of moving from the uninteresting cases of logic

and its preoccupation with the recognition of the truth of propositions, moving instead

> to show how thought as such produces something interesting when it
> accedes to the infinite movement that frees it from truth as supposed
> paradigm and reconquers an immanent power of creation. But to do
> this it would be necessary to return to the interior of scientific states
> of affairs or bodies in the process of being constituted, in order to
> penetrate into consistency [that is, the zone of indiscernibility, the
> "area *ab*"], that is to say, into the sphere of the virtual, a sphere that is
> only actualized in them. It would be necessary to go back up the path
> science descends, and at the very end of which logic sets up its camp.
> (WP 140/QP 133)

It is at this point that Deleuze and Guattari broach the subject
of a transcendental logic. A transcendental logic will not follow the
path of science and history; nor will it, as with logic, set up its camp
where this path ends. To the contrary, a transcendental logic will
"go back up the path science descends." As Deleuze and Guattari
made this point in the "Geophilosophy" chapter, philosophy moves
not towards territories but towards the earth (see Chapter 4). In
their "Prospects and Concepts" chapter, it is life – or A LIFE – that
serves as the earth and deterritorializing plane of immanence, the
life inseparable from the "world of the lived" – "If the world of the
lived is like the earth, which must found and support the science
and logic of states of affairs, it is clear that apparently philosophical
concepts are required to carry out this first foundation" (WP 141/
QP 134). It is through the creation of concepts that the infinite
movements of thought and the "immanent power of creation" are
accessed and one is able to think and create new objects of thought,
new ways of thinking, in the very act of creating the conditions of
reference. It is precisely here that Deleuze and Guattari introduce
a transcendental logic:

> A transcendental logic (it can also be called dialectical) embraces the
> earth and all that it bears, and this serves as the primordial ground
> for formal logic and the derivative regional sciences. It is necessary
> therefore to discover at the very heart of the immanence of the lived to
> a subject, that subject's acts of transcendence capable of constituting
> new functions of variables or conceptual references: in this sense the
> subject is no longer solipsist and empirical but transcendental. (WP
> 142/QP 135)

Deleuze and Guattari acknowledge the significance of Husserl
and the phenomenological tradition in opening the doors to the

possibilities of a transcendental logic. Notwithstanding their praise, however, Deleuze and Guattari are quick to caution that despite the move to the constitutive conditions of thought itself, what the phenomenologists claim one comes to upon moving up the path science descends is a lived world – a *Lebenswelt* – and it is this lived world that is the common basis for thought. What the lived world gives us, Deleuze and Guattari claim, is a fundamental *Urdoxa* which mirrors the common, everyday opinions and *doxa*, and it is this that becomes the focal point of the analytic tradition.[14] It is for this reason, Deleuze and Guattari claim, that "phenomeno- logical concepts . . . are tolerated in homeopathic doses – hence the strangest hybrids of Frego-Husserlianism, or even Wittgensteino- Heideggerianism" (WP 143/QP 136). In other words, the phenom- enological turn to a philosophy of the lived world (*Lebenswelt*) is an acceptable complement to philosophy departments (especially departments in America, Deleuze and Guattari note) because it does not challenge the already constituted common sense that it is the task of analytic philosophy to recognize and further discern. In short, the transcendental logic, as exemplified in the phenomenol- ogy of the lived world, is another of the many instances of the "long denaturation of the plane of immanence" (ibid.). That is, the tra- dition that accepts the "denaturation of the plane of immanence" does not affirm a Spinozist naturalism and embrace an absolute, infinite substance, but rather it reduces nature to the limits of a finite, bounded *Urdoxa* of the lived world. As Deleuze and Guattari would pursue a transcendental logic, however, it will not involve a return to and affirmation of opinion (*doxa*), but would involve instead a "counter-actualization" of opinion that challenges and problematizes it – philosophy, and philosophical concepts, will thus continually invoke *para-doxa* rather than *doxa*.

§3

Despite Deleuze and Guattari's critique of opinion, they are fully cognizant of the fact that opinion is pervasive and essential. As they argue, opinion entails "a particular relationship between an external perception as state of a subject and an internal affection as passage from one state to another (exo- and endoreference)" (WP 144/QP 137). In particular, an opinion is the result of two simultaneous, *convergent* processes. With respect to perception, first, there is the process of picking out "a quality supposedly common to several objects that we perceive," and with respect to internal affections, and second, there is the process of picking out "an affection supposedly common to several subjects who experience it and who, along with us, grasp that quality" (ibid.). "Opinion," Deleuze and Guattari argue, "is the rule of the correspondence of one to the other; it is a function or a proposition whose arguments are perceptions and affections" (ibid.). When I see my cat Charlie, for example (and to extend Deleuze and Guattari's own example), I do not see Charlie but I "grasp a perceptual quality common to cats." An identifiable perceptual quality, although it presupposes disparity and the heterogeneity of difference as its sufficient reason, nonetheless cancels and hides (in a "true cover up") this difference within the common perceptual quality, even though the disparity and difference remain inseparable from this quality. At the same time there is the affect associated with this quality, "a certain feeling that makes us like or hate" cats. There are "cat people" and "dog people," and thus inseparable from an opinion is a shared group identity – a shared affect.

We can now gain added insight into the reason behind Deleuze and Guattari's claim that they flee from discussion, for discussion, as they see it, "bears on the choice of the abstract perceptual quality and on the power of the generic subject affected" (WP 145/QP 138). Opinion, in other words, reflects the choice or power of the already constituted, or that which is there to be held in common, and thus opinion is a thought that "is closely molded on the form of recognition – recognition of a quality in perception (contemplation), recognition of a group in affection (reflection), and recognition of a rival in the possibility of other groups and other qualities (communication)" (WP 145–6/QP 139). Discussion does not move back up the path towards the processes of constitution and individuation; to the contrary, discussion largely avoids the fact that "opinion is already political" (WP 145/QP 138) and moves instead within the parameters already laid down by constitutive, political processes. The discussion of opinions, therefore, does nothing to problematize the already constituted parameters of opinion and hence it does not open the field for creative encounters with the objectivity of a problem. As with the reductionism of logic, opinion is also, Deleuze and Guattari claim, a reductionist form of thought. Just as logic is a form of thought that prioritizes the recognition of the already constituted objects of reference without truly addressing the conditions of reference itself – that is, the inseparability and indiscernibility of intensional conditions – so too does opinion reduce thought to the common, shared, already constituted nature of thought rather than turn towards the constitutive, political conditions for this thought. With this argument in place, Deleuze and Guattari return to the theme of discussions and colloquia, or to the reasons why they would prefer not to engage in "pleasant or aggressive dinner conversations at Mr. Rorty's" (WP 144/QP 138):

> The essence of opinion is will to majority and already speaks in the name of a majority. . . . This is still only the first step of opinion's reign: opinion triumphs when the quality chosen ceases to be the condition of a group's constitution but is now only the image or "badge" of the constituted group that itself determines the perceptive and affective model, the quality and affection, that each must acquire. . . . Ours is the age of communication, but every noble soul flees and crawls far away whenever a little discussion, a colloquium, or a simple conversation is suggested. (WP 146/QP 139)

With respect to the lived, therefore, or with respect to the movement towards A LIFE (earth) that defines a transcendental logic for Deleuze and Guattari, the task is one of moving "up the path" science and history descend in order to think the very condition of a group's constitution, the problematic substance that is the sufficient reason for the constituted group. This transcendental logic, moreover, is not to be confined simply to human affairs, to the "opinions" of social groups. As readers of *A Thousand Plateaus* will know, Deleuze and Guattari extend their analyses well beyond human matters to include issues such as the territoriality of birds, evolutionary theory, and the sedimentation of sandstone rocks, among many other things. In *What is Philosophy?*, the topics Deleuze and Guattari cover do not span the same diverse range of subjects that they cover in *A Thousand Plateaus*. In *What is Philosophy?*, Deleuze and Guattari's focus remains largely limited to philosophical themes, though it is clear that the transcendental logic they propose here is precisely what they were doing in *A Thousand Plateaus*. If transcendental logic is moving up the path from the constituted, from the realm of opinion, the lived, and so on, to the problematic conditions of this constitution, then all that is constituted is a form of opinion and thus subject to a transcendental logic. This is just what Deleuze and Guattari claim:

> we have opinions on everything that we see or that affects us, to the extent that the human sciences can be seen as a vast doxology – but things themselves are generic opinions insofar as they have molecular perceptions and affections, in the sense that the most elementary organism forms a proto-opinion on water, carbon, and salts on which

its conditions and power depend. Such is the path that descends from the virtual to states of affairs and to other actualities: we encounter no concepts on this path, only functions. (WP 155/QP 147)

To the extent that everything entails a process of selection and filtering – a molecular perception or contemplation – that constitutes the conditions for the individuation of the quality or property that then gets taken up by bodies as their power to affect and be affected by other bodies, then everything is opinion. Every determinate thing, in other words, is a generic opinion that is conditioned by the constitutive conditions of the multiplicity and problematic substance that is able to move towards chaos without undermining the possibility of individuation. In *A Thousand Plateaus*, Deleuze and Guattari express this point by arguing that "politics precedes being."[15] A transcendental logic, therefore, will move up the path science descends and seek to address the conditions of the problem that made the constituted generic opinions possible. In *A Thousand Plateaus*, we saw this transcendental logic in action. In *What is Philosophy?*, Deleuze and Guattari not only show how what they were doing in *A Thousand Plateaus* was philosophy rather than science, but also, more importantly they are arguing that a philosophy that pursues a transcendental logic as they understand it will be ineluctably led to follow the promiscuous path one witnesses in *A Thousand Plateaus*, for, since everything is a generic opinion, then everything becomes fair game to Deleuze and Guattari's transcendental logic.

§4

A further consequence of Deleuze and Guattari's claim that "things themselves are generic opinions" is that everything has lived experience. "Even when they are nonliving, or rather inorganic," Deleuze and Guattari claim, "things have a lived experience because they are perceptions and affections" (WP 154/QP 146); or, to say it again, they are generic opinions. A transcendental logic, however, begins with these lived experiences and moves to the immanence of A LIFE or earth that is filtered and contemplated (at infinite speeds) in order to constitute the generic opinions. What this move entails is moving from the lived and livable to the unlivable, and it is precisely events that are unlivable:

> The event is not the state of affairs. It is actualized in a state of affairs, in a body, in a lived [*un vécu*], but it has a shadowy and secret part that is continually subtracted from or added to its actualization: in contrast

with the state of affairs, it neither begins nor ends but has gained or kept the infinite movement to which it gives consistency. . . . The event is immaterial, incorporeal, unlivable: pure reserve. (WP 156/QP 148)

The event, in other words, is what constitutes the intensional conditions of reference, of identity, and it is precisely these conditions that the logic of Frege and Russell, and the Anglo-American philosophers who followed in their wake, set out to determine. Unfortunately, although this logic began, as it must, with the constituted givens of lived experience, it in the end simply returned to a more fine-grained reaffirmation of lived experience. This logic remained within the grips of an opinion that was perfectly suited to the shared, communicative efforts of philosophy colloquium and late-night discussions around the table, beer in hand. Unless philosophy moves towards the unlivable event it will never really provoke the conditions of a problem that generate thought, generate learning, and hence the creation of concepts that are the responses to these conditions. What we have instead is an exchange of opinion, moves in a game where the rules are already established and remain unquestioned. It is indeed the nature of the lived to follow opinion (*doxa*), to move within the realm of the rules and expectations of lived experience, but this is not the nature of philosophy. Philosophy's task is to counter opinion, to invoke *para-doxa* and to be, as Nietzsche sought to be in his own writings, untimely.

This movement towards the event that is the task of philosophy is not, however, done in isolation or in ignorance of the findings of science or the facts of the matter regarding states of affairs in the world. Although science concerns itself with functions, as we saw in Chapter 5, and despite the fact that the "virtuality" of the event "goes beyond any possible function" (WP 157/QP 149), Deleuze and Guattari argue that it is necessary to engage in both science and philosophy. As they put it, "It is necessary to go back up to the event that gives its virtual consistency to the concept, just as it is necessary to come down to the actual state of affairs that provides the function with its references" (WP 159/QP 150). This is also why Deleuze and Guattari close their "Prospects and Concepts" chapter by recognizing that if "philosophy has a fundamental need for the science that is contemporary with it, this is because science constantly intersects with the possibility of concepts and because concepts necessarily involve allusions to science that are neither examples nor applications, nor even reflections" (WP 162/QP 153). In other words, in the efforts of science "not to distance itself too much from chaos," it draws towards the problematic, absolutely infinite substance that motivates the creation of concepts, even though, in the end, science sets limits and parameters that define the plane of reference that enables the creation of scientific functives. As for philosophy, as it moves towards the deterritorializing of the event, there is simultaneously the movement of reterritorialization that brings the event and the philosophical concept back down to actual states of affairs, and it is here that the findings of contemporary science become especially relevant. The examples from contemporary science one finds throughout Deleuze and Guattari's texts are thus not just examples but are rather thought of as conditioned by a problem that remains unresolved and irreducible to the actualized state of affairs. The examples from science, in short, are certainly the subject that is being thought, but for philosophy the task is not one of creating functives that establish determinate relationships between a set of determinate states of affairs and objects; instead, it creates concepts that address the "true substantive" of the examples – namely, the problematic substance and multiplicity. Philosophy turns to science, but it does not do science; nor should it. Deleuze and Guattari are clear on this point: "it is always unfortunate when scientists do philosophy without really philosophical means or when philosophers do science without real scientific means (we do not claim to have been doing this)" (WP 161/QP 152). Both philosophy and science, therefore, offer contrasting approaches in addressing the problematic nature of substance, or they both offer contrasting approaches towards learning.

As we turn now to the final chapter, we will turn to art as the third of the major efforts to address the objectivity of a problem, or to address the problem of learning. Whereas philosophy creates concepts in the face of the objectivity of a problem, and science creates functives, art creates "*a bloc of sensations, that is to say, a compound of percepts and affects*" (WP 164/QP 154). Some have criticized Deleuze and Guattari for reducing human efforts to just these three categories. Most notably, Alain Badiou has argued that it was a mistake for Deleuze and Guattari not to classify politics as one of the creative endeavors of human beings.[16] As we have seen, however, Deleuze and Guattari argue that everything is a generic opinion and hence *everything is political.* The creative tasks of philosophy, science, and art each presuppose the political conditions of their state of affairs, and it is in response to the problematic substance inseparable from these states of affairs that their creative tasks begin. For philosophy, science, and art, therefore, the political is always near at hand.[17] Others have argued that Deleuze and Guattari artificially compartmentalize the multiplicity of creative processes that may result during the encounter with the objectivity of a problem. This would indeed be a damning criticism if philosophy, science, and art were to be understood as a category type with the assumption being that the three are mutually exclusive kinds of process. This is not what Deleuze and Guattari are doing. By offering the trilogy of creative processes associated with philosophy, science, and art, Deleuze and Guattari are creating a concept of learning, and this concept has three components – philosophy, science, and art. These three components, moreover, are not distinct, categorical types but rather they are the inseparable components of the concept learning, and *What is Philosophy?* in the end provides us with an example of "the inseparability of intensional components (zone of indiscernibility)" (WP 138/QP 131) that is involved with the philosophical concept of learning. What Deleuze and Guattari are doing in *What is Philosophy?*, therefore, and what they admit to doing in their introduction, is offering a "pedagogy of the concept" (WP 12/QP 17). This pedagogy of the concept, however, presupposes a concept of learning, and it is the task of *What is Philosophy?* to create this concept. As we turn, then, to the final chapter and the Conclusion, the inseparability of the three components – philosophy, science, art – will become more apparent, as will their role in effectuating a pedagogy of the concept. It is to this that we now turn.

Example 11

Perhaps no philosopher in the Western European tradition is as well known as Socrates for encouraging reflective enquiry into one's own life as essential to a well-lived life. In the *Apology*, Socrates defends himself against charges of not believing in the gods of Athens and corrupting the youth. During his defense Socrates admits that he "did not care for the things that most people care about . . . [namely] making money, having a comfortable home, high military or civil rank, and all the other activities . . . which go on in our city".[18] What Socrates set out to do instead with the people he would meet was to persuade each "not to think more of practical advantages than of his mental and moral well-being."[19] What Socrates thinks is necessary to attend to one's "mental and moral well-being," however, or at least as this is commonly assumed, is to distinguish between opinion and knowledge and to live in accordance with knowledge rather than opinion. In the *Euthyphro*, for instance, after having been given a few examples of pious acts, Socrates reminds Euthyphro:

> Now call to mind that this is not what I asked you, to tell me one or two of the many holy acts, but to tell the essential aspect (ειδος [often translated as Idea or Form]), by which all holy acts are holy; for you said that all unholy acts were unholy and all holy ones holy by one aspect.[20] (6e)

Since Socrates' interlocutors were unable to give a universal definition that could apply to all examples of the term – such as piety in the *Euthyphro* (justice in the *Republic*, beauty in the *Phaedrus*, and so on) – the conclusion Socrates comes to is that although he came across many people who claimed to possess knowledge, in the end they lacked knowledge and simply had opinions. This led Socrates to his famous conclusion that if he is indeed the wisest of all men, then it is only because he knows he knows nothing, or he knows that he lacks knowledge rather than thinking he possesses knowledge when he does not.

For Deleuze and Guattari, however, this characterization of Plato is not quite on the mark. Their reasoning is rather simple: if opinion is, as Deleuze and Guattari argue, a function of perceptions and affections that are "supposedly common to several objects . . . [or] common to several subjects who experience it" (WP 144/QP 137), and if it is this which enables us to refer to objects of our shared experience, and do so accurately, then it would appear that opinion is not only not divorced from truth but is rather a precondition for it. Deleuze and Guattari thus ask how, if knowledge "takes a truth value, could opinion be something entirely for the sophists?" (WP 147/QP 140). The best way to understand the relationship between knowledge and opinion, therefore, and the subsequent effort to attain the knowledge necessary for a well-lived life, is thus to find within opinions those that are "most plausible by reference to the quality they extracted and which opinions were the wisest by reference to the subject who advanced them" (ibid.). Moreover, Deleuze and Guattari argue that Plato and Aristotle already recognized this fact. Aristotle, for instance, recognized that it was necessary to begin with opinions in a dialectic that eventually leads to scientific propositions, and Plato had already recognized that it is "'true opinion'" that is a "prerequisite for knowledge and the sciences. Even Parmenides," Deleuze and Guattari note, "did not pose knowledge and opinion as being two disjunctive pathways" (ibid.), and they cite Heidegger's and Beaufret's studies of Parmenides as exemplary in their recognition of this fact.[21]

What, then, is the relation between ideas (ειδος) and *doxa*, between opinions and the knowledge inseparable from a well-lived life? The Platonic solution, according to Deleuze and Guattari, is that one must "choose the quality that was like the unfolding of the Beautiful in any lived situation, and [. . .] take as generic subject Man inspired by the Good" (WP 148/QP 140–1). As Deleuze and Guattari clarify this point, the "beautiful in Nature and the good in minds define philosophy as a function of the variable life . . . [and thus] the beautiful and the good are functions whose truth value is opinion" (WP 148/QP 141). In other words, just as the concept was understood by Frege to be a function (see our discussion in this chapter), so too is the Beautiful and the Good a function on Deleuze and Guattari's reading. For example, Frege offered the example of "the capital of x" as an example that expresses a function or concept, and "if we take the German Empire as the argument, we get Berlin as the value of the function," the value that renders the concept true.[22] So if we take the capital-function, $f(c)$ (capital of x), then this function awaits a value to replace the x variable that will render the function either true or false, Berlin being the value that renders it true. Now in the case of the Beautiful and the Good as functions, if we take the Beautiful-function, $f(b)$ (x is beautiful), and similarly, if we take our lives as lived in a given situation as the argument, then the Beautiful-function awaits a value – a particular quality in the case of the Beautiful-function or a particular subject or person in the case of the Good-function – that gives a true opinion as the resulting value of the function. The problem with this approach, however, according to Deleuze and Guattari, is that it leads to an aporia, "the very one expressed in the most astonishing dialogue, the *Theaetetus*" (ibid.). As Deleuze and Guattari state the aporia, "Knowledge must be transcendent; it must be added to and distinguished from opinion in order to make opinion true. But knowledge must be immanent for opinion to be true as opinion" (ibid.). With respect to the Beautiful-function, for example, the knowledge that enables the extraction of the particular quality that results in a true opinion must be transcendent for it is precisely this quality that renders the particular opinion true when the opinion participates in this quality and this quality thereby makes the opinion a true opinion; or it is the Good that the subject participates in that renders opinions about the subject true. At the same time, however, it is the opinion that is true, not the transcendent form or idea, and with this move the immanence of opinion becomes an immanence that is immanent to a form or idea (an εἶδος), and hence transcendence is introduced into the mix (see the Introduction and example 3). Deleuze and Guattari thus conclude that "The beautiful and the good continue to lead us back to transcendence. It is as if true opinion still demanded a knowledge that it had nevertheless deposed" (WP 148–9/QP 141).

Deleuze and Guattari then argue that phenomenology follows a similar path to the Platonists and it too ends up leading to transcendence rather than restoring the "full rights of immanence" (WP 49/QP 47 [see example 3]). According to Deleuze and Guattari, in its "search of original opinions" phenomenology also "needs the beautiful and the good so that the latter [original opinions] are not confused with variable empirical opinion and so that perception and affection attain their truth value" (WP 149/QP 142). In its effort to avoid psychologism – that is, the reduction of opinions and thoughts to being "nothing more than an empirical opinion as psychosociological type" (ibid.) – phenomenology turns to art and culture as the expression of a true, proper beauty and good that are the immanent basis for the empirical, routine opinions of everyday life. "Phenomenology needs art as logic needs science," Deleuze and Guattari claim. But in their battle against the rule of the everyday, the rule of opinion, phenomenology turns to a transcendental subject (see example 3) and to a proto-opinion (*Urdoxa*) that can save us from a life consigned to mere opinion and cliché, but with this turn the transcendent returns. To "fight against perceptual and affective clichés," Deleuze and Guattari argue, we must "also fight against the machine that produces them" (WP 150/QP 142). The effort of phenomenology to do this by "invoking the primordial lived, by making immanence an immanence to a subject" (ibid.), albeit a transcendental subject, ultimately results in the restoration of transcendence rather than immanence. The turn to art and culture in order to find a way of "deepening opinion and of discovering original opinions" will only succeed, Deleuze and Guattari claim, if one also finds and creates a concept, and a concept that is not limited to a limited plane of reference and its functional role of delivering truth values, but a concept that embraces "infinite movement" (ibid.). Only then, Deleuze and Guattari conclude, will we be able to overturn opinion.

Suggested reading for example 11
   Plato, *The Sophist*
   Maurice Merleau-Ponty, *The Primacy of Perception*

Example 12

With Badiou we find a recent attempt to do precisely what Deleuze and Guattari call for in the close of the previous example – namely, to overturn opinion by embracing the infinite movement of the concept. Badiou, moreover, begins with the function – or with Cantorian set theory, to be precise (see example 10) – and from there he raises the function to the uncountably infinite, a move whereby Badiou appears to affirm the concept that overturns everyday opinions and prepares the way for truly new and novel ways of thinking and being. Despite the moves Badiou makes in this direction, moves Deleuze and Guattari have much sympathy for, in the end Badiou ultimately restores the power of transcendence rather than the full "rights of immanence."

Deleuze and Guattari readily admit that "Badiou's theory is very complex; we fear we may have oversimplified it" (WP 228, fn. 11/QP 144), and Badiou heartily agrees that not only have they oversimplified his theory, but also they have misunderstood it. Without delving into the numerous issues that both Deleuze and Badiou touch upon (issues that have been discussed elsewhere[23]), there is a key claim from example 12 that bears closer scrutiny, and which is particularly relevant to the themes of *What is Philosophy?* – namely, Deleuze and Guattari's claim that "It seems to us that the theory of multiplicities does not support the [Badiou's] hypothesis of any multiplicity whatever" (WP 152/QP 144). What Deleuze and Guattari are referring to here is Badiou's understanding of a multiplicity that is uncountable, which Badiou arrives at by way of Cantor's method of arriving at non-denumerable sets. In particular, and as we have seen (in example 10), for each set, whether finite or infinite, a countable set is one where elements can be placed in relation to other elements. An infinite set, for instance, consists of a set that has the same power as a subset of this set – the infinite integers have the same power as the subset of even integers. Following Cantor's argument that the set of all sets, the power set, does not have the same power as the sets of which it is the set, Badiou comes to the conclusion that there are what he calls "inconsistent" multiplicities, or sets that cannot be subject to a "count-as-one" function. Badiou is clear on this point and he argues quite explicitly that an "inconsistent multiplicity . . . [is] anterior to any one-effect,"[24] and more importantly, that "the inconsistent multiple is actually unthinkable as such. All thought supposes a situation of the thinkable, which is to say a structure, a count-as-one, in which the presented multiple is consistent and denumerable."[25] The event, for Badiou, is what happens when an inconsistent multiplicity that cannot be placed into a determinate situation, into a historical context, presents a rupture within a situation – that is, with a determinate, namable situation that can be thought in accord with the principle of the "count-as-one."[26] This is the multiplicity that Deleuze and Guattari are referring to when they speak of "any multiplicity whatever," for it is a multiplicity without determinate, "count-as-one" characteristics so one cannot say what or where it is but only that it is. In *Being and Event*, Badiou will refer to this as the indiscernibility of the event, which constitutes the rupture or void of a determinate situation but is not a determinate part of this situation; rather, it is "the indiscernible part, [and] by definition, solely possesses the 'properties' of any part whatsoever. It is rightfully declared generic, because, if one wishes to qualify it, all one can say is that its elements are. . . ."[27]

For Badiou, it is only by way of these inconsistent sets and events that cannot be determinately counted within a situation that we can truly account for the new without reducing it to being merely a fold or continuation of the already created. It is for this reason that Badiou calls for "the absolute ontological separation of the event, the fact that it occurs in the situation without being in any way virtualizable . . . the basis of the character of truths as irreducibly original, created, and fortuitous."[28] In other words, Badiou argues against Deleuze's claim that the virtual is indiscernible and insepa-rable from the actual, for by doing this Deleuze fails to account for the eruption of novel truths within any determinate situation. For Badiou, by contrast, the truth of the event is completely separate from, and discontinuous with, any determinate situation and it is only by a "faithful" procedure of being attuned to the void in the situation – the unnamable inconsistent multiplicity – whereby the void becomes determinate and named. As Badiou puts it,

> For what the faithful procedure thus rejoins is none other than the truth of the entire situation, insofar as the sense of the indiscernible is that of exhibiting as one-multiple the very being of what belongs insofar as it belongs. Every nameable part, discerned and classified by knowledge, refers not to being-in-situation as such, but to what language carves out therein as recognizable particularities. The faith-ful procedure, precisely because it originates in an event in which the void is summoned . . . disposes, in its infinite states, of the being of the situation.[29]

The faithful procedure thus identifies the event that becomes a new determinate situation by virtue of imposing a "count-as-one" function on the generic "any part whatsoever"; in this way, the determinate naming can literally begin with any multiplicity whatever, and from there the multiplicity becomes increasingly determinate and historicized, much as the rupture that was Haydn's music, to refer to Badiou's own example, became historicized as the beginning of the classical tradition in music. The resulting task for philosophy, as Deleuze and Guattari read Badiou, consists of executing the faithful procedure in the wake of the rupturing void of the event; hence they conclude that "philosophy seems to float in an empty transcendence" (WP 152/QP 144), awaiting a rupturing void that, because of the "absolute ontological separation of the event," transcends any given determinate reality. It is precisely this separation that causes problems for Badiou's theory, and problems similar to what we have found with previous attempts to reduce the philosophical concept to a function (see example 11), even if this is a function of the infinite, as in the case of Badiou.

An even more significant reason for Deleuze and Guattari's claim that they cannot "support the hypothesis of any multiplicity whatever" is that, rather than there being a generic multiplicity, "There must be at least two multiplicities, two types, from the outset" (ibid.). In clarifying this claim, Deleuze and Guattari argue that there must be two multiplicities "not because dualism is better than unity but because the multiplicity is precisely what happens between the two" (ibid.). To recall an earlier example and chapter (example 3 and Chapter 2), multiplicities are precisely the working parts of an abstract machine, and the abstract machine consists of the two limits, the two types of multiplicities, that a working multiplicity must stave off. On the one hand, we have the multiplicity of stratification, the multiplicity that locks patterns into unchanging, rigidified patterns and as a result stifles the life of a working multiplicity; and on the other hand, we have the multiplicity of absolute deterritorialization and its undermining of the connections and consistency necessary for a working multiplicity to continue to work. In both cases, a multiplicity as a working part entails the two multiplicities as the life of the multiplicity, the two limits that a living, working multiplicity must flirt with but not actualize. How this process unfolds becomes most clear for Deleuze and Guattari in art, and it is therefore no surprise that art becomes the central focus and concern of the last chapter and example of *What is Philosophy?*

Suggested reading for example 12
  Alain Badiou, *Being and Event*

NOTES

1. See Gilles Deleuze, *Difference and Repetition*, trans. Paul Patton (New York: Columbia University Press, 1994), p. 228: "It is not surprising that, strictly speaking, difference should be 'inexplicable'. Difference is explicated, but in systems in which it tends to be cancelled . . . [i]t [difference] is cancelled in so far as it is drawn outside itself, in extensity and in the quality which fills that extensity. However, difference creates both this extensity and this quality." In other words, difference is the sufficient reason for all that appears, for extensive qualities and properties.
2. Recall Ladyman and Ross's claim regarding the universal world-structure: "the 'world-structure' just is and exists independently of us and we represent it mathematico-physically via our theories" (*Every Thing Must Go*, Oxford: Oxford University Press, 2007, p. 158).
3. See Frege's essay, "Concept and Function," in *Collected Papers on Mathematics, Logic, and Philosophy*, ed. Brian McGuinness (Oxford: Basil Blackwell, 1984).
4. Ibid., p. 147
5. Ibid., p. 146.
6. W. V. O. Quine, "On What There Is," in *From a Logical Point of View* (Cambridge, MA: Harvard University Press, 1980).
7. Meinong, for instance, argues that there really are entities that make statements such as "Sagittarius is a centaur" meaningful. See Alexius Meinong's *Theory of Objects*, trans. J. N. Findlay (Oxford: Oxford University Press, 1933). Frege and Husserl, among others, set out to limit the types of objects that exist.
8. Saul Kripke, "A Puzzle about Belief," in *Meaning and Use*, ed. A. Margalit (Dordrecht: D. Reidel), p. 241.
9. Ibid., p. 266.
10. For a recent defense of Russell's solution, see David Chalmers, *Constructing the World* (Oxford: Oxford University Press, 2012).
11. For Kripke's critique, see his *Naming and Necessity* (Cambridge, MA: Harvard University Press, 1980). For a recent critique of Chalmers's solution and defense of the Fregean puzzle, see Jason Stanley's "Constructing Meanings," in *Analysis* 74, no. 4 (2014): 662–76.
12. *Difference and Repetition*, p. 166: "solutions tend to abruptly replace the movement of problems with the rigidity and stasis of a true cover up."
13. The first is from Russell, "On Denoting," *Mind* 14, no. 56 (1905), pp. 483–5 (Russell also responds to Meinong in this essay); the second is a well-known example, first presented in David Wiggins's "On Being in the Same Place at the Same Time," *Philosophical Review* 77 (1968): 90–5, though more commonly known from Peter Geach, *Reference and Generality* (Ithaca, NY: Cornell University Press, 1980).

14. Beginning, most notably, with G. E. Moore's common-sense philosophy – see his "Defence of Common Sense," in *Philosophical Papers* (New York: Collier, [1925] 1966) – though this is a widely adopted by view among most philosophers in the analytic tradition.

15. Gilles Deleuze and Félix Guattari, *A Thousand Plateaus: Capitalism and Schizophrenia*, trans. Brian Massumi (Minneapolis: University of Minnesota Press, 1987), p. 203.

16. Recall my earlier footnote: Chapter 4, fn. 18.

17. Science may not be expressly involved in political affairs, though in many ways science and politics are mutually and reciprocally involved with one another. Bruno Latour, for instance, has shown how important the drawing together of allies and connections are if one is to support a given scientific proposition (see my *Deleuze's Hume: Philosophy, Culture and the Scottish Enlightenment* [Edinburgh: Edinburgh University Press, 2009]). From a practical perspective, much of scientific research is dependent upon some form of government funding, and subsequently political concerns are very much part of the process involved in selecting research projects.

18. Plato, *Five Dialogues: Euthyphro, Apology, Crito, Meno, Phaedo*, 2nd edn, trans. G. M. A. Grube, revised John M. Cooper (Indianapolis: Hackett, 2002), 36c.

19. Ibid.

20. Ibid., 6e.

21. Heidegger, *Parmenides*, trans. Andre Schuwer and Richard Rojewicz (Bloomington: Indiana University Press, 1998); Jean Beaufret, *Le Poème* (Paris: P.U.F., 1986), pp. 31–4.

22. Frege, *Collected Papers*, p. 147.

23. See Dan Smith's "Mathematics and the Theory of Multiplicities: Badiou and Deleuze Revisited," *Southern Journal of Philosophy* 41, no. 3 (2003), 411–50, and my "Charting the Road of Inquiry: Deleuze's Humean Pragmatics and the Challenge of Badiou," *Southern Journal of Philosophy* 44, no. 3 (2006) 399–425.

24. Alain Badiou, *Being and Event*, trans. Oliver Feltham (London: Bloomsbury, 2007), p. 33.

25. Ibid., p. 34.

26. Badiou discusses the case of Haydn in *Ethics: An Essay on the Understanding of Evil*, trans. Peter Hallward (London and New York: Verso, 2001). As Badiou puts it, Haydn's music is "absolutely detached, or unrelated to, all the rules of the situation. Hence the emergence of the classical style, with Haydn, . . . concerns the musical situation and no other, a situation then governed by the predominance of the baroque style. It was en event for this situation . . . [an event that] was not comprehensible from within the plenitude achieved by the baroque style; it really was a matter of *something else*" (p. 68).

27. *Being and Event*, p. 339.

28. Alain Badiou, *Deleuze: The Clamor of Being,* trans. Louise Burchill (Minneapolis: University of Minnesota Press, 2000), p. 79.
29. Ibid., p. 339.

7

Philosophy and Art

As we turn to discuss Deleuze and Guattari's philosophy of art in this final chapter we will begin to draw a number of the themes of this book together, in particular the importance of philosophical "taste" for creating concepts. This return to the notion of taste is quite natural, given the importance of Hume for Deleuze's project and the importance for Hume of the role of taste in accounting for aesthetic judgments. For Hume, the faculty of taste is able to generate aesthetic judgments regarding objects that are reducible neither to the variations of our sentiments nor to a universal rule that applies to all objects of a certain type. Although there may be various sentiments, emotions, and physiological reactions that one might have, both positive and negative, in response to an actual work of art, the judgments of the faculty of taste may be related to but are not reducible to these physiological reactions and sentiments. Nor are judgments of taste to be understood as the application of a universal, abstract rule to a given particular (for example, a given art object). With respect to concepts and the creation of concepts, similarly, the role of taste is essential to co-adapting the various processes in a way that is irreducible to a functional relation between a concept and a set of objects that give the function a truth value. In short, the use of the faculty of taste enables us to avoid a Fregean view of concepts as we have discussed this earlier (see Chapter 5), where, for Frege, "It must be determinate for every object whether it falls under a concept or not. . . ."[1] A concept is meaningless, Frege claims, if one cannot clearly demarcate what objects do and do not fall under the concept. At the same time, a concept is not an abstract universal detached from the particulars to which it applies, as a reading of Plato might understand it.

One of the ongoing themes of this book has been to detail the manner in which concepts are real in a way that is irreducible either to being an abstract entity distinct from its material content or to being nothing more or less than the material content alone. In other words, we have been implicitly addressing the *quid facti* and *quid juris* questions (see Chapter 3, §3 for our earlier discussion of Maïmon). On the one hand, we have been concerned to show that determinate facts and elements are constitutive of each particular concept, and thus it is important to discern these elements (hence the significance of the *quid facti* question); and yet, on the other hand, we have been careful, following Deleuze and Guattari, to note that a concept is irreducible to these determinate elements and, as a result, the question of whether the concept applies to these elements or not necessarily arises (and with it the *quid juris* question). In their chapter "Percept, Affect, and Concept," Deleuze and Guattari begin with these questions and turn to the work of art in order to provide an explanation that addresses both the *quid facti* and *quid juris* questions. In doing this, Deleuze and Guattari also provide a final accounting of what philosophy is and how it relates to other creative efforts of thought – namely, science and art. By turning to art, we will show how Deleuze and Guattari draw together the threads of earlier chapters and argue that a thoughtful engagement in the world involves a process of learning, and how the concept of learning itself that underlies this thoughtful engagement involves three inseparable, intensional components – to wit, philosophy, science, and art.

§1

As Deleuze and Guattari begin their chapter on art, they make quite a bold claim: "art," they say, "preserves, and it is the only thing in the world that is preserved" (WP 163/QP 154). This is a rather remarkable statement coming from Deleuze and Guattari, given the fact that throughout their careers they had stressed the importance and inevitability of becoming, continuous variation, and change. In *A Thousand Plateaus*, for instance, they argue that "there is no genetics without 'genetic drift'," and they add that "a code," whether this be a genetic code or any axiomatized coding of a process, "has an essential margin of decoding."[2] It would seem, then, that for Deleuze and Guattari there is nothing that is preserved and, no matter what is, whether art or anything else, it entails a process whereby it becomes other and no longer is; thus any individuated entity always involves "an essential margin of decoding" that does not preserve this entity but rather undoes it. Deleuze and Guattari's claim that art "is the only thing in the world that is preserved" thus appears surprising, if not outright inconsistent with their project as a whole. An assumption that likely contributes to this element of surprise is the belief that to be preserved is to maintain a continuous self-identity. If this were what it means to be preserved for Deleuze and Guattari, then indeed their claim about art would be problematic.

What is preserved, however, is not a continuously self-identical, unchanging entity. To understand what is preserved in art, along with the other moves Deleuze and Guattari make in this chapter, we can begin by placing their understanding of taste into the context of traditional arguments related to the nominalism/realism debate. For both the nominalists and realists, what is preserved is a self-identical entity. For the nominalists, individuals are the self-same entities that persist and to which names are applied that group these entities according to relations of similarity, use, and so on. In the case of art, for instance, aesthetic terms, such as beauty, sublimity, or even the term art itself, can be taken to be names attached to various objects and to the various sentiments and reactions one has in the social-cultural context within which one encounters these objects. The history of twentieth-century art, for example, is replete with challenges to the traditional application of the term "art" to objects – think of Marcel Duchamp's famous display of the urinal as an artwork, named *Fountain*, or Andy Warhol's Brillo boxes. From the nominalist perspective, art is to be understood in terms of the entities that are called art objects, and whether or not such entities are referred to as art draws its legitimacy from the social context in which the object is placed. From this perspective, however, the appropriateness of the use of aesthetic terms is not preserved but subject to variation as the experience of avant-garde art in the twentieth century has taught us. It is only the individual object that is preserved, not the name or label applied to it.

From the perspective of the realists, what is preserved is a universal category regarding beauty, form, and so on that determines whether a particular object is a work of art or not if it exemplifies these categories. As was discussed earlier, however, the Humean argument for the theory of taste refuses to accept the notion that there are universal rules or categories that are the unchanging arbiters of what is or is not to be considered an artwork, beautiful, and so on. At the same time, however, for Hume, the use of aesthetic terms is irreducible to the determinate, individuated entities and elements that comprise the content of an aesthetic judgment (that is, the qualities of the object as well as the passions and affects associated with this object). It is this irreducibility that gives traction to the arguments of the realists who claim there is a concept or universal category that is real and irreducible to the distinct and determinate elements and entities that fall under the scope of this concept. The use of the concept or term "phone," for instance, as a general term, is irreducible to any single phone and in fact the meaningfulness of this term persists even after the loss or destruction of this phone or even all individual phones, much as the use of the term "dodo bird" is meaningful even though there are no dodo birds left. There is thus something preserved and ever present in the nature of universals and concepts, the realists argue, that is irreducible to the determinate entities to which these terms refer. Deleuze and Guattari, however, reject both the notion that what is preserved is the reality of the self-same individual objects, and the view that it is the nature of the concepts themselves as universals that is preserved. What Deleuze and Guattari argue for instead is an aesthetic realism that claims it is neither a concept nor an individuated object that is preserved. What, then, is preserved, and preserved only in art?

The primary aim of the "Percept, Affect, and Concept" chapter is to answer this question. In their initial foray towards an answer, Deleuze and Guattari claim that what is preserved in art and only in art is not to be confused with the qualities and properties of the objects themselves, nor with the relations these objects have to the subjects and institutions that support artists and promote our perceptions of what is to be considered an object worthy of aesthetic admiration.[3] For Deleuze and Guattari, art "preserves and is preserved in itself (*quid juris?*), although actually," they add, "it lasts no longer than its support and materials – stone, canvas, chemical color, and so on (*quid facti?*)" (WP 163/QP 154). There is thus a *quid juris* question regarding the nature of the aesthetic reality that is preserved in itself and that is irreducible to the "support and materials" upon which this reality depends. What is the relationship between this aesthetic reality and its "support and materials"? Since this aesthetic reality "lasts no longer than its support and materials," while remaining preserved in itself and irreducible to this support, the *quid facti* question of the nature of this support and materials also comes into play. The aesthetic reality that is irreducible to the pose and gestures of a 5,000–year-old statue of a young girl is indeed the reality of the young girl's pose and gestures, but this reality, Deleuze and Guattari stress, "became independent of its 'model' from the start" (ibid.); that is, regardless of how faithful or accurate the sculptor's representation of the model – in this case, a young girl and her actual pose, gestures, smile, and so on, the aesthetic reality of the sculpture is inseparable from these elements while irreducible to them. Although the *quid facti* question is important, the fact remains, for Deleuze and Guattari, that the aesthetic reality of an artwork is independent of the elements that come to be identified in the process of addressing this question. At the same time, however, Deleuze and Guattari argue that the aesthetic reality that is preserved in itself is "no less independent of the viewer or hearer, who only experience it [the aesthetic reality] after, if they have the strength for it" (WP 164/QP 155). And, finally, this aesthetic reality "is independent of the creator through the self-positing of the created, which is preserved in itself" (ibid.). The reality of Deleuze and Guattari's aesthetic realism, therefore, is independent of creator, created, and all those who may come and bear witness to that which was created. It may appear, then, that Deleuze and Guattari's aesthetic realism turns on an appeal to mystical transcendence, to a reality beyond the reach of all except, perhaps, the mystically attuned artist who is unable to state precisely what it is they have done or how they did it. For reasons to be clarified more fully below, this mystical reading is mistaken.

The first indication that the mystical reading is mistaken can be seen in Deleuze and Guattari's blunt statement that what is preserved in itself in an artwork is "*a bloc of sensations, that is to say, a compound of percepts and affects*" (ibid.). Far from being a transcendent reality that is beyond percepts and affects, the aesthetic reality is nothing less than a bloc or compound of percepts and affects. "The work of art," Deleuze and Guattari argue, "is a being of sensation and nothing else: it exists in itself" (ibid.). The compound of percepts and affects, or the being of sensation, is not, however, to be confused with the perception of the artwork, or with the feelings and emotions of the viewer. The being of sensation is inseparable from these perceptions and feelings, but the task of the artist is to extract from these perceptions and feelings a bloc and compound of percepts and affects, a being of sensation. This is no easy task for "the artist's greatest difficulty is to make it [the bloc or compound of percepts and affects] stand up on its own" (ibid.). The artist's task is not to represent a model or adequately portray a possible or actually existent life or state of affairs, or even a dramatic transition between states of affairs; to the contrary, the artist's task, and one that is exceedingly difficult, is to extract A LIFE and being of sensation from the model and from the possible or actually lived states of affairs, and it is this life that is, in the end, preserved in itself. Sensations and feelings, as well as the material within which and through which artworks circulate, are the medium through which the artist attempts such extractions. As Deleuze and Guattari put it,

> By the means of the material, the aim of art is to wrest the percept from perceptions of objects and the states of a perceiving subject, to wrest the affect from affections as the transition from one state to another: to extract a bloc of sensations, a pure being of sensations. (WP 167/ QP 158)

When art does this, the resulting "percept," Deleuze and Guattari claim, "is the landscape before man, in the absence of man" (WP 169/QP 159). The percept is thus beyond the relationship between a perceiver and an object but expresses a reality that is able to "stand up on its own," and this is precisely the "landscape before man, in the absence of man." Similarly, in extracting an affect from the transition from one state to another, one moves beyond the Spinozist theory of joy and sorrow wherein, as Spinoza argued, the affects of joy and sadness express how humans feel as they transition either from lesser to greater power (joy), or from greater to lesser power (sadness). Rather than extracting human joy or sadness, therefore, what the artist extracts instead are *"Affects [that] are precisely these nonhuman becomings of man,* just as percepts . . . are *nonhuman landscapes of nature"* (ibid.). The artist then works to create a being of sensation that is a reality that stands on its own and is independent of human relationships while all the while being inseparable from such relationships and the material that actualizes the being of sensation. To understand this move, as well as its implications for art, along with its connections to the themes of earlier chapters in *What is Philosophy?*, we need to explore in more detail the nature of the life that artists extract from perceptions and affections.

§2

Returning to the task of the artist, and to the difficult task of forging a bloc and compound of percepts and affects in order to create a work that is preserved in itself and able to "stand up on its own," what an artist essentially does is to extract A LIFE from the lived.

What is involved in doing this, Deleuze and Guattari claim, is that "the artist, including the novelist, goes beyond the perceptual states and affective transitions of the lived" (WP 171/QP 162). In doing so, the artist extracts a percept from perceptual states and an affect from affective transitions. This leads us to the obvious question: how can an artist, beginning with perceptual states and affective transitions, extract "a being of sensation" that "exists in itself"? Deleuze and Guattari tackle this question head on – "How can a moment of the world be rendered durable or made to exist by itself?" (WP 172/QP 162) – and they argue that Virginia Wolf provides us with the answer:

> "Saturate every atom," "eliminate all waste, deadness, superfluity," everything that adheres to our current and lived perceptions, everything that nourishes the mediocre novelist; and keep only the saturation that gives us the percept. "It must include nonsense, fact, sordidity: but made transparent"; "I want to put practically everything in; yet to saturate." (WP 172/QP 163)[4]

Let us unpack Woolf's answer by focusing on the notion of saturation. Understood in its usual sense, a solution of a particular substance is saturated, for instance, when no more of that substance can be dissolved in the solution. This point of maximum concentration, the saturation point, is a point at the edge of a phase transition, and the addition of more of the substance into the solution can initiate a process of transition of the solution into a form of precipitate such as crystal. It is this point of maximum concentration, the point that conditions processes of actualization and individuation, that interests Deleuze and Guattari. On Deleuze and Guattari's reading of Woolf, a text is saturated not because it accurately portrays a scene from a life as lived but rather because it saturates such a scene with the instability that comes with the point of saturation, and it is this unstable state at the edge of chaos that allows for the possibility of new affects. As Deleuze and Guattari put it, "A great novelist is above all an artist who invents unknown or unrecognized affects and brings them to light as the becoming of his characters" (WP 174/QP 165); and it is the point of saturation that is the condition for the becoming of characters and for the actualization of "unknown or unrecognized affects."

For the sake of clarification, we can contrast the artist's efforts to saturate their work with a recent account of metaphysical saturation. In his book, *Writing the Book of the World,* Ted Sider also stresses the significance of saturation for understanding the nature of reality, the reality independent of human affairs that is able to "stand up on its own." Carrying forward Frege's argument that a concept is a function that is unsaturated when it does not have an argument to give the function a truth value, Sider will argue that there simply is a metaphysical difference between unsaturated sentences such as, "New York is between," "in the National League," and "Jeff," and their saturated versions – "New York is between Washington and Boston," "The Dodgers are in the National League," and "Jeff is an American." As Sider puts it, "Some kind of joint in nature separates (saturated) facts . . . from (unsaturated) properties and relations. . . ."[5] As for the nature of this joint, Sider argues that it is a "complete sentence in a fundamental language," whereby in this fundamental language "sentences are always, 'metaphysically complete' – saturated."[6] In short, Sider offers a representational theory that claims it is the complete (saturated) sentences of a fundamental language that represent the structure of reality and carve reality at the joints. Sider is forthright in his assertion that this is precisely the aim of his project. In the first paragraph of the Preface to *Writing the Book of the World*, Sider claims, "The world has a distinguished structure, a privileged description. For a representation to be fully successful, truth is not enough; the representation must also use the right concepts so that its conceptual structure matches reality's structure."[7]

For reasons that should be clear by now, Deleuze and Guattari's aesthetic realism does not entail a saturation that allows for the representation of "reality's structure." The reason for this is that Sider's understanding of saturation presupposes an already individuated and actualized reality, and a sentence or "privileged description" is saturated if it matches and successfully represents this reality. For Deleuze and Guattari, however, the reality that stands up on its own is precisely the saturated edge of chaos state that is the condition for the actualization and individuation of determinate states of affairs, including the perceptual states and affective transitions of our determinate lives as lived. To extract such saturated states is to extract A LIFE from the lived, and the representations of the lived states presuppose the saturation (A LIFE) that made them possible; this saturation remains as the problematic substance that is never fully represented or actualized within determinate lived states and it is therefore the artist's efforts at saturation that bring about the problematization of these lived states, such that previously unknown or new affects become possible. This is the great novelist's and artist's task.

§3

At this point we return to an earlier theme, to one of the ritornellos of this work. In the first chapter, "What is a Concept?," Deleuze and Guattari argue that concepts have components that are "distinct, heterogeneous, and yet not separable," and this is what "defines the consistency of the concept" (WP 19/QP 25). With respect to the components themselves, however, there is something more, "something [that] passes from one to the other, something that is undecidable between them. There is an area *ab* that belongs to both *a* and *b*, where *a* and *b* 'become' indiscernible" (WP 19–20/QP 25). This area *ab*, as we have been arguing throughout this book, is precisely the plane of consistency that is the condition for the possibility of differentiating between individuated elements – that is, *a* and *b*. In the context of the current chapter on art, we again find this motif recurring, and understandably so, given the importance it has relative to Deleuze and Guattari's arguments. When Virginia Woolf sought to "saturate every atom," she did so in order to give us the percept and affect that facilitate the becoming of characters and the possibility of "unknown or unrecognized affects." The percepts and affects themselves, however, entail, Deleuze and Guattari argue,

> a zone of indetermination, of indiscernibility, as if things, beasts, and persons (Ahab and Moby Dick, Penthesilea and the bitch) endlessly reach that point that immediately precedes their natural differentiation. This is what is called an affect. (WP 173/QP 164)

To drive the point home, Deleuze and Guattari add that it is "Life alone [that] creates such zones . . . and only art can reach and penetrate them in its enterprise of co-creation" (ibid.). To take the example of a Rodin sculpture, the art of such a sculpture, Deleuze and Guattari claim, "lives on these zones of indetermination," and as a result the creative process of sculpting is more than a matter of the application of "the skill of the draftsman who notes resemblances between human and animal forms and gets us to witness their transformation" (ibid.). In other words, rather than being a relationship between an artist and their work, or a relationship of resemblance between artworks and animal and human forms, and so on, art lives on a co-creation where *a* and *b* (artist and work, representation and represented, animal and human) become indiscernible. This is the life of an artwork, what Deleuze and Guattari call the power of a ground that can dissolve forms and impose the existence of a zone in which we no longer know which is animal and which human, because something like the triumph or monument of their nondistinction rises up – as in Goya or even Daumier or Redon. (ibid.)

That which exists in itself and is able to stand up on its own in art is A LIFE, a pure immanence and zone of indetermination that is irreducible to all determinate forms and relationships between forms for it is the very power presupposed by the individuation of forms, as well as the power that can dissolve these forms. This is what Deleuze and Guattari refer to as the "triumph or monument" (WP 173/QP 164) of art, and it runs counter to the life as lived, to common sense and the life of opinion.

When it comes to the relationship between art and opinion, Deleuze and Guattari could not be clearer: "Art does not have opinions" (WP 176/QP 166), they claim. This conclusion follows naturally from Deleuze and Guattari's argument that "opinions are functions of lived experience" (WP 174/QP 165), meaning that they involve functional relations between determinate states of lived experience, and to what is common in experience and thereby able to be adequately represented and shared through discourse and conversation. The indiscernible event, however, the point of saturation, is "unlivable," a "pure reserve," as Deleuze and Guattari put it (WP 156/QP 148). It is this "pure reserve," this point of saturation in "every atom" and every sentence, that "makes the standard language," the language and discourse of opinion, "stammer, tremble, cry, or even sing: this is the style . . . the foreign language within language that summons forth a people to come" (WP 176/QP 166; see our earlier discussion of the 'people to come' in Chapter 4). This foreign language within language highlights a key difference between concepts and artworks, between the components and conceptual personae of a concept and the percepts and affects of artworks. While both concepts and percepts/affects presuppose an indiscernible area *ab* or "zone of indetermination," the becoming of philosophical concept grasps "heterogeneity . . . in an absolute form," while the "sensory becoming" of artworks involves an "otherness caught in a matter of expression" (WP 177/QP 167). And this is why Deleuze and Guattari refer to an artwork as a monument, for as a monument an artwork is not "the virtual event," the event that forever "eludes what is"; nor does it actualize such events, as concepts do, but rather the artwork as monument "incorporates or embodies it [the event]: it gives it a body, a life" (WP 177/QP 168).

What is the difference between a concept that actualizes an event that forever eludes what is and a monument that incorporates or embodies an event, giving it a body, a life? To answer this question we need to return to the question with which we began this chapter – namely, what is meant by saying not only that "art preserves," as Deleuze and Guattari do, but that "it is the only thing in the world that is preserved" (WP 163/QP 154)? Deleuze and Guattari do not claim that concepts are preserved, nor scientific functions, but only art. We can now begin to unpack their reasons for the privileging of art in this regard. Put simply, Deleuze and Guattari are materialists, but materialists who argue that what is, what is preserved in art, is A LIFE, and this life is the continual becoming-other of matter, or "the moving matter of a continuous variation,"[8] as Deleuze and Guattari put it in *A Thousand Plateaus.* Understood in this way, matter is not to be confused with the determinate, already individuated states of affairs of life as lived and the opinions that are functions of the lived; nor is matter to be confused with the already actualized and individuated states to which science refers, and which Sider presupposed, as we saw in his arguments for metaphysical saturation. Nor is the continual becoming-other of matter to be confused with concepts, for while concepts actualize the virtual event that eludes what is, the becoming of art does not elude what is but causes what is to tremble, to stutter and stammer; it is the foreign language within language.

Caution is necessary at this point, for by privileging the preservative powers of art it may seem that Deleuze and Guattari, in the vein of the phenomenological tradition – and Merleau-Ponty in particular – are advocating for their own particular version of the primacy of art and perception.[9] To the contrary, Deleuze and Guattari explicitly criticize the reliance of the phenomenological tradition on a fundamental *Urdoxa* as the condition that guarantees in advance the unity and integrity of perceptual phenomena. By basing perceptual experience upon the foundation of *Urdoxa*, perception becomes a function of the lived rather than the lived itself presupposing A LIFE as the condition for determinate perceptual states and affective transitions of our lives as lived. By moving late in his career to the concept of flesh, Merleau-Ponty was able, Deleuze and Guattari note, to free perception from "the lived body, the perceived world, and the intentionality of one toward the other" (WP 178/QP 168–9). In other words, with the notion of the flesh and chiasmus, Merleau-Ponty does not presuppose the already constituted identities of a perceiving subject and perceived world, nor the intentional relationship between these already determined identities and an *Urdoxa* that predetermines the unity of perceptual experience. The concept of the flesh, in other words, is Merleau-Ponty's attempt to account for the identity of and hence relationship between a perceiving subject and their world, much as the zone of determination serves to account for the "natural differentiation" (WP 173/QP 164) between humans and animals, Ahab and Moby Dick, and so on. Despite Merleau-Ponty's moves in this direction, however, Deleuze and Guattari argue that the notion of the flesh, as Merleau-Ponty understands it, is "too tied to experience" (WP 178/QP 169), where experience itself has become a home base or unitary starting point rather than a unity that needs to be accounted for rather than presupposed. It is in this sense, then, that Deleuze and Guattari continue with Deleuze's early efforts to develop a transcendental empiricism that sets out to understand the conditions of real experience rather than presuppose such experiences as unquestioned givens. In other words, Deleuze and Guattari set out to understand the processes that are inseparable from the identities that presuppose a matter that is continually becoming-other. Crucial to this effort is the concept of the refrain (*ritournelle*).

Deleuze and Guattari dedicate an entire chapter of *A Thousand Plateaus* to the concept of the refrain, and in an interview, when asked what concept Deleuze and/or Deleuze and Guattari had created, Deleuze replied: "we formulated a concept of the ritornello in philosophy."[10] Deleuze thus recognizes the significance of this concept for his own work and for his work with Guattari, and the first few lines of the refrain plateau in *A Thousand Plateaus* relate directly to the themes that have been central to this chapter – namely, the nature of that which is preserved, and only preserved, in art. The chapter begins as follows:

> A child in the dark, gripped with fear, comforts himself by singing under his breath ... Lost, he takes shelter, or orients himself with his little song as best he can. The song is like a rough sketch of a calming and stabilizing, calm and stable, center in the heart of chaos. ... Now we are at home. But home does not preexist: it was necessary to draw a circle around that uncertain and fragile center, to organize a limited space.[11]

As is clear from this passage, we do not begin with a home, with a calm and stable center in the heart of chaos. A circle needs to be drawn around an uncertain and fragile center, and this fragile center is sketched without a plan, with no home or *Urdoxa* already in place from which we can safely and calmly draw another home. It is the song, the refrain and "singing under his breath," that embody the chaos and verge upon lines of flight and deterritorialization into the infinite speeds of chaos. Art, in other words, embodies the chaos that could very well undermine it, much as learning draws planes of consistency within a milieu and plane of immanence (problematic substance) that may well subvert the process and send it careening into the chaos of failure or back to the already established, well-worn routines (recall Deleuze's claim that there is always "something fatal about all education"[12]). When successful, a refrain creates the stable place amidst the absolutely infinite chaos from which a limited space may be drawn, a home, and it is this stable place that is able to stand up on its own – it is that which is preserved and only preserved in art. Deleuze and Guattari are quite explicit on this point: "The whole of the refrain is the being of sensation. Monuments are refrains" (WP 184/QP 175).

A refrain is inseparable from a territory, and from a process of territorialization that equally implies a deterritorialization. It is for this reason that Deleuze and Guattari propose that "Perhaps art begins with the animal, at least with the animal that carves out a territory and constructs a house" (WP 183/QP 174). The "territory-house system," Deleuze and Guattari claim, "transforms a number of organic functions," such as "sexuality, procreation, aggression, feeding" (ibid.). In contrast to Konrad Lorenz's argument that these transformations are the result of functional relationships to an animal's home/territory, Deleuze and Guattari argue that it is the emergence of the territory and house itself that explains the transformation of the animal's functions, and this emergence is itself dependent upon the refrain, or upon "pure sensory qualities . . . that cease to be merely functional and become expressive features, making possible a transformation of functions" (ibid.).[13] In other words, it is the animal's territorialization process – the bird-song, or the Australian bird who turns leaves over "so that the paler, internal side contrasts with the earth" (WP 184/QP 174) – that allows for the emergence of a stable place, a home, and it is only then that functions become transformed in relation to this established place. When the turned-over leaves provide a contrast with the surrounding earth, the result is a "pure sensory quality" or being of sensation that can stand up on its own, in that it is independent of functional relationships to a home or to an animal that inhabits and defends this home through aggressiveness. The pure sensory qualities are refrains that create the stable space amidst the chaos and it is this stable space that is the condition for the possibility of an identifiable home, and for the functional relationships between animal and home/territory, or, to connect this with art, the relationship between a perceiver and creator of art and the artwork itself. This is why Deleuze and Guattari claim that perhaps "art begins with the animal," for with the animal we have the emergence of pure sensory qualities which are "already art" (WP 184/QP 175). And with the artist's efforts to forge compounds of percepts and affects, they too seek a refrain – "Everything begins with refrains" (WP 189/QP 179). From the infinite speeds of chaos a stable space is necessary for connections to be made, for an attachment to a home to begin, and with this process we have all we need for art to begin. With Paul Klee's work in mind, Deleuze and Guattari make this point explicitly:

> All that is needed to produce art is here: a house, some postures, colors, and songs – on condition that it all open onto and launches itself on a mad vector as on a witch's broom, a line of the universe or of deterritorialization – *Perspective on a Room with Occupants* (Klee). (WP 184–5/QP 175)

§4

We can now turn to the reasons why Deleuze and Guattari structured their work around philosophy, science, and art. Some have criticized this move for foisting upon thought an artificial division that runs counter to the general tenor and rhythms of Deleuze's and Deleuze and Guattari's thought. Others such as Badiou, as we have seen, have criticized Deleuze and Guattari for the incomplete nature of their typology, pointing to politics as a fundamental mode of thought that ought to have been included. As Deleuze and Guattari come towards the end of the chapter on art, they define what they refer to as "thought in its three great forms," and what is integral to them is the relationship each bears to the infinite – that is, to chaos:

> What defines thought in its three great forms – art, science, and philosophy – is always confronting chaos, laying out a plane, throwing a plane over chaos. But philosophy wants to save the infinite by giving it consistency: it lays out a plane of immanence that, through the action of conceptual personae, takes events or consistent concepts to infinity. Science, on the other hand, relinquishes the infinite in order to gain reference: it lays out a plane of simply undefined coordinates that each time, through the action of partial observers, defines states of affairs,

functions, or referential propositions. Art wants to create the finite that restores the infinite: it lays out a plane of composition that, in turn, through the action of aesthetic figures, bears monuments or composite sensations. (WP 197/QP 186)

With this passage Deleuze and Guattari provide a succinct summation of much of the territory we have traversed throughout this book. As has been a guiding theme on this journey, we have developed the implications of a "pedagogy of the concept," as Deleuze and Guattari set this out at the end of their Introduction. This in turn led us to unpack the concept of learning as this gets put to work throughout Deleuze's and Deleuze and Guattari's work. In *Difference and Repetition*, for instance, the example of learning to swim was highlighted as an important example to illustrate how learning involves a process of conjugating and drawing together signs. In the context of the current chapter, we can restate this process as being the effort to sketch a calm and stabilizing center "in the heart of chaos." This is done by bringing together points of saturation (or signs[14]) into a refrain, and from here everything begins once a home and territory become established. A consistent theme in all these discussions, as the extended quotation above acknowledges, is the relationship of the process of learning to chaos – this is where there is always "something fatal about all education" – and integral to Deleuze and Guattari's understanding of chaos is the claim that chaos consists of the infinite speeds that undermine the connections necessary for the emergence of an individuated entity, or for successful learning.[15] To use the example of the refrain, within the context of chaos a single note appears and disappears too quickly to establish a relation or conjugation with other notes, and without such connections we have no melody, and hence no refrain. Similarly to the example of the monkey learning to find its food under boxes of a particular color, learning occurs when there is a shift from random, unconnected behaviors to a paradoxical point – what we have referred to here as the consistent area *ab* – when the monkey makes fewer mistakes but does not yet "know" or possess the rule that would enable it to find the food consistently. The monkey, in essence, is sketching a stable, consistent zone of behavior within a chaos of random, unconnected behaviors, and this is precisely the process of learning that allows for the possibility of knowledge.

With this brief summary in place, we can now turn to the relationship between the three great forms of thought. As we saw in

Chapter 1, and as Deleuze and Guattari remind us, philosophy sets out to create concepts that affirm the infinite speeds of chaos while at the same time providing for a consistency that provokes a creative process in thought, a thought that develops in continual response to the problematic that is the condition for the consistency associated with the concept. A concept embraces infinite speeds, moreover, by providing for the incorporeal transformation of the components of the concept on a problematic plane of immanence into a plane of consistency, and it does so at once, or at infinite speed. Hume's concept of belief, for example, transforms a series of repeated events, A followed by B, into a belief in the necessary connection between A and B, and it does so by bringing A and B together at once, or at infinite speed, as well as the series of events where A is followed by B, and through contemplation this produces the habit or concept of belief in the necessary connection between A and B. This concept, however, remains inseparable from the problematic substance that continues to provoke new thoughts in response to it. Deleuze and the Deleuze and Guattari extend, as we have seen, Hume's example to the point of claiming, following Plotinus, that all is contemplation. "The plant," Deleuze and Guattari claim, "contemplates water, earth, nitrogen, carbon, chlorides, and sulphates, and it contracts them in order to acquire its own concept and fill itself with it (enjoyment)" (WP 105/QP 101). In short, a concept entails an incorporeal transformation and as such it is an event that is irreducible to the actualized states of affairs and phenomena that are transformed. The concept of belief in the necessary connection between A and B, for example, is irreducible to A or B, and the concept a plant acquires is irreducible to the elements that are contemplated and contracted.

As an assemblage and multiplicity of incorporeal transformations, a concept forever eludes the actualized states of affairs with which concepts become associated. As Deleuze and Guattari put it, and as discussed above, "conceptual becoming," or the incorporeal transformations of concepts, "is the action by which the common event itself eludes what is" (WP 177/QP 167). As a result, concepts provide the problematic basis for the actualization and individuation of phenomena in a way that does not predetermine what will or will not come to be. As Deleuze says, the eye is a solution to a light problem, but the problem is only apparent with the solution, and thus the problematic basis does not predetermine the manner in which the various contemplations and solutions (such as eyes) will arise.[16] Science, by contrast, sets out to establish functives

229

that do map relationships between what is and what will or will not come to be. To do this, however, science must relinquish the infinite and embrace instead the partial observer on the plane of reference. The plane of reference, as we saw, must limit the infinite speeds, slow them down and freeze-frame the chaos so that one can then establish functional relationships between phenomena.[17] From the scientific perspective, creative thought entails "a 'higher' taste" which consists of "choosing the good independent variables, installing the effective partial observer on a particular route, and constructing the best coordinates of an equation or function" (WP 133/QP 127). The result will be the creation of functives that map independent variables to states of affairs, but only on the condition that the infinite is relinquished in order to establish a plane of reference. As for art, it sets out, like philosophy, to affirm the infinite but it does so through finite works of art rather than through the incorporeal transformation and infinite speeds of concepts. It is for this reason that "art preserves, and it is the only thing in the world that is preserved" (WP 163/QP 154). A philosophical concept does not preserve and is not preserved, for although it affirms the infinite, it does so through the incorporeal transformation that "is the action by which the common event itself eludes what is," and therefore it eludes being anything to be preserved. Scientific functives do not preserve for they relinquish the infinite in order to establish a plane of reference; in doing so, however, they relinquish the real itself, for what is real, Deleuze and Guattari claim, following Spinoza, is an absolutely infinite, problematic substance – multiplicity, recall, is for Deleuze the "true substantive, substance itself."[18] The functives science creates may thus be understood, to follow Spinoza again, as useful fictions but not as representations that preserve reality.[19] This leaves us, then, with art. By beginning with the refrain – in fact, "everything," as we saw Deleuze and Guattari argue, "begins with refrains" (WP 189/QP 179) – art sets out to create compounds of percepts and affects that instill a foreign language within language, a stabilized chaos (refrain) that allows for an artwork to begin and which is in fact inseparable from an artwork, from "its support and materials." It is this stabilized chaos that restores the infinite in a way that is inseparable from something that is – namely, an artwork. It is therefore only with art that we have something that is preserved.

This brief summary of what Deleuze and Guattari refer to as "thought in its three great forms" may lead one to the conclusion that art is the privileged form of thought since it is the only one that restores the infinite by way of something that is – it is the only one that preserves – while scientific functions and philosophical concepts do not. This would be a mistake. Deleuze and Guattari are quite forthright in arguing that art "should not be thought to be like a synthesis of science and philosophy" (WP 198/QP 187); that is, art is not a Hegelian synthesis that preserves both the infinite (*à la* philosophy) and the finite (*à la* science). To the contrary, each of the three great forms of thought is to be "distinguished by the nature of the plane and by what occupies it" (ibid.). "Thinking," Deleuze and Guattari go on to argue, "is thought through concepts, or functions, or sensations and *no one of these thoughts is better than another, or more fully, completely, or synthetically 'thought'*" (WP 198/ QP 187, emphasis added). The three great forms of thought "do intersect and intertwine but without synthesis" (WP 198–9/QP 187); that is, it is the differentiation between these forms, as difference, that generates a thought – "thought as heterogenesis" (WP 199/QP 188), as Deleuze and Guattari put it. Therefore, although Deleuze and Guattari recognize that there are "culminating points, where sensation itself becomes sensation of concept or function, where the concept becomes concept of function or of sensation, and where the function becomes function of sensation or concept" (ibid.), these culminating points do not achieve identity or synthesis but mark irreducible differences – again, the irreducible differences that characterize "thought as heterogenesis."

To return to where we began, if thought is learning, and if learning is a matter of sketching a refrain in the heart of chaos, then we can see that the three great forms of thought involve culminating points that are the singularities drawn from the problematic substance and plane of immanence that is A LIFE, and they are to be drawn into the plane of consistency necessary for learning, for learning to live a life that is not simply living but involves extracting A LIFE from the lived. A life well lived, therefore, is a thoughtful life, a life of learning where, in the midst of living, one extracts A LIFE from the lived. Deleuze and Guattari, therefore, can be seen to be developing a concept of learning as they set forth a pedagogy of the concept. This concept, moreover, has three distinct components or forms, distinguished by the planes they cast over chaos and by what occupies these planes; and yet the concept of learning, as a concept, entails the incorporeal transformation of these three distinct components, and while they remain distinct, "something passes from one to the other, something that is undecidable between them" (WP 19–20/QP 25). This something is precisely the indiscernible, indeterminate zone that belongs to philosophy, science, and art – in short, this something is A LIFE and it is precisely what is extracted from our lives as lived when we become thoughtful learners. But learning is forever at risk – there is always "something amorous – but also something fatal – about all education."[20] As Deleuze and Guattari state this risk in closing their chapter on art, the effort to draw the culminating points of philosophy, science, and art together (the heterogenesis of thought), is an effort that risks "two extreme dangers: either leading us back to the opinion from which we wanted to escape or precipitating us into the chaos that we wanted to confront" (WP 199/QP 188).

Example 13

Deleuze and Guattari's turn to music in the final example converges in significant ways with Nietzsche's own preoccupation with music. Nietzsche's interest in music was not simply an expression of his own personal love of music (although this is certainly true[21]), but it reflects more profoundly on his efforts to understand process and becoming without reducing it to being a relationship between identifiable states of affairs. Deleuze and Guattari share Nietzsche's concerns on this front. Music is particularly appropriate for both Nietzsche's and Deleuze and Guattari's efforts, for it is both dynamic and chaotic, and, if done well, it entails an order or form that is inseparable from it. Put in other words, art and music, as understood by Nietzsche, cannot be reduced to a predetermining identity such as the 'truth' of beauty and the rules proper for art. Moreover, music especially can play a part in the process of attempting to think beyond the Fregean either/or of categorical concepts – that is, a determinate extension either does or does not fall under a given concept. As Nietzsche states the relevant point in an early note from 1872: "Music as a supplement to language: many stimuli and entire states of stimulation which cannot be expressed in language can be rendered in music."[22]

The most notable point of convergence between Nietzsche and Deleuze and Guattari on music is with respect to the role music plays, or the refrain for Deleuze and Guattari, in drawing an order or plane of consistency within chaos that does not presuppose a predetermining identity that guides the ordering process. Just a few lines before they begin their thirteenth and final example, Deleuze and Guattari claim that "everything comes to an end at infinity in the great Refrain" (WP 189/QP 190); everything begins with the refrain as well ("Everything begins with refrains" [WP 189/QP 179]), or "the whole of the refrain is the being of sensation" (WP 184/QP

175). In particular, from the midst of the infinite speeds of chaos, the refrain allows for the stable space necessary for connections to be made, and hence for determinate, individuated entities and processes to appear. The refrain, in short, entails "sonorous blocs . . . or framing forms each of which must join together to secure a certain closing-off" (WP 189/QP 179–80); that is, the refrain as "sonorous bloc" and "being of sensation," provides for the stability with which individuation begins and ends. And for Deleuze and Guattari, this musical "closing-off" occurs in three forms:

> the melodic *air*, which is a monophonic refrain; the *motif*, which is already polyphonic, an element of a melody entering into the development of another and creating counterpoint; and the *theme*, as the object of harmonic modifications through melodic lines. (WP 189/QP 180)

The air, motif, and theme are each distinct ways in which a stable sonorous bloc takes shape. The melodic air is the lead part in a composition, the solo line and sequence that provides the refrain with which other elements and variations connect. The "air is a vibration," Deleuze and Guattari argue, for it provides the basis for a rhythmic, compositional structure to take shape, which is what occurs with the motif. With the motif the musical vibration of the air comes to take on the salient form of a recurring, identifiable sequence that then becomes an integral element within a musical composition. This is why Deleuze and Guattari claim a motif is "a clinch, a coupling" (WP 190/QP 180), for it is what connects the vibration of the melody to the thematic structure of a musical composition.[23] In the case of the theme, it provides both for the structure of a musical composition but it also, Deleuze and Guattari claim, does not do so "without also unclenching, splitting, and opening" (ibid.). In other words, by beginning with the refrain, a musical theme allows for the drawing together of the motifs and melodic airs into a musical composition, but at the same time this musical composition opens on to the infinity (chaos) from which the refrain gets its start and it thereby sets music off down continually differing musical paths.

This process is clearly exemplified, Deleuze and Guattari argue, by the sonata form in music. On the one hand, the sonata form initially appears to be "a particularly rigid enframing form" (ibid.) that it is built upon two themes. In the first movement of a multi-movement piece, the sonata begins first with the "exposition of the first theme, transition, exposition of the second theme, developments on the first or second, coda, development of the first with modulation, and so on" (ibid.).[24] The sonata itself "is an entire house with its rooms" (ibid.), Deleuze and Guattari claim, by which they mean that it is an enframed musical composition from which subsequent movements then develop. And it is with the development of the subsequent movements that the themes developed in the sonata open out onto the infinity from which the refrain arises and thus they open "onto an ever more limitless plane of composition" (ibid.). It is for this reason that Deleuze and Guattari argue that the "sonata appears then rather like a crossroads form where the opening of a plane of composition is born from the joining of musical sections" (ibid.). The sonata form is thus both an enframing, the house and refrain from which everything begins, and the opening onto the "limitless plane of composition" that deframes the initial themes and initiates the experimental efforts of musicians (Deleuze and Guattari cite the "*compositional studies*" of Chopin, Schumann, and Liszt as examples of this process). The result of these efforts, Deleuze and Guattari claim, is that the

> creative labor [of musicians] no longer bears on sonorous compounds, motifs, and themes . . . but on the contrary bears directly on the plane of composition itself, so that it gives birth to much freer and deframed compounds, to almost incomplete or overloaded aggregates, in permanent disequilibrium. (WP 190–1/QP 180)

The creative labor of musicians that bears "directly on the plane of composition itself" is evidenced in the work of Arnold Schoenberg, who admits to creating musical *compositions* rather than *musical* compositions. The point for Schoenberg is not to construct a musical composition from musical, tonal elements, or from sonorous blocs, as Deleuze and Guattari might put it; rather, one begins with a composition, a plane of consistency and coherence from which one then carves out the relevant musical phrases and elements. Schoenberg makes this point explicitly in the opening pages of his *Fundamentals of Musical Composition*:

> A composer does not, of course, add bit by bit, as a child does in building with wooden blocks. He conceives an entire composition as a spontaneous vision. Then he proceeds, like Michelangelo who chiseled his Moses out of the marble without sketches, complete in every detail, thus directly forming his material.[25]

For Schoenberg, therefore, the task of a musical composer is not one of building an assemblage of musical refrains from already individuated pieces and elements – melodies, motifs, and themes, for instance – but rather it involves pushing the refrains to the plane of composition itself and to the "spontaneous vision" from which one then returns with a deframed or atonal assemblage of musical elements. Deleuze and Guattari will find similar compositional approaches in the work of Mahler, Berg, Bartók, and Stockhausen. The latter, in particular, takes the "House to the Cosmos" (WP 191/ QP 180) theme as an integral part of his work. In the liner notes, for instance, to his last electronic work, *Cosmic Pulses*, Stockhausen spoke of the process of working with twenty-four layers of sound. He said that

> For the first time, I have tried out superimposing 24 layers of sound, as if I had to compose the orbits of 24 moons or 24 planets . . . if it is possible to hear everything, I do not yet know – it depends on how often one can experience an 8–channel performance. In any case, the experiment is extremely fascinating.[26]

For Stockhausen, as for Schoenberg, Bartók, Messiaen, and others, Deleuze and Guattari find in their work the effort to extract A LIFE from the lived, a pure immanence and cosmos from the house and the refrain. Their work may be challenging, but this is precisely the result of deframing and deterritorializing the creature comforts of home in a process that sends us on a line of flight to the infinite cosmos, or chaosmos as Deleuze and Guattari refer to it. The challenge, as Deleuze and Guattari note in closing the "Percept, Affect, and Concept" chapter, is that this deframing line of flight may result in "either leading us back to the opinion from which we wanted to escape [the life as lived] or precipitating us into the chaos that we wanted to confront" (WP 199/QP 188). The effort to steer this course between the Scylla and Charybdis of life as lived and chaos becomes the theme of the conclusion to *What is Philosophy?*, and with this they close out their meditation on a life well lived.

Suggested reading for example 13
   John Cage, *Silence: Lectures and Writings by John Cage*

NOTES

1. Gottlob Frege, "Comments on Sinn and Bedeutung," in *The Frege Reader*, ed. Michael Beaney (Oxford: Blackwell, 1997), p. 178.
2. Gilles Deleuze and Félix Guattari, *A Thousand Plateaus: Capitalism and Schizophrenia*, trans. Brian Massumi (Minneapolis: University of Minnesota Press, 1987), p. 53.

3. This sentence is, in essence, a short summary of George Dickie's institutional theory of art. See George Dickie, "Defining Art," *American Philosophical Quarterly* 6, no. 3 (1969).

4. Deleuze and Guattari are citing Virginia Woolf, *The Diary of Virginia Woolf*, ed. Anne Olivier Bell (London: Hogarth Press, 1980), vol. 3, pp. 209, 210.

5. Theodore Sider, *Writing the Book of the World* (Oxford: Oxford University Press, 2011), p. 253.

6. Ibid., p. 254.

7. Ibid., p. vii.

8. *A Thousand Plateaus*, p. 340.

9. An allusion to Maurice Merleau-Ponty's *The Primacy of Perception*. For more on the contrast between Deleuze and Merleau-Ponty, see my *The Problem of Difference: Phenomenology and Poststructuralism* (Toronto: University of Toronto Press, 1998).

10. Gilles Deleuze. *Two Regimes of Madness: Texts and Interviews 1975–1995*, ed. David Lapoujade, trans. Ames Hodges and Mike Taormina (New York: Semiotext[e], 2006), p. 381.

11. *A Thousand Plateaus*, p. 311.

12. Gilles Deleuze, *Difference and Repetition*, trans. Paul Patton (New York: Columbia University Press, 1994), p. 23.

13. For their critique of Lorenz, see *A Thousand Plateaus*, pp. 315–16: "The marking of a territory is dimensional, but it is not a meter, it is a rhythm. It retains the most general characteristic of rhythm, which is to be inscribed on a different plane than that of actions. But now the distinction between the two planes is between territorializing expressions and territorialized functions. That is why we cannot accept a thesis like Lorenz's, *which tends to make aggressiveness the basis of territory*" rather than, as Deleuze and Guattari argue, making the process of territorialization the basis for understanding aggressiveness.

14. Recall our earlier discussion of signs in Chapter 1.

15. Recall the important passage from WP 42/QP 44 cited earlier (see p. ??): "Chaos is characterized less by the absence of determinations than by the infinite speed with which they take shape and vanish."

16. See *Difference and Repetition*, p. 211: "An organism is nothing if not a solution to a problem, as are each of its differentiated organs, such as the eye which solves a light 'problem'."

17. Recall Mark Wilson's arguments, discussed in Chapter 5, regarding the necessity of limiting parameters in order to provide for successful, truth-tracking descriptions of phenomena. This was an example, we argued, of drawing upon partial observers in order to install a plane of reference on chaos.

18. *Difference and Repetition*, p. 182.

19. For Spinoza on mathematics, see his famous letter on the infinite (letter 12).

20. *Difference and Repetition*, p. 23.
21. Nietzsche even wrote some piano music that has been performed and recorded.
22. Friedrich Nietzsche, *Philosophy and Truth*, ed. and trans. Daniel Breazeale (Atlantic Highlands, NJ: Humanities Press International, 1992), p. 40.
23. See Rudolph Reti, *The Thematic Process in Music* (New York: Macmillan, 1951).
24. For more on sonata form, see Charles Rosen, *Sonata Forms* (New York: Norton, 1988).
25. Arnold Schoenberg, *Fundamentals of Musical Composition*, ed. Gerald Strang (London: Faber & Faber, 1967), pp. 1–2.
26. Karlheinz Stockhausen, *Cosmic Pulses* CD Liner Notes (Kürten: Stockhausen-Verlag, 2007).

Conclusion

"There is a crack in everything.
That's how the light gets in."

Leonard Cohen, *Selected Poems, 1956–1968*

In drawing *What is Philosophy?* to a close, Deleuze and Guattari provide an Aristotelian reading of the context in which to place "thought in its three great forms – [namely] art, science, and philosophy" (WP 197/QP 186). As was stated somewhat boldly in the Introduction, *What is Philosophy?* should be read as a meditation on a life well lived, and more to the point, such a life is one where one lives, as Aristotle argued, with an "eye on the mean and working towards it . . . [as the] good artists do their work"; in doing this, one thus lives a life whereby "nothing can be subtracted from or added to [it]."[1] The life of moderation, therefore, the life well lived, is a life that avoids both excess and deficiency. For Deleuze and Guattari, the three great forms of thought are similarly tasked in that, while they are integral to a thoughtful life, to a life well lived, what this involves – as we have seen throughout this text and as the Conclusion reminds us – is that a life well lived avoids the excess of chaos (pole of deterritorialization) and the deficiency of opinion (pole of stratification [see Chapter 2, §1]).

As Deleuze and Guattari begin the Conclusion, they are quite forthright in their assertion that "We require just a little order to protect us from chaos" (WP 201/QP 189). What is critical to this understanding of chaos, as we have seen, is *not* that it consists of a disorganized mess of determinate, already individuated entities; to the contrary, chaos is characterized by the infinite speeds that

238

undermine and yet condition the very individuation that allows for the presence of determinate individuals in the first place. The effect of such infinite speeds on thought is that it can undermine thought itself, or as Deleuze and Guattari put it, we have "a thought that escapes itself . . . ideas that fly off, that disappear hardly formed, already eroded by forgetfulness" (ibid.). It is precisely the "infinite variabilities" or "infinite speeds" that account for this disappearance of thought, and hence we have the need for "just a little order to protect us from chaos." Hume's theory of the association of ideas, for instance, is, for Deleuze and Guattari, an example of putting "some order into ideas" so as to prevent thought from disappearing into a realm of fantasy and delusion. The association of ideas thus provides thought with the "protective rules – resemblance, contiguity, causality" (ibid.) that keep thought in check. These rules serve, then, as a source of opinions, and opinions, Deleuze and Guattari argue, are "like a sort of 'umbrella', which protects us from chaos" (WP 202/QP 190).

At the same time that opinions protect us from chaos, they also go too far in stifling the creative vitality inseparable from chaos, and thus there is a complementary struggle, Deleuze and Guattari claim, a struggle that "takes on more importance – the struggle *against opinion*, which claims to protect us from chaos itself" (WP 203/QP 191). It is the three great forms of thought – philosophy, science, and art – that struggle against both chaos and opinion, and thus they are critical to a thoughtful life, or a life, *à la* Aristotle, that seeks to avoid both the excesses of chaos and the deficiencies of opinion. As Deleuze and Guattari put it, if opinions are like the images on the underside of an umbrella, "a firmament on the umbrella, like the figures of an *Urdoxa* from which opinions stem," then "Philosophy, science, and art want us to tear open the firmament and plunge into the chaos" (WP 202/QP 190). To echo the sentiment expressed in the lyrics of the Leonard Cohen song that heads this Conclusion, philosophy, science, and art, as thoughtful engagements, force a crack into the firmament that allows the light of chaos in, but a light and chaos that becomes consistent, a "chaosmos" or "chaoid," as Deleuze and Guattari put it. Philosophy, as we have argued, lets the light of infinite speeds shine through and renders the infinite consistent in the creation of concepts, a concept being a "chaoid," as Deleuze and Guattari put it in the Conclusion. Deleuze and Guattari are clear on this point: "A concept is . . . a chaoid state par excellence; it refers back to a chaos rendered consistent, become Thought, mental chaosmos" (WP 208/QP 196). Similarly for art,

Deleuze and Guattari claim that it "takes a bit of chaos in a frame in order to form a composed chaos that becomes sensory, or from which it extracts a chaoid sensation as variety" (WP 206/QP 194). The being of sensation, as discussed in the previous chapter, is the consistency of the area *ab*, and this is precisely the chaoid that resists both the determinate images of opinions on the firmament and the chaos that leads to the disappearance of our thoughts and ideas. For science as well, Deleuze and Guattari claim that it "takes a bit of chaos in a system of coordinates and forms a referenced chaos that becomes Nature, and from which it extracts an aleatory function and chaoid variables" (ibid.). In clarifying this point, Deleuze and Guattari note that the emphasis in "modern mathematical physics" on strange or chaotic attractors is an example of science using the cracks in the firmament in order to construct the chaoids that are central to work in dynamic systems theory, or in what Deleuze and Guattari will also refer to as nomad science in contrast to royal science, the latter being in the business of manufacturing scientific opinion.[2] In contrast to these efforts, Deleuze and Guattari argue that one can readily find "pseudosciences" that remain content to stay within the stable orbit of the world of common-sense opinion. According to Deleuze and Guattari,

> As for pseudosciences that claim to study the phenomena of opinion, the artificial intelligences of which they make use maintain as their models probabilistic processes, stable attractors, an entire logic of the recognition of forms; but they must achieve chaoid states and chaotic attractors to be able to understand both thought's struggle against opinion and its degeneration into opinion. (WP 207/QP 194–5)

This last point is key, for a thoughtful life, a life where thought is extracted from the everyday, lived states of affairs, from the common discourse of shared opinions, is a life that lets the light of chaos in but this light is rendered consistent and ordered, a cha-osmos or chaoid that is a chaos "become Thought" (WP 208/QP 196). It is this relationship to chaos that accounts, as Deleuze and Guattari argue in the embedded citation, for "both thought's struggle against opinion and its degeneration into opinion." The tendency for thought, in its struggle against chaos, is towards the static and determinate states of affairs represented by common opinion; conversely, by letting the light of chaos in through the cracks of the firmament so as to struggle against the tendency of thought to degenerate into opinion, there is the resulting struggle against losing thought altogether in the chaos ("a thought that escapes itself" [WP 201/QP 189]). This is the Aristotelian effort of Thought in its three great forms – that is, avoid the excess of infinite, creative movements that occur when one submerges into the chaos whereby one's ideas fly off, and avoid the deficit of opinion where creative processes come to be reduced to the static state of what has always already been determined. A thoughtful life is thus a creative life that hews close to the chaos that is the very life of creative process, or it is A LIFE as we have referred to it throughout this book, and it avoids the excess of chaos and the deficit of opinion so as to maintain a creative, chaoid state. As Deleuze and Guattari put it, "chaos has three daughters, depending on the plane that cuts through it: these are the *Chaoids* – art, science, and philosophy – as forms of thought or creation" (WP 208/QP 196).

With this turn to understanding philosophy, science, and art as forms of thought or creation that involve chaoids, and with these forms understood as forms of the creative, thoughtful life, we come to the vitalism that Deleuze readily recognized to be an important feature throughout his own work, as well as in his work with Guattari. Deleuze and Guattari acknowledge the vitalist nature of their project in the conclusion to *What is Philosophy?* They are careful to note, however, that vitalism "has always had two possible interpretations" (WP 213/QP 201). On the one hand, there is vitalism as a life or "Idea that acts, but is not"; that is, it is a life that is not to be confused with the determinate, living things that are. Bergson's *élan vital*, for instance, is not to be identified with the determinate lives this active force (*élan vital*) makes possible. On the other hand, there is vitalism understood as "a force that is but does not act – that is therefore a pure internal Awareness" (ibid.). In addition to citing Leibniz and Ruyer as figures who fall into this tradition, Deleuze and Guattari will admit that the "second interpretation [of vitalism] seems to us to be imperative." Their reasoning for this imperative follows for Deleuze and Guattari because it was Hume, they claim, who showed that in the processes of habit formation the active, "progressive integrations, from one test to another, the tests or cases, the occurrences, must . . . be contracted in a contemplating 'imagination' while remaining distinct in relation to actions and to knowledge" (ibid.). What we must find, then, "beneath the noise of actions, [are] those internal creative sensations or those silent contemplations that bear witness to a brain" (ibid.). It is precisely this Humean vitalism that is critical to Deleuze and Guattari's project in *What is Philosophy?* and to Deleuze's project more generally.[3]

To return to a recurring theme or motif – that is, refrain or ritornello (*ritournelle*) – of this book, the "silent contemplations that bear witness to a brain" refers to the Humean argument, extended by Deleuze, whereby elements in a problematized state (plane of immanence, A LIFE) are brought to a state of synthesis (plane of consistency) by "silent contemplations" that do not play an active role in synthesizing the elements, and contemplations that are not to be confused with the elements themselves. This process is what Deleuze called "passive synthesis" in *Difference and Repetition*, and it is Hume's work that sets the stage for Deleuze's own extension of this process. We have already detailed how Deleuze and Deleuze and Guattari go about extending Hume's work (see Chapter 2, §4 and Chapter 5, §3), but in the Conclusion Deleuze and Guattari go even further and invoke Plotinus's claim that "all is contemplation" in order to justify their vitalism, or what they call "an inorganic life of things" (WP 213/QP 200). As was discussed in Chapter 2, the Humean contemplations are precisely the syntheses that are external to the elements synthesized and which make active syntheses possible as these passive syntheses are picked up by an active synthesis. For example, in *Difference and Repetition*, Deleuze offers thirst as an example of the interplay between passive and active synthesis. Since contemplation is understood by Deleuze, and Deleuze and Guattari, to be the processes of contraction associated with passive synthesis, Deleuze thus follows through on Plotinus's claim that "all is contemplation" and argues that "We are made of contracted water, earth, light and air . . . Every organism, in its receptive and perceptual elements, but also in its viscera, is a sum of contractions, of retentions and expectations."[4] Deleuze then adds that "each contraction, each passive synthesis, constitutes a sign which is interpreted or deployed in active synthesis."[5] This is where the thirsty organism comes in, for it is by way of signs that are constituted by the "sum of contractions, of retentions and expectations" that are then taken up by "an animal [who] 'senses' the presence of water" and then sets out to get to the water. These signs or contemplations, however, "do not resemble," Deleuze stresses, "the elements its thirsty organism lacks."[6] To clarify, we can refer to the mental state of thirst, C, as the contemplation or passive synthesis and contraction of elements that then allows for the possibility that the animal will actively seek the presence of water through an activity, A, that now involves an active synthesis that is made possible by the contemplation C. To restate this in the context of Deleuze and Guattari's claim that we need "to discover, beneath the noise of actions, those internal creative sensations or those silent contemplations," we can say that beneath the action, A, of seeking the presence of water there is the passive synthesis, contraction, and contemplation of elements, C, that constitutes the sign that is then taken up by A. In the Conclusion to *What is Philosophy?*, Deleuze and Guattari refer to this contemplation of elements, C, that allows for the possibility of active, determinate relations, A, as the brain. The "silent contemplations . . . bear witness to a brain," Deleuze and Guattari claim.

In Deleuze and Guattari's discussion of the brain, the brain is not to be confused with the bodily organ; rather, the brain is the plane of immanence or problematic substance (A LIFE) where the process of contraction and contemplation, or C, takes place and makes it possible for a determinate subject to have a determinate thought, or A. It is for this reason that Deleuze and Guattari claim that "It is the brain that thinks and not man – the latter being only a cerebral crystallization" (WP 210/QP 197–8). Deleuze and Guattari then add that they "will speak of the brain as Cézanne spoke of the landscape: man absent from, but completely within the brain" (ibid.). In other words, an active thinking subject is not to be confused with the contemplations and passive syntheses of contractions and retentions that made this active subject possible. The subject is completely within the brain, therefore, for the subject is nothing over and above the process of contemplation and contraction that constitutes the signs that are then taken up in a process of active synthesis. In the case of a plant, for instance, Deleuze and Guattari return in the conclusion to an example they used earlier and argue that the "plant contemplates by contracting the elements from which it originates – light, carbon, and the salts – and it fills itself with colors and odors that in each case qualify its variety, its composition: it is sensation in itself" (WP 212/QP 200). For the plant, then, the passive synthesis draws together a subset of heterogeneous elements such as water, nitrogen, carbon, chlorides, and sulphates that is nothing less than the retention and expectations of cellular wall-weakenings and relations – in short, the brain as understood here is the plane of immanence (recall Deleuze and Guattari's claim that "the plane of immanence is like a section of chaos and acts like as a sieve" [WP 42/QP 44]) that makes it possible for the passive synthesis and contemplation that draw these elements into a plane of consistency, "an area *ab*."[7] This passive synthesis then constitutes the sign that is taken up and leads to a new active synthesis, such as a plant's being phototropic, or its being filled with the "colors and odors" that are in turn taken up as the signs that lead to the active syntheses and behaviors of wasps, bees, and birds, and so on. The brain, in other words, is the plane of immanence or problematic substance, or what we have repeatedly referred to as A LIFE, that initiates the processes of learning or passive synthesis whereby elements are drawn into planes of consistency and hence emerge as the signs that are then taken up by the active, spatio-temporal processes of individuation. It is this view of the brain that leads Deleuze and Guattari to the final formulation of their vitalism:

> Not every organism has a brain, and not all life is organic, but everywhere there are forces that constitute microbrains, or an inorganic life of things. (WP 213/QP 200)

Deleuze and Guattari thus take Plotinus's claim that "all is contemplation" quite to heart. In this context, Plotinus's claim becomes the claim that everywhere there are microbrains or "an inorganic life of things." This inorganic life is not to be confused with the determinate lives of animal species, or even with organic life itself; rather, this life is the problematic, infinite substance – A LIFE – that allows for the passive syntheses and contraction of elements – that is, the "silent contemplations" – that make possible the emergence and individuation of determinate entities, whether organic or not, living or not. The microbrains, in short, are the very life of things, the life that allows for the very determinate existence of things at all. With respect to our own lives, moreover, our lives as lived within determinate contexts and states of affairs, the task, as Deleuze and Guattari see it, is to extract A LIFE from our lives as lived, and this entails engaging with the chaos through the cracks in the firmament. The result is a thoughtful life, a life that extracts "thought in its three great forms" as philosophy, science, and art; or, as Deleuze and Guattari put it, the task is to extract the "Thought-brain" from our determinate lives as lived:

> Philosophy, art, and science are not the mental objects of an objectified brain but the three aspects under which the brain becomes subject, Thought-brain. They are the three planes, the rafts on which the brain plunges into and confronts the chaos. (WP 210/QP 198)

With this effort to extract the "Thought-brain" from our lives as lived we return to one of the central concepts of this book – namely, the importance of learning, or the "modest task of a pedagogy of the concept" (WP 12/QP 17) that was the project of *What is Philosophy?* as Deleuze and Guattari understood it. In what may appear to be a surprising move, it is only as they bring *What is Philosophy?* to a close (it is in the last paragraph of the book, in fact!) that they finally come to the issue of teaching, and then only to push it aside in favor of a pedagogy as contemplation (contemplation understood in the Plotinian/Humean sense). There is good reason for this, however, for the pedagogies associated with philosophy, art, and science, Deleuze and Guattari argue, do not consist of forming "those of us who are not artists" (WP 218/QP 205), philosophers, or scientists. The pedagogy they are concerned with is not a matter of passing on an already established knowledge or practice to one who lacks it. To the contrary, for Deleuze and Guattari, the pedagogies they have in mind

> [m]ust [in the case of art] awaken us and teach us to feel, and [. . .] philosophy must teach us to conceive, or [. . .] science must teach us to know. Such pedagogies are only possible if each of the disciplines is, on its own behalf, in an essential relationship with the No that concerns it. (ibid.)

This "No" that concerns the pedagogies of philosophy, science, and art is, in each case, to be "found where the plane confronts chaos" (ibid.). For philosophy, then, where the plane of immanence confronts chaos, we have nonphilosophy; for art, the confrontation of the plane of composition with chaos is nonart; and for science, the result of the plane of reference's confrontation with chaos is nonscience, or it is, to recall our earlier discussion of Mark Wilson's work [see Chapter 5, §1], where Wilson argued that the scientific effort to provide truth-tracking descriptions encounters its limits [namely, chaos], and leads to the breakdown of these descriptions. The pedagogy that is made possible by the "No," therefore, is precisely the brain and contemplations – or it is the plane of immanence and A LIFE that is "unlivable" (see our earlier discussions of the "unlivable" life, Chapter 6, §4, and Chapter 7, §3) – that draws the chaoid that protects us from the chaos while also resisting the stasis and determinate nature of opinion. As for the relationship between philosophy, science, and art, or "thought in its three great forms" (WP 197/QP 186), they are to be understood as determinate only insofar as their respective planes allow for the possibility of distinct chaoids (concepts, functives, and percepts/ affects), and yet the "Thought-brain" is "*the junction* – not the unity – *of the three planes*" (WP 208/QP 196). In other words, in living a thoughtful life we are to attempt to extract the "Thought-brain" from each of our determinate efforts, and in doing so the determinate and determinable nature of the three great thought forms will become indiscernible as they become submerged in the pedagogy and problematic substance of the "Thought-brain." Our three great efforts and forms of thought, in other words, encounter their non-thinking condition, and a life well lived is a life where we are open to learning, where the actualization of determinate forms of thought is left undetermined and undecidable. "It is here," as we confront the chaos in our pedagogical effort to extract A LIFE from the lived that we encounter the "nonthinking thought" (WP 218/QP 206) at the basis of all thought and where "concepts, sensations, and functions become undecidable, at the same time as philosophy, art, and science become indiscernible" (ibid.). The "Thought-brain" one extracts from one's determinate efforts and lives as lived is itself fundamentally and essentially related to the "nonthinking thought" that allows for the learning that in turn conditions the possibility of the three great forms of thought. The three chaoids and "daughters" of chaos that are inseparable from the learning associated with philosophy, science, and art are thus made possible by the effort to chart an Aristotelian path between the Scylla of chaos and the Charybdis of opinion. Consequently, in their meditation and contemplation upon a life well lived, what Deleuze and Guattari offer us in *What is Philosophy?* is the conceptual resources associated with learning whereby our lives are to be thought of not as consisting of being a coordination and composition of philosophy, science, and art, but rather as lives wherein these three forms become indiscernible, and where our lives become inseparable from creative, learning processes that allow for the emergence of forms of thought that we have not even anticipated. These emergent forms of thought, finally, will in turn be inseparable from the lives we live, and thus a life well lived may well help us to usher in a "people to come" that will bring to the stage a radical transformation in the way we live our lives. As Socrates argued long ago (see *The Apology*[8]), the point is not simply to live life but to bring about the changes necessary to live life well.

NOTES

1. Aristotle, *Nichomachean Ethics,* trans. Hippocrates Apostle (Grinnell: Peripatetic Press, 1984), 1097a36–7.
2. For more on this aspect of Deleuze and Guattari's project, see my *Philosophy at the Edge of Chaos: Gilles Deleuze and the Philosophy of Difference* (Toronto: University of Toronto Press, 2006), along with the work of John Protevi and Manuel DeLanda (Manuel DeLanda, *A Thousand Years*

of Nonlinear History [New York: Zone, 1997]). Protevi, in particular, has developed the implications of a dynamical systems approach and has applied this to aid in our understanding of both political processes (see Protevi, *Political Affect: Connecting the Social and the Somatic* [Minneapolis: University of Minnesota Press, 2009]; *Life, War, Earth: Deleuze and the Sciences* [Minneapolis: University of Minnesota Press, 2013]) and recent work in extended cognition.

3. Again, see my *Deleuze's Hume: Philosophy, Culture and the Scottish Enlightenment* (Edinburgh: Edinburgh University Press, 2009).

4. Gilles Deleuze, *Difference and Repetition*, trans. Paul Patton (New York: Columbia University Press, 1994), p. 73.

5. Ibid.

6. Ibid.

7. There is a close parallel with Deleuze's understanding of the relationship between passive and active synthesis and Jessica Wilson's use of what she calls the powers-based subset, powers strategy, to lay out a theory of mental phenomena that is nonreductive to physical phenomena and yet nothing over and above this physical phenomenon. As she argues, mental phenomena can be understood nonreductively if they are a proper subset of physical powers. To restate Deleuze's example of thirst in Wilson's terms, the mental phenomenon of thirst is a determinable subset of determinate powers, and what is crucial is the relevance of the subset as a sign that is then taken up by the action of seeking water. The determinable subset is thus multiply realizable in that a different subset of heterogeneous elements can be taken up as a sign for the same active processes (for example, searching for water). For Deleuze, similarly, the signs constituted by contemplation and passive synthesis are also multiply realizable upon the plane of immanence. The plane of immanence or sieve, in other words, can draw from many different elements; what is important is the relevance of the sign as it is taken up by an active synthesis. For Wilson's work, see Jessica Wilson, "How Superduper Does a Physicalist Supervenience Need to Be?," *Philosophical Quarterly* 49, no. 194 (1999): 33–52; "Non-Reductive Realization and the Powers-Based Subset Strategy," *The Monist (Issue on Powers)* 94, no. 1 (2011): 121–54; and "Fundamental Determinables." *Philosophers' Imprint* 12, no. 4 (2012).

8. *Apology* 30a-b: Socrates claims to be "doing nothing else than urging you, young and old, not to care for your persons or your property more than for the perfection of your souls, or even so much; and I tell you that virtue does not come from money, but from virtue comes money and all other good things to man, both to the individual and to the state." This immediately precedes the passage where Socrates argues that he is a gadfly the gods have given to the people of Athens, a gadfly who stirs the people into action so as to become better than they would be otherwise.

Bibliography

Aristotle. *Nichomachean Ethics.* Trans. Hippocrates Apostle. Grinnell: Peripatetic Press, 1984.

Augustine, St. "The Teacher." In *Augustine: Earlier Writings.* Westminster: John Knox Press, 1953.

Badiou, Alain. *Deleuze: The Clamor of Being.* Trans. Louise Burchill. Minneapolis: University of Minnesota Press, 2000.

—. *Ethics: An Essay on the Understanding of Evil.* Trans. Peter Hallward. London and New York: Verso, 2001.

—. *Being and Event.* Trans. Oliver Feltham. London: Bloomsbury, 2007.

Baierlein, Ralph. *Atoms and Information Theory: An Introduction to Statistical Mechanics.* New York: W. H. Freeman, 1971.

Barnett, Vincent. *Kondratiev and the Dynamics of Economic Development.* London: Macmillan, 1998.

Beaufret, Jean. *Le Poème.* Paris: P.U.F., 1986.

Beiser, Frederick C. *The Fate of Reason: German Philosophy from Kant to Fichte.* Cambridge, MA: Harvard University Press, 1987.

Bell, Jeffrey A. *The Problem of Difference: Phenomenology and Poststructuralism.* Toronto: University of Toronto Press, 1998.

—. *Philosophy at the Edge of Chaos: Gilles Deleuze and the Philosophy of Difference.* Toronto: University of Toronto Press, 2006.

—. "Charting the Road of Inquiry: Deleuze's Humean Pragmatics and the Challenge of Badiou." *Southern Journal of Philosophy* 44, no. 3 (2006): 399–425.

—. *Deleuze's Hume: Philosophy, Culture and the Scottish Enlightenment.* Edinburgh: Edinburgh University Press, 2009.

—. "Whistle While You Work." In *Deleuze and Ethics.* Ed. Nathan Jun and Daniel W. Smith. Edinburgh: Edinburgh University Press, 2011.

Benardete, José A. *Infinity: An Essay in Metaphysics.* Oxford: Clarendon Press, 1964.

Boltanski, Luc, and Eve Chiapello. *The New Spirit of Capitalism.* Trans. Gregory Elliot. London: Verso, 2007.

Boyer, Carl. *The History of the Calculus and its Development.* New York: Dover, 1959.

Brandom, Robert B. *Articulating Reasons: An Introduction to Inferentialism.* Cambridge, MA: Harvard University Press, 2001.

Braudel, Fernand. *On History.* Trans. Sarah Matthews. Chicago: University of Chicago Press, 1982.

Brouwer, René. *The Stoic Sage: The Early Stoics on Wisdom, Sagehood and Socrates.* Cambridge: Cambridge University Press, 2014.

Cage, John. *Silence: Lectures and Writings by John Cage.* Hanover, NH: Wesleyan University Press, 1961.

Cantor, Georg. "Foundations of a General Theory of Manifolds: A Mathematico-Philosophical Investigation into the Theory of the Infinite." In *From Kant to Hilbert: A Source Book in the Foundations of Mathematics,* vol. II. Ed. W. B. Ewald. Oxford: Oxford University Press, 1996.

Chalmers, David. *Constructing the World.* Oxford: Oxford University Press, 2012.

Cohen, Leonard. *Selected Poems, 1956–1968.* New York: Jonathan Cape, 1969.

Cusa, Nicholas of. "On Learned Ignorance." In *Nicholas of Cusa: Selected Spiritual Writings.* Trans. H. Lawrence Bond. Mahwah, NJ: Paulist Press, 2005.

DeLanda, Manuel. *A Thousand Years of Nonlinear History.* New York: Zone, 1997.

—. *Intensive Science and Virtual Philosophy.* London: Bloomsbury Academic, 2005.

Deleuze, Gilles. "I Have Nothing to Admit." Trans. Janis Forman. *Semiotext(e)* 2, no. 3 (1977): 111–16.

—. *Expressionism in Philosophy: Spinoza.* Trans. Martin Joughin. New York: Zone, 1990.

—. *Empiricism and Subjectivity.* Trans. Constantin Boundas. New York: Columbia University Press, 1991.

—. *The Fold: Leibniz and the Baroque.* Trans. Tom Conley. Minneapolis: University of Minnesota Press, 1993.

—. *Difference and Repetition.* Trans. Paul Patton. New York: Columbia University Press, 1994.

—. *Essays Critical and Clinical.* Trans. Daniel Smith and Michael A. Greco. Minneapolis: University of Minnesota Press, 1997.

—. "Immanence: A Life." In *Pure Immanence: Essays on A Life.* Trans. Anne Boyman. New York: Zone, 2001.

—. *Desert Islands and Other Texts 1953–1974.* Trans. Michael Taormina. New York: Semiotext(e), 2004.

—. *Two Regimes of Madness: Texts and Interviews 1975–1995.* Ed. David

Lapoujade. Trans. Ames Hodges and Mike Taormina. New York: Semiotext(e), 2006.

Deleuze, Gilles, and Félix Guattari. *Anti-Oedipus: Capitalism and Schizophrenia*. Trans. Mark Seem and Robert Hurley. Minneapolis: University of Minnesota Press, 1977.

—. *Kafka: Toward a Minor Literature*. Trans. Dana Polan. Minneapolis: University of Minnesota Press, 1986.

—. *A Thousand Plateaus: Capitalism and Schizophrenia*. Trans. Brian Massumi. Minneapolis: University of Minnesota Press, 1987.

—. *Qu'est-ce que la philosophie?* Paris: Les Éditions de minuit, 1991.

—. *What is Philosophy?* Trans. Hugh Tomlinson and Graham Burchell. New York: Columbia University Press, 1994.

Della Rocca, Michael. *Spinoza*. New York: Routledge, 2008.

—. "Taming of Philosophy." In *Philosophy and its History*. Ed. Mogens Lærke, Justin E. H. Smith, and Eric Schliesser. Oxford: Oxford University Press, 2013.

Descartes, René. "Meditations on First Philosophy." In *The Philosophical Works of Descartes*, trans. Elizabeth S. Haldane and G. R. T. Ross (Cambridge: Cambridge University Press, 1967), p. 144.

—. *Discourse on Method*. Indianapolis: Hackett, 1998.

Dickie, George. "Defining Art." *American Philosophical Quarterly* 6, no. 3 (1969): 253–6.

Dostoevsky, Fyodor. *Notes from Underground*. Trans. M. Ginsburg. New York: Bantam, 1992.

Fontenelle, Bernard le Bovier de. *Conversations on the Plurality of Worlds*. Trans. H. A. Hargreaves. Berkeley: University of California Press, 1990.

Foucault, Michel. *The Archaeology of Knowledge*. Trans. Rupert Swyer. New York: Random House, 1972.

—. *Fearless Speech*. New York: Semiotext(e), 2001.

Frege, Gottlob. "Concept and Function." In *Collected Papers on Mathematics, Logic, and Philosophy*. Ed. Brian McGuinness. Oxford: Basil Blackwell, 1984.

—. *The Frege Reader*. Ed. Michael Beaney. Oxford: Basil Blackwell, 1997.

Friedman, Michael. *A Parting of the Ways: Carnap, Cassirer, and Heidegger*. Chicago: Open Court, 2000.

Geach, Peter. *Reference and Generality*. Ithaca, NY: Cornell University Press, 1980.

Gordon, Peter. *Continental Divide: Heidegger, Cassirer, Davos*. Cambridge, MA: Harvard University Press, 2012.

Halmos, Paul R. *Naive Set Theory*. Princeton: Van Nostrand, 1991.

Hawking, Stephen. *The Grand Design*. New York: Bantam, 2012.

Hawthorne, John, and Brian Weatherson. "Chopping up Gunk." *The Monist* 87, no. 3 (2004): 339–50.

Hegel, G. W. F. *The Jena System, 1804–1805: Logic and Metaphysics*. Trans.

John W. Burbidge and George di Giovanni. Montreal: McGill–Queen's University Press, 1986.

—. *Lectures on the Philosophy of History*. Trans. J. Sibree. New York: Dover Philosophical Classics, 2004.

—. *Hegel's Science of Logic*. Trans. A. V. Miller. Atlantic Highlands, NJ: Humanities Press International, 1995.

Heidegger, Martin. *An Introduction to Metaphysics*. Ed. Ralph Manheim. New Haven: Yale University Press, 1959.

—. *Early Greek Thinking*. San Francisco: Harper, 1985.

—. *Kant and the Problem of Metaphysics*. Trans. Richard Taft. Bloomington: Indiana University Press, 1997.

—. *Parmenides*. Trans. Andre Schuwer and Richard Rojewicz. Bloomington: Indiana University Press, 1998.

Holt, Edwin B., Walter T. Marvin, W. P. Montague, Ralph Barton Perry, Walter B. Pitkin, and Edward Gleason Spaulding. "The Program and First Platfrom of Six Realists." *Journal of Philosophy, Psychology and Scientific Methods* VII, no. 14 (1910): 393–401.

—. *The New Realists*. New York: Macmillan, 1912.

Hume, David. *A Treatise of Human Nature*. Ed. L. A. Selby-Bigge and P. H. Nidditch. Oxford: Clarendon Press, [1739] 1978.

—. *An Enquiry Concerning Human Understanding*. Ed. Tom Beauchamp. Oxford: Oxford University Press, [1748] 2005.

Husserl, Edmund. *Cartesian Meditations*. Trans. Dorion Cairns. Boston: Martinus Nijhoff, 1988.

Hylton, Peter. *Russell, Idealism, and the Emergence of Analytic Philosophy*. Oxford: Oxford University Press, 1993.

Kafka, Franz. *The Trial*. Trans. Willa and Edwin Muir. New York: Schocken, 1964.

Kant, Immanuel. *Groundwork of the Metaphysics of Morals*. Trans. Mary Gregor. Cambridge: Cambridge University Press, 1998.

—. *Critique of Pure Reason*. Trans. Norman Kemp Smith. London: Macmillan, 1929.

—. *Prolegomena to Any Future Metaphysics*. Trans. Gary Hatfield. Cambridge: Cambridge University Press, 2004.

Kierkegaard, Søren. *Stages on Life's Way*. Trans. Howard Vincent Hong and Edna Hatiestad Hong. Princeton: Princeton University Press, 1988.

—. *Fear and Trembling*. Trans. C. Stephen Taylor. Cambridge: Cambridge University Press, 2006.

Kirk, G. S., and J. E. Raven. *The Presocratic Philosophers: A Critical History with a Selection of Texts*. Cambridge: Cambridge University Press, 1984.

Kripke, Saul. "A Puzzle About Belief." In *Meaning and Use*. Ed. A. Margalit, 239–83. Dordrecht: D. Reidel, 1979.

—. *Naming and Necessity*. Cambridge, MA: Harvard University Press, 1980.

Kuhn, Thomas. *The Structure of Scientific Revolutions*. Chicago: University of Chicago Press, [1962] 2012.

Ladyman, James, and Don Ross. *Every Thing Must Go.* Oxford: Oxford University Press, 2007.

Laërtius, Diogenes. *Lives of Eminent Philosophers.* Trans. R. D. Hicks. Vol. II, Books 6–10, Cambridge, MA: Loeb Classical Library, Harvard University Press, 1925.

Leibniz, Gottfried Wilhelm. *Monadology.* La Salle: Open Court, 1988.

Leibniz, G. W. F. *New Essays on Human Understanding.* Cambridge: Cambridge University Press, 1996.

Martin-Jones, David. *Deleuze and World Cinemas.* London: Continuum, 2011.

McDowell, John. *Mind and World.* Cambridge, MA: Harvard University Press, 1994.

—. "What Myth?" In *Inquiry* 50, no. 4 (August 2007), 338–51.

Mackay, Robin (eds), *Collapse Vol. II: Speculative Realism* (Falmouth: Urbanomic, 2007).

McNeill, William. *Plagues and Peoples.* New York: Anchor, 1977.

Meinong, Alexius. *Theory of Objects.* Trans. J. N. Findlay. Oxford: Oxford University Press, 1933.

Merleau-Ponty, Maurice. *Phenomenology of Perception.* Trans. Colin Smith. New York: Routledge & Kegan Paul, 1958.

—. *The Primacy of Perception.* Trans. James M. Edie. Evanston: Northwestern University Press, 1964.

Moore, G. E. "External and Internal Relations." In *Proceedings of the Aristotelian Society*, New Series, vol. 20 (1919–1920): 40–62.

—. "A Defence of Common Sense." In *Philosophical Papers*, 32–59. New York: Collier, [1925] 1966.

Nietzsche, Friedrich. *Beyond Good and Evil.* Trans. Walter Kaufmann. New York: Vintage, 1966.

—. *Philosophy and Truth.* Ed. and trans. Daniel Breazeale. Atlantic Highlands, NJ: Humanities Press International, 1992.

—. *Untimely Meditations.* Trans. R. J. Hollingdale. Cambridge: Cambridge University Press, 1997.

Pascal, Blaise. *Pensées.* New York: Penguin, 2003.

Patton, Paul. *Deleuzian Concepts: Philosophy, Colonization, Politics.* Palo Alto: Stanford University Press, 2010.

Péguy, Charles. *Clio.* Paris: Gallimard, 1931.

—. *Temporal and Eternal.* Trans. Alexander Dru. Indianapolis: Liberty Fund, 2001.

Plato. *The Collected Dialogues of Plato.* Trans. Lane Cooper. Ed. Edith Hamilton and Huntington Cairns. Princeton: Princeton University Press, 2005.

—. *Five Dialogues: Euthyphro, Apology, Crito, Meno, Phaedo*, 2nd edn. Trans. G. M. A. Grube, revised John M. Cooper. Indianapolis: Hackett, 2002.

—. *Parmenides.* Trans. Mary Louise Gill and Paul Ryan. Indianapolis: Hackett, 1996.

Post, H. R. "Correspondence, Invariance and Heuristics: In Praise of

Conservative Induction." *Studies in History and Philosophy of Science Part A* 2 (1971): 213–55.

Prigogine, Ilya, and Isabelle Stengers. *Entre le temps et l'éternité.* Paris: Fayard, 1988.

Protevi, John. *Political Affect: Connecting the Social and the Somatic.* Minneapolis: University of Minnesota Press, 2009.

—. *Life, War, Earth: Deleuze and the Sciences.* Minneapolis: University of Minnesota Press, 2013.

Quine, W. V. O. "On What There Is." In *From a Logical Point of View,* 1–19. Cambridge, MA: Harvard University Press, 1980.

Reti, Rudolph. *The Thematic Process in Music.* New York: Macmillan, 1951.

Rosen, Charles. *Sonata Forms.* New York: Norton, 1988.

Russell, Bertrand. "On Denoting." *Mind* 14, no. 56 (1905): 479–93.

—. "Some Explanations in Reply to Mr. Bradley." *Mind* 19, no. 75 (1910): 373–8.

—. *Mysticism and Logic and Other Essays.* London: George Allen & Unwin, 1910.

—. *The Problems of Philosophy.* Oxford: Oxford University Press, 1959.

Schoenberg, Arnold. *Fundamentals of Musical Composition.* Ed. Gerald Strang. London: Faber & Faber, 1967.

Sellars, Wilfrid. *Empiricism and the Philosophy of Mind.* Cambridge, MA: Harvard University Press, [1956] 1997.

Sartre, Jean-Paul. *The Transcendence of the Ego: An Existentialist Theory of Consciousness.* Trans. Forrest Williams and Robert Kirkpatrick. New York: Farrar, Strauss & Giroux, 1961.

—. "The Humanism of Existentialism." In *Essays in Existentialism.* Secaucaus, NJ: Citadel Press, 1964.

Seneca, *Epistles* 1–65. Trans. Richard Gummere. Cambridge, MA: Loeb Classical Library, Harvard University Press, 2006.

Sider, Theodore. *Writing the Book of the World.* Oxford: Oxford University Press, 2011.

Simondon, Gilbert. *L'Individuation: À la lumière des notions de forme et d'information.* Grenoble: Millon, 2013.

Smith, Daniel W. "Mathematics and the Theory of Multiplicities: Badiou and Deleuze Revisited." *Southern Journal of Philosophy* 41, no. 3 (2003): 411–50.

—. *Essays on Deleuze.* Edinburgh: Edinburgh University Press, 2012.

Spinoza, Benedict de. *Collected Works of Spinoza,* Vol. 1. Trans. and ed. Edwin Curley. Princeton: Princeton University Press, 1985.

—. *The Letters.* Trans. Steven Barbone, Lee Rice and Jacob Adler. Ed. Samuel Shirley. Indianapolis: Hackett, 1995.

Stanley, Jason. *Knowledge and Practical Interests.* Oxford: Oxford University Press, 2005.

—. "Constructing Meanings." *Analysis* 74, no. 4 (2014): 662–76.

Stanley, Jason, and John Krakauer. "Motor Skill Depends on Knowledge of Facts." *Frontiers in Human Neuroscience* (August 29, 2013).

Stockhausen, Karlheinz. *Cosmic Pulses* CD Liner Notes. Kürten: Stockhausen-Verlag, 2007.

Sudnow, David. *Ways of the Hand.* Cambridge, MA: Harvard University Press, 1978.

Wallerstein, Immanuel. *The Modern World System, 3 Volumes.* New York: Academic Press, 1974.

Wang, Hao. *A Logical Journey: From Gödel to Philosophy.* Cambridge, MA: MIT Press, 2001.

Whitehead, Alfred North. *Process and Reality.* Boston: Free Press, 1969.

Wiggins, David. "On Being in the Same Place at the Same Time." *Philosophical Review* 77 (1968): 90–5.

Wilson, Jessica. "How Superduper Does a Physicalist Supervenience Need to Be?" *Philosophical Quarterly* 49, no. 194 (1999): 33–52.

Wilson, Jessica M. "Non-Reductive Realization and the Powers-Based Subset Strategy." *The Monist (Issue on Powers)* 94, no. 1 (2011): 121–54.

—. "Fundamental Determinables." *Philosophers' Imprint* 12, no. 4 (2012).

Wilson, Mark. "Predicate Meets Property". *Philosophical Review* XCI, no. 4 (October 1982), pp. 549–50.

—. "This Thing Called Pain." *Pacific Philosophical Quarterly* 66, no. 3–4 (1985): 227–67.

—. "Theory Façades." *Proceedings of the Aristotelian Society*, New Series, vol. 104 (2004): 273–88.

—. *Wandering Significance: An Essay on Conceptual Behavior.* Oxford: Oxford University Press, 2006.

Woolf, Virginia. *The Diary of Virginia Woolf.* Ed. Anne Olivier Bell. London: Hogarth Press, 1980.

Index